British Housing Design

Dedication

For Helen, Andrew, and especially Iain, but for whose arrival this book might have been finished a lot sooner.

Other titles in this series

Social Housing and the Social Services by Paul Spicker

Housing Finance by David Garnett, Barbara Reid and Helen Riley

Housing Practice and Information Technology by David Hunter

The Housing Service of the Future edited by David Donnison and Duncan Maclennan

Maintaining Home Ownership: the Agency Approach by Philip Leather and Sheila Mackintosh

Effective Sheltered Housing by Imogen Parry and Lyn Thompson

Longman/Institute of Housing

The Housing Practice Series

BRITISH HOUSING DESIGN

Duncan Sim

Published by the Institute of Housing (Services) Ltd, Octavia House, Westwood Business Park, Westwood Way, Coventry CV4 8JP and Longman Group UK Ltd, 6th Floor, Westgate House, The High, Harlow, Essex CM20 1YR

Telephone (0279) 442601; Fax (0279) 444501

Published in the IOH/Longman Housing Practice Series under the General Editorship of Peter Williams

A catalogue record for this book is available from the British Library

ISBN 0-582-10248-0

Typeset by Anglia Photoset Ltd, 34A St Botolphs, Church Walk, St Botolphs Street, Colchester, Essex CO2 7EA.
Printed in Great Britain by BPCC Wheatons Ltd, Exeter

Contents

Acknowledgements

In writing this book, I am particularly indebted to Professor Peter Williams of the University of Wales College of Cardiff. He encouraged me to draw up the original proposal, offered support during the writing stage and provided detailed comments on earlier drafts. I am also indebted to John Perry of the Institute of Housing for his comments, to my colleagues at Stirling, Douglas Robertson, Mary Taylor and Alan Ferguson, for both comments and support, to John Gilbert for detailed architectural advice, and to my family for their help and support and for putting up with my periods of short temper and general grumpiness.

Finally, for typing the manuscript, my deepest thanks go to Sarah Pugh and Sally Armstrong-Payne, of the University of Stirling.

Stirling, February 1993.

Introduction

There is an urgent need for a book on British housing design, written from a housing perspective. Although there are a substantial number of design texts, they approach the subject from quite different standpoints. Some take a social or historical angle (Burnett 1986, Gaskell 1987, for example) while there are a number of texts which focus on particular house types (Muthesius 1982, Worsdall 1979). From an architectural perspective there are useful books such as Scoffham (1984), although this is concerned only with the postwar period.

Recently, there have been a number of books which have reported on specific projects or research findings, of which one of the most influential has been Coleman (1985). There is too a burgeoning literature on community architecture, the work of co-operatives and the work of self-builders.

As well as seeking to provide a housing perspective on design, and a link to housing management, this book seeks also to respond to the very rapid changes taking place in housing education, the growth of new courses and the restructuring of existing ones. The aims of the book can therefore be summarised as follows:

(i) to provide an up-to-date text for practitioners and students on housing design;

(ii) to ensure that practitioners and students are aware of the current debates taking place regarding design issues, for example in the area of community architecture and in the debate over the influences of design on resident behaviour;

(iii) to bring together material which currently exists in a variety of disparate sources, including the housing, architectural and planning press, and to make this more accessible to housing students;

(iv) to provide student support for a wide range of courses, particularly new courses being developed by the Institute of Housing.

The book begins by taking a historical approach to design, beginning with the development of local styles and vernacular architecture during the eighteenth and nineteenth century. Different forms of housing ranging from back-to-backs to Tyneside flats and Scottish tenements are discussed. This first chapter goes on to explore the influences of new thinkers such as Salt, Cadbury and Lever with their philanthropic approach to housing and the development of model villages, and Ebenezer Howard and the Garden City pioneers.

Chapters Two and Three continue the chronology of design through the interwar and postwar periods. There are similarities in that both periods begin with a government report seeking to promote design improvements and to provide better housing — homes fit for heroes. In both periods, the good intentions were not always realised, with the 1930s characterised by a move back to cheaper, flatted property and away from the generously proportioned Wheatley Act dwellings. In the 1950s, there was a similar shift from the high space standards of the postwar Labour government to the smaller 'People's Houses' of Macmillan. In housing design, as elsewhere, history has a habit of repeating itself.

From Chapter Four onwards, the chapters take specific themes, beginning with the issue of system-built and high rise housing. Although often regarded as an example of design failure, there are many positive aspects to high rise housing and a number of blocks have been successfully adapted. The chapter explores the history of the high rise approach, as well as the current debate surrounding this particular house type.

Chapter Five moves outside the dwelling to look at issues of road layout and neighbourhood planning, at open space and the housing environment. A number of research studies have demonstrated that, for many tenants, the external appearance and layout of an estate can be more important than that of the house itself, and these findings are discussed at length.

The next three chapters all take as their focus the issue of 'good' design and the importance of involving local people in decisions about the design of their housing. Defensible space is now seen as being an important element in design and its absence is blamed for deviant resident behaviour. The work of Oscar Newman and Alice Coleman is associated with this viewpoint and their research is reported extensively in Chapter Six. Coleman's work has been particularliy influential and has led to government funding of design adaptations in certain housing estates; this work is discussed in the chapter.

Chapters Seven and Eight then look at what might be construed as 'good' design, first by exploring the influence of local authority advice as expressed through Design Guides and second by examining the attitudes of tenants to design. In recent years, there have been significant changes in the levels of user participation in design and the growth of significant technical aid and community architecture movements. These are discussed at length.

Most house designs relate, of course, to mainstream provision and there are numerous groups who may find themselves excluded. These range from the elderly and the disabled, who may have particular support needs, through to those who have found themselves unable to influence the design process to any real extent, including most women, young and single people. Chapter Nine examines the particular needs of these various groups and emphasises that good quality design should be for everyone.

Finally, Chapter Ten looks at some of the current issues in housing design, including the debate about space standards, the growth of design and build packages, and the greater attention now being paid to energy efficiency and 'green' housing design.

Changes in attitudes to design have been remarkably rapid and the 1980s saw a number of new initiatives launched, substantial research carried out and a significant growth in user participation. Change is likely to be equally fast in the 1990s and a book such as this can easily become out-of-date. Hopefully, although some of the emphases may change, the basic ideas about 'good' design and the need to involve tenants are unlikely to be very different in ten years' time. The key, however, will always be resources and one of the themes which runs through the book is the need to spend money if design is to be successful. Only if adequate resources are made available will we be able to design quality housing that will stand the test of time.

Chapter 1
Housing design before the First World War

Introduction

The rich variety of housing which existed in the first half of the nineteenth century was a product partly of class and partly of geography. Class influences were important, with speculative builders adopting quite different designs for middle class as opposed to working class housing while, even within the middle class housing sector, there was experimentation with a range of different styles. Geography was also important and, with industrial production being highly localised, housing styles too were localised, varying tremendously across the country and ranging from cellar dwellings to four storey tenements to single storey cottages.

This chapter will explore the differences between housing types and between the various parts of the country, identifying the regional and local variations in style. The influences of mid-nineteenth century legislation, particularly in health, will be explored, as well as the role of the Victorian philanthropists in designing housing for their workforces. Many of the settlements which they founded, such as Port Sunlight and Bournville, formed the basis for the Garden City movement at the end of the century, with which Ebenezer Howard is associated. The chapter will end with an assessment of the influence of this movement in the period leading up to the First World War.

Middle Class Housing

At the beginning of the nineteenth century, the most common middle class urban house type was the terrace. Partly this was a reflection of the limited public transport which existed and the necessity for building at relatively high density, in fairly close proximity to the town centre. Georgian terraces were anything from twenty to thirty feet wide with a staircase on one side and, on each floor, two rooms, one at the front and one at the rear. They were frequently of three or four storeys, including a basement.

The layout of such terraces was influenced by two factors, of which the first was local legislation. The London Building Act of 1774, for example, set out certain minimum standards regarding fire protection and the building of party walls. There were fines for non-compliance with the Act and all buildings were inspected by official surveyors both during construction and on completion (Muthesius 1982). In the newly-established town of Southport, typical of resort development of the Victorian period, the local lords of the manor, the Bolds, imposed strict controls on new building, including street widths, and prevented certain forms of housing from being constructed. As a result, most houses had gardens and the spacious street grid allowed for maximum daylighting and ventilation (Bell and Bell 1972, p137).

The second important influence was that of the landowner, who might impose certain restrictions regarding the development of his land. Thus, Edward Willes of Leamington Spa, who decided in the 1820s to develop his estate on the east side of the town. In 1826, Peter Robinson, his architect, drew up a series of plans for the whole estate, the emphasis being on terraced housing. The estate was eventually laid out by John Nash in similar fashion to his work in Regents Park in London.

In Scotland, an added control was exercised through the feudal land system and the restrictive clauses contained within feu charters. Land was therefore leased or sold on very strict conditions. In Glasgow, for example, a feu charter was granted in 1850 to a local builder for the development of Kew Terrace in the city's West End. Restrictions were placed on the building materials to be used (polished ashlar fronts and slate roofs), on the building line (at least 70 feet from Great Western Road), and the provision of access through the carriage drive and a mews lane.

> It was this stringent application of the feudal superior's ancient rights which ensured success for the West End as an exclusively upper-middle-class suburb.
>
> (Simpson et al. 1977)

The exercise of such controls did, however, lead to the danger that the housing, when completed, would be monotonous. Developers tried to avoid such problems through the introduction of squares and crescents into their layouts, together with small areas of open space, and good examples are provided not only in London but in cities like Bath and Edinburgh.

As the nineteenth century progressed, cities expanded and the location of middle class housing became crucial. Partly this was for social reasons but, at a more practical level, the wealthier merchants and businessmen felt it was important to move away from the noise, dirt and insanitary conditions of the inner areas. Newer suburbs began to be developed, further from the city centre, and house styles began to change.

First indications of change had come in the late 1820s with John Nash's development of Regents Park. Although the bulk of the housing was terraced, some villas were erected, including a small enclave called Park Village which, according to Edwards (1981) was 'the first piece of suburbia to be built'.

For the Victorians villas had certain advantages. The physical separation of home from work and the outward movement from the city centres encouraged the development of new kinds of social life, with the home becoming, for women, the centre of existence.

> It was of the essence of the new code of conduct that social interaction should be ordered and regulated by a ritual of 'calls', 'At Homes', teas, dinners and parties, and not left to possibly embarrassing chance encounters. This therefore implied that the house itself should be as separate as possible from its neighbours and, at all costs, from neighbouring areas of an inferior social status. For these reasons, terraces became increasingly out of favour as the century progressed, and the detached house increasingly the ideal; the semi-detached was a compromise solution typically employed in the inner suburbs where land costs were relatively high.
>
> (Burnett 1986, p105)

Victorian villas were primarily of brick construction, with bay windows and a fair degree of ornamentation, including turrets, finials and chimney stacks. Gardens were frequently large with the plot consisting of half an acre or more. In most large cities, large suburbs of villas were developed, such as Brondesbury in London, Mossley Hill in Liverpool and Edgbaston in Birmingham. In some places, villas were developed several miles from the cities so that the middle classes could retreat entirely from the urban smoke and squalor. Liverpool businessmen built villas to the north in Waterloo and Blundellsands and to the west on the Wirral; on Clydeside, towns like Innellan, Helensburgh and Skelmorlie were developed in this period. Public transport — in the form of suburban railways and expanding tramway systems — now made such suburbs possible.

Not all middle class Victorian housing, however, was in the form of villas. In certain parts of the country, local traditions prevailed, none more so than the Scottish tradition of tenement building. Many of the middle class suburbs in the West End of Glasgow, therefore, were not villas or semi-villas but speculative estates of tenements, laid out mainly in gridiron fashion but often incorporating, as in the Hyndland development, squares of open space, bowling greens etc. Like the villas, the tenements were stone-built, with ornamental features such as oriel or bay windows, pillared doorways and tiled entrance halls and staircases. Some were very large, of seven, eight or more rooms but, because they were flatted, had no separate access to gardens or drying greens.

Working Class Housing

By any standards, the accommodation available to the working classes in the mid-nineteenth century was at best poor, at worst appalling. At its lowest level was the cellar dwelling, dark and damp, with virtually no natural light and often inhabited by recent immigrants to the city, unable to secure any alternative. The problem was at its worst in cities with high levels of immigration and in Liverpool, for example, the then Medical Officer of Health estimated that there were 40,000 people living in such dwellings around 1840. Most were below terraced housing, with a floor area of around 12 feet square and ceilings 6 feet in height.

Another house type — if cellar dwellings can be so described — and one similarly characteristic of cities like Liverpool was the court dwelling. In an attempt to cope with the rapid population growth, speculative builders built housing in blocks of around three storeys but arranged around courts. These courts were between six and fifteen feet wide, accessed through an archway or narrow passage and with the other end closed by the back or side of an adjacent building. They therefore formed culs-de-sac with narrow openings (Edwards 1981). Sometimes, courts were joined by alleys to make an interconnecting system of passage ways, which Burnett (1986) suggests became something like an irregular secondary street system. The courts were however, dark and dismal places which were subsequently attacked by the Victorian health reformers for their lack of fresh air and daylight.

Inseparably linked to the development of court housing was the spread of back-to-back housing, and the two frequently went together. These houses were built in double rows, but with each house having only one aspect, to the front. The rear and side walls were shared with other houses and there were no doors or windows except on the front face. As a result the houses could generally only be one room deep, as natural light could not penetrate to an inner room, and there was generally only one room per floor. In some instances, however, there were two, smaller, rooms on the upper floor (Figure 1.1).

The major problem with back-to-back housing was its lack of through ventilation in the absence of a rear door or windows. Consequently, they were much criticised by the health reformers.

> Confined communal space between the rows of houses may have encouraged socialising, gossip, child care and games but it adversely affected hygiene, since unsupervised and irregularly cleaned communal privies in close proximity to eating, sleeping and playing areas and to a shared water tap assisted the transmission of diseases in the congested maze of housing.
>
> (Rodger 1989, p34)

Back-to-back housing was geographically concentrated in the north of England, particularly in the West Riding of Yorkshire. By 1886, Leeds had 49,000 such houses, representing 71 per cent of the total, and built at densities of 70–80 per acre. Leeds back-to-backs, however, tended to be on the large side with a plot size of 15 feet square and with a cellar and attic as well as the two main storeys. In Sheffield rooms tended to be around 12 feet square (Burnett 1986).

During the mid to late nineteenth century, many cities, under pressure from their Medical Officers of Health, passed bye-laws which banned the building of further back-to-back housing. Such bye-laws came into effect in 1844 in Manchester, 1864 in Liverpool and 1876 in Birmingham. But in Yorkshire, back-to-back housing continued to be built, albeit with the introduction of basement toilets and restrictions on street widths, until 1937. At the time of writing, around 20,000 such dwellings still remain in Leeds and, at the present rate of renewal, are likely to remain in use until the end of the twenty-first century. With modernisation and improvement, back-to-backs have, somewhat ironically, found an important niche in the private housing market, forming an accessible first step on the ladder of home ownership.

Elsewhere in the north of England, working class housing took different forms. In Sunderland, such housing was built in rows of single-storey cottages, about 20 feet in width, comprising a large front room and, at the rear, a smaller room and a kitchen. By the mid-nineteenth century, extensions to the rear of the property, for a toilet or for an extra bedroom, were becoming common. Other urban concentrations of single storey housing, however, are almost unknown, although the design is not unlike early miners' housing.

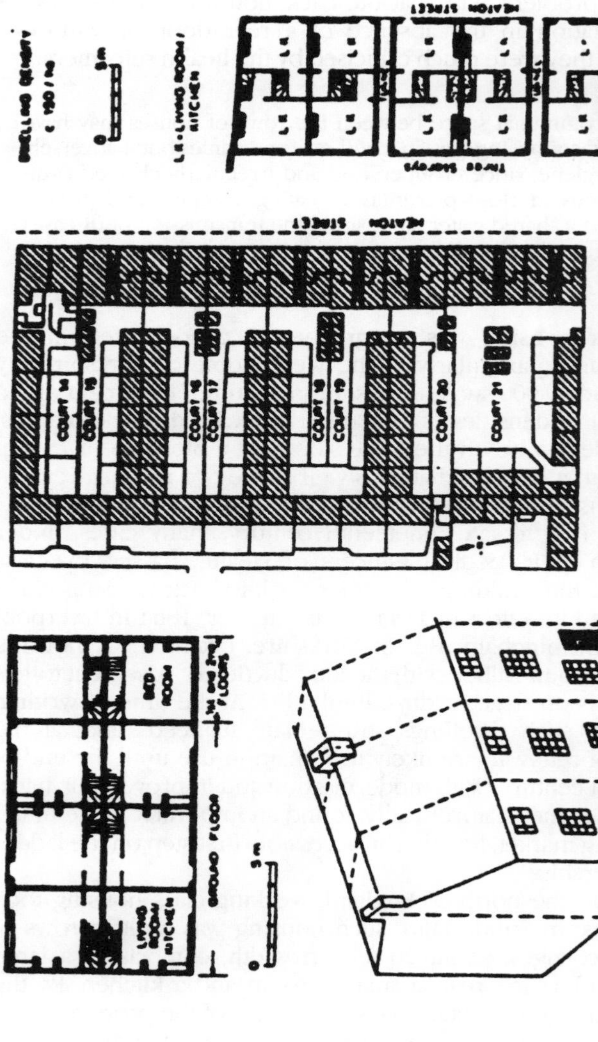

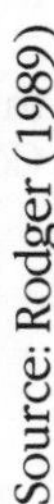

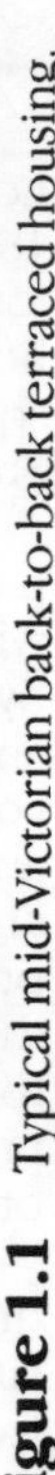

Figure 1.1 Typical mid-Victorian back-to-back terraced housing. Source: Rodger (1989)

The other house design characteristic of the north east — and constructed on a much wider scale — was the Tyneside flat. The type seems to have originated on the riverside where houses were crowded on the steep hillsides of Newcastle and Gateshead. A tendency for multi-storey structures emerged with the upper part of the property gaining access from the rear (Muthesius 1982, p130). The fashion spread and by the mid-nineteenth century, almost all working class housing was of this type. Indeed by 1911, almost two-thirds of Tyneside dwellings were flats.

The basic elements of the Tyneside flat were as follows. The street frontage consisted of one room, belonging to the ground floor flat, and two doors. One door led into the lower flat which would also have two rooms at the rear. The other door led straight on to a staircase, providing access to the upper flat which usually had an extra room (over the front door). Both flats had access through back doors and outside stairways, to a yard where the toilet was situated (Figure 1.2).

The type became common throughout Tyneside and as far north as Ashington in Northumberland. Many of the later properties were built with inside toilets and bathrooms for artisans and wealthier working class families, although the basic layout remained the same.

Flatted properties were similarly common north of the border. In Edinburgh, the Co-operative Building Society adopted a solution similar to the Tyneside flat but with the upper flats accessed through an external rather than an internal stair. In 1861, they developed a scheme of eleven parallel blocks in the Stockbridge area of the City with this upstairs–downstairs arrangement fairly reminiscent of the architecture of fishing villages (McWilliam 1975, p155). Known locally as 'colony' flats, there are examples in other parts of Edinburgh such as Gorgie and Abbeyhill.

The characteristic Scottish house type is, however, the tenement, stone-built and of three or four but sometimes five storeys. The origins of the Scottish tenement seem to lie in the country's feudal system of land tenure, although some debate still surrounds this issue (Daunton 1983). Essentially the original owner or 'feu superior' would grant land to a vassal in return for a fixed annual feu duty or ground rent. If the ground rent was high, then the erection of cottages at a reasonable rent would be simply uneconomic and it became necessary to build at a higher density. In addition, building costs in Scotland were higher than in England, and this would have encouraged speculators to build at high densities, to maximise rental income and hence profits.

Tenements were built, like terraced houses, in long rows with, at intervals, an entrance leading directly off the street into a communal passageway called the 'close'. Ground floor flats were accessed from

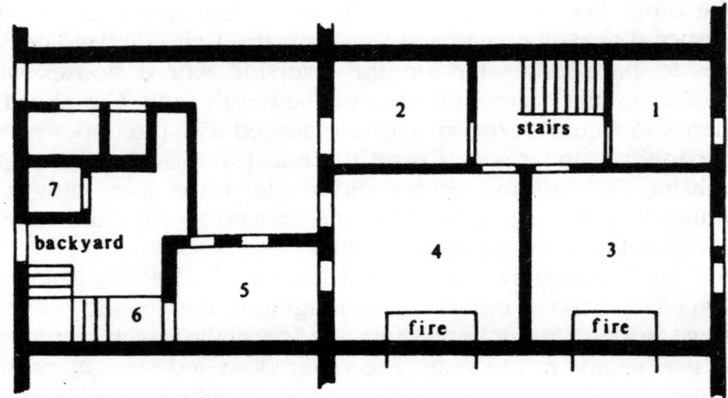

Plans of Tyneside flats in Park Terrace, Swalwell
Upstairs accommodation comprising front bedroom (1), back bedroom (2), main bedroom (3), living room (4), kitchen or scullery (5), and the backyard in which is situated the coalhouse (6) and toilet (7).

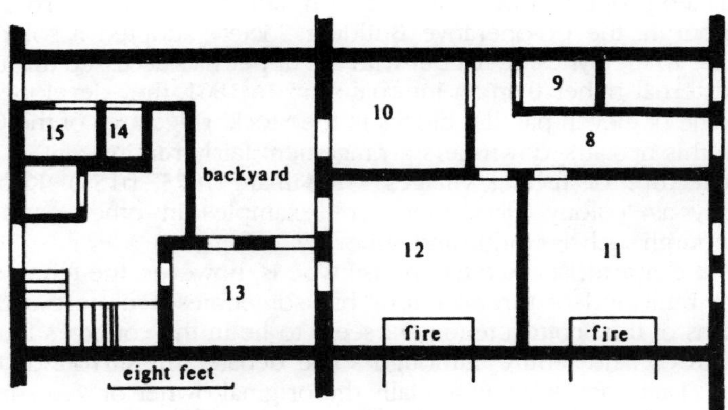

Downstairs accommodation comprising the passage (8), cupboard under the stairs (9), back bedroom (10), front bedroom (11), living room (12), kitchen (13), and the backyard in which is situated the coalhouse (14) and the toilet (15).

Figure 1.2 Source: Turnbull & Womack (nd)

the close, while at the rear was the main stairway providing access to the upper storeys. It was common for between four and six flats to be served by each landing so that one tenement close could consist of around 20 flats. The average house size was small, being frequently of one or two rooms; in Glasgow, one-roomed flats were known as 'single-ends', although they were often not at the ends but in the middle of the landings. In the 1970s when the comprehensive rehabilitation of such tenements began, the single-end was frequently split, to provide bathrooms for the two-roomed flats on either side (Figure 1.3).

The cramped internal conditions and the overshadowing effect of adjacent tenements combined to create living conditions of appalling quality. The properties were dark, poorly ventilated and had the absolute minimum in terms of sanitation. 'Water pumping and storage were expensive in tenements and this contrasted strongly with the ground level supplies available to English terraced houses. Until the 1880s therefore, WCs were usually located at ground level, one or at best two being shared by the entire tenement.' (Rodger 1989, p37). Later, brick lavatory towers were added to the backs of tenements to provide toilets on each landing, many surviving almost to the present day.

Health Legislation and Bye-Law Housing

Although Britain had evolved a rich variety of different types of working class housing, they were all characterised by deficiencies of light, ventilation and sanitation. Throughout the mid-Victorian period, therefore, newly appointed Medical Officers of Health joined with reformers like Edwin Chadwick and the Poor Law Board to press for legislation on public health and standards of building.

Some local legislation was passed during the 1840s, culminating in the 1848 Public Health Act. The Act is generally regarded as the first step in the reform of sanitary legislation and it provided for the establishment of local Boards of Health in individual towns, as well as providing a national framework for local legislation — 'bye-laws' — which could follow the national model. Ten years later, the Local Government Act 1858 laid down strict conditions regarding street widths, and this had important effects on town plans and housing layouts. But still no regulations existed which would prevent a speculative builder from building back-to-back housing or which would make it mandatory for rooms to be of a minimum size, although gradually the quality of the housing itself was becoming a major political issue.

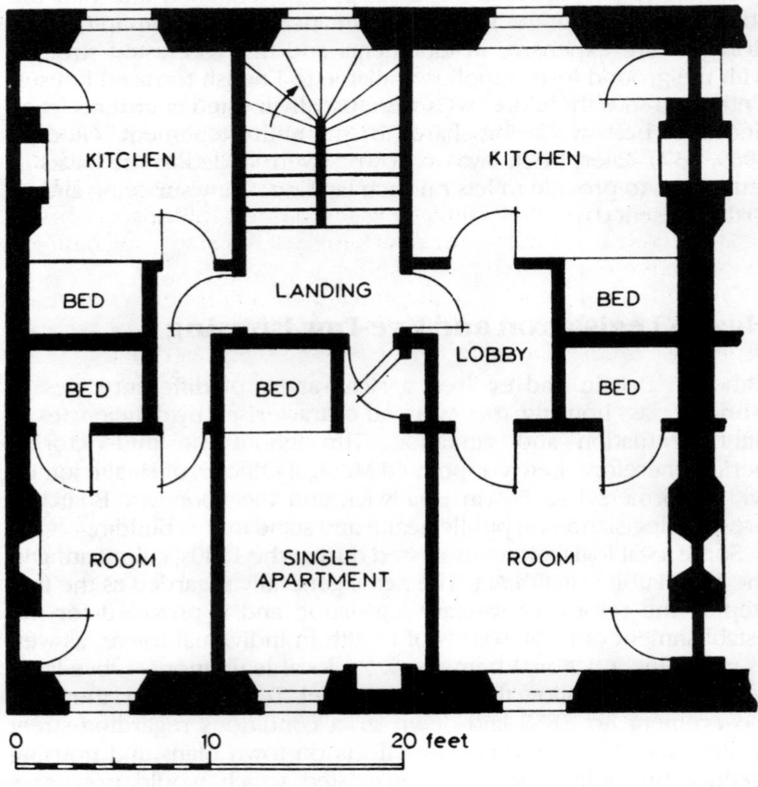

Figure 1.3 Upper floor plan of a typical Victorian working-class tenement. There was no internal sanitation in this example.
Source: Worsdall (1979)

Following local legislation promoted by Manchester City Council in 1867, the first bye-laws came into being, regulating the building of new houses in Manchester, laying down minimum sizes for rooms and windows and providing for space around the house. Finally, eight years later, the Public Health Act 1875 was passed and a major landmark in housing standards was reached.

Section 157 of the Act empowered (but not compelled) local authorities to make bye-laws with regard to street widths, the construction of new buildings, the regulation of space around them, and their sanitation. The Government produced a set of model bye-laws as a guide to local authorities and these were circulated in 1877 by the Local Government Board as its 'New Code of Model Bye-Laws'.

The model bye-laws required that almost all new streets had to be at least 36 feet wide and had to have a side opening within a 100 yard stretch. These relatively wide streets with frequent intersections were intended to aid the circulation of air within a housing development. New housing had to have an open space such as a yard at the rear of the building (thus preventing back-to-back housing) and a minimum space between the rear of the house and the premises opposite. In practice, not all authorities adopted such bye-laws and those that did frequently watered down their provisions. It was this leniency which allowed back-to-back housing to be built for so long in the West Riding of Yorkshire.

During the last decades of the nineteenth century therefore, new housing development consisted almost exclusively of what became known as 'bye-law housing'. Much criticised in later years for its monotony, such housing took the form of repetitive terraces, the houses generally opening directly off the street and with small walled yards at the rear, containing an outside toilet and shed. The yard would normally have a back gate opening on to a lane, or 'ginnel' as it was sometimes called in parts of northern England (Figure 1.4). These rear access arrangements could be highly variable, with wide road-like accesses in parts of the north giving way to narrow, often tortuous, alleys in the south. Where these back lanes were fairly wide, residents tended to use them for normal access to their houses, while the main streets and front doors were used only for special occasions such as weddings and funerals.

Internally, houses were generally not large. They were between 15 and 20 feet wide with a front and a back room and a small kitchen or scullery projecting into the back yard. A staircase facing the front door led up to two bedrooms upstairs, although in some houses there was a third bedroom extending over the kitchen. There were still no internal bathrooms. In the 1960s and 1970s such neighbourhoods were frequently declared General Improvement Areas and modernised with internal bathrooms (Gibson and Langstaff 1982).

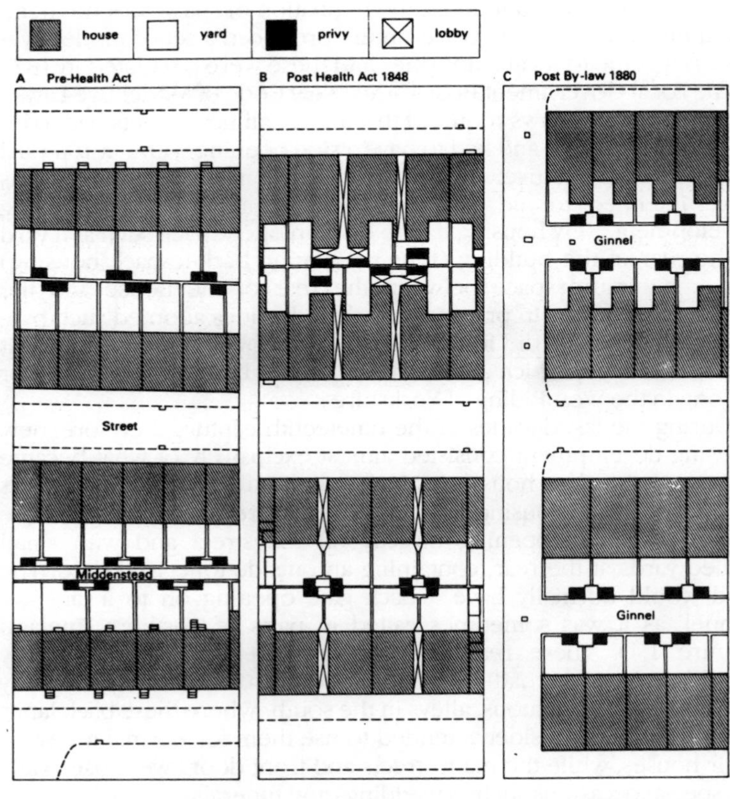

A: With privies in back yards, reached either through the houses (top), or by way of a middenstead (bottom).

B: Post 1848 Health Act, with privies reached by lobbies between every two houses leading to yards.

C: Post 1880 bye-laws, with privies in back yards reached by back lanes or ginnels.

Figure 1.4 Three layouts of houses in Preston.
Source: Quiney (1989)

Bye-law housing is familiar to us on our television screens in 'Coronation Street'.

Although there is undoubtedly a uniformity and monotony about bye-law housing, the model bye-laws were important as a first attempt to ensure that new housing then being built was at least healthy, adequately constructed and well ventilated.

Early Philanthropy – Industrial Housing

At the same time that health reformers like Chadwick were campaigning for legislative change, others were beginning to take the initiative in the actual provision of better quality housing for the working classes. Partly, this was due to the need for decent houses for one's own workforce but partly it was from acts of philanthropy.

One of the early philanthropists was George Peabody, an American, who in 1862 created the Peabody Trust, aimed at benefiting the London poor, particularly in the area of housing. The following year, the Trustees (mainly business associates and colleagues) acquired a site in Spitalfields and work began on a block of shops and dwellings. The building was four storeys high with shops on the ground floor, housing (mostly two-roomed flats) above and with communal lavatories and washing facilities. The Trustees apparently argued that communal lavatories were sensible because they were capable of easy supervision and as they were not situated near living areas they helped to create a healthier environment (Tarn 1973, p46). After Spitalfields, further developments followed at Islington, Shadwell, Westminster and Chelsea. All the estates were tenemental in style and all had a rather grim and forbidding outward appearance.

It is important to note, however, that, despite the barrack-like design, the developments were significant steps towards improved housing provision:

> The importance of this group of estates built by a new agency was undoubtedly much greater at the time they were built than would now appear. First, because they were so much larger than any previous venture either philanthropic or commercial; secondly, because they set a standard of accommodation and construction which established a definite point of view . . .; thirdly, because Peabody made his gift at a psychologically sound time when men were looking for fresh inspiration to continue striving for better

> conditions and when the poor themselves needed to see that someone cared for their wellbeing.
>
> (Tarn 1973, p47)

Parallel with the work of the Peabody Trust was that of Sydney Waterlow, who founded in 1863 the Improved Industrial Dwellings Company. A politician, and later Lord Mayor of London, Waterlow was concerned with social problems and built a small block of dwellings in 1863 in Finsbury. Later developments were larger, tenemental in form but linear, often occupying the sites of former terraced housing, but on a grander scale. The Company did not, however, develop such large housing schemes as the Peabody Trust.

Nevertheless, the contribution of the Company to the numerical solution of London's housing problem was important. Tarn (1973) indicates that by 1895, the Peabody Trust had built 5,100 houses, the Improved Industrial Dwellings Company 5,350 and the Artisans', Labourers' and General Dwellings Company, founded by the builder William Austin, 6,500.

Outwith London, however, the picture was fairly bleak with a general lack of activity in the provision of working class housing. The exception to this was in the establishment of company towns, such new settlements being necessary in order to attract labour to new factory sites outside existing towns. Across the north of England and South Wales were numerous instances of cottages for miners and millworkers but early examples were often of fairly poor quality.

By the 1840s, however, employers were becoming more enlightened, none more so than the newly established railway companies. Railway towns like Swindon, Crewe, Wolverton and Eastleigh sprang up alongside junctions and engine works. In Crewe, there was an hierarchical system of housing provision ranging from villa-style houses for the senior management to small cottages for labourers, but all were of good quality and design, with almost all houses having gardens:

> . . . even in the 1870s, after much speculative building to standards well below the railway's had begun to crowd in the centre, the people of Crewe boasted proudly that they had no slums — unlike Chester and Nantwich. The railway had discovered at the very beginning that if they wanted anything, they would have to provide it, and so had laid on sewerage and water, gas and roads, education, refuse-collection, even policemen. All this meant that in the 1840s Crewe represented the ideal against which men like Chadwick judged the squalor of the rest of industrial England
>
> (Bell and Bell 1972, p202)

Elsewhere, as in Swindon and Wolverton, houses tended to be

terraced with access to a back lane and often with fairly wide streets. Although constructed in the 1840s and 1850s, they were of a quality which was not generally seen elsewhere until the better bye-law housing began to be built in the 1880s.

Later Philanthropy — the Company Town

The railway companies were not alone, however, in recognising the need for workers to be adequately housed. There were other Victorian industrialists who had realised the importance of good quality housing. Thus:

> In the second half of the century several schemes were pioneered which were larger both in scale and in concept, sometimes involving the total planning of new communities on utopian lines, and designed not only to ensure to the employer an efficient and contented labour force, but to point the way towards a new relationship of capital and labour and the creation of a new kind of physical environment in which men and machines could live harmoniously together.
>
> (Burnett 1986, p179)

Among the earliest examples of such schemes are two model villages built near Halifax by local mill-owner Edward Akroyd. The first, Copley, was largely comprised of terraced back-to-back housing although with gardens and allotments and accompanied by a school, library and local church. The second village, Akroydon, was more ambitious and was designed in a Gothic style by George Gilbert Scott. Housing was ranged around a village green and was stone built with slate roofs. Room sizes were fairly generous with a living room of 15 feet by 13 feet, a scullery and two bedrooms, one of 15 feet by 11 feet and one of 11 feet by 6½ feet. Later houses had parlours and extra bedrooms (Burnett 1986). All had small yards, accessed from a back lane, the pattern which later became typical of bye-law housing.

Not far from Halifax, one of Akroyd's contemporaries, Titus Salt, had recently completed new mills on the outskirts of Bradford in 1853. Anxious to surround his mill with accommodation for his workers, Salt had acquired an adjacent site, on which his architects laid out a settlement of 22 streets, 805 houses, churches, public baths, hospital and school. Taking its name from its founder and the adjacent river, the village was christened Saltaire. Houses were of different sizes (of two, three and four bedrooms) reflecting the different sizes of family, and this helped to provide enough variety to avoid monotony of design. Each house had a living room of 14 feet by 13 feet, a scullery, and sometimes, a parlour, in addition to the bedrooms. Most had an outside lavatory and few had gardens.

In almost complete contrast to Saltaire was the village of Bromborough on the Wirral, founded in 1853 by the Price's Patent Candle Company, recently relocated from Battersea. Although small, consisting of a mere seventy-six houses, they had the distinction of being semi-detached or in blocks of four, as opposed to the more usual terraced design. Internally the houses had a living room, kitchen and scullery and two or three bedrooms above and, in that respect, were similar to Saltaire. But all had front and back gardens and the generous open-space provision, with also a cricket field and bowling green, provides Bromborough with a claim to be the first garden suburb. The village remained a company settlement until 1987 when it was handed over to Merseyside Improved Houses.

The provision of open space for gardening, sport and recreation was increasingly seen as important for the creation of a healthy workforce and later settlements tended to be 'greener', and at lower densities. Close to Bromborough was the village of Port Sunlight, founded by the soap manufacturer William Lever, where such trends could be seen. Founded in 1888, the first housing was completed the following year, the settlement taking its name from its founder's most successful brand of soap. By 1909, 720 houses had been built although building continued into the 1920s. At the time of Lever's death in 1925, the village consisted of 890 houses, plus village hall, schools, churches, shops, hotel, cottage hospital and, perhaps most famously, a Technical Institute and the Lady Lever Art Gallery. The scale of Port Sunlight was remarkable.

A number of architects worked on the village over the years, including Sir Edwin Lutyens, but mostly architects were local, and all combined to produce a harmonious whole, albeit one which harks back to some 'Olde England' past. 'Although built for industrial workers [the houses] have the appearance of country cottages, the dwellings of the English yeoman or tenant farmer. Lever aspired to recreate the conditions of an idyllic rural past where a man's home and work were not irrevocably apart, but were two aspects of one contented life' (Sellers 1988, p16).

Originally, all the houses were to have been semi-detached with gardens, but the demand for accommodation prevented this and a number of small terraces were built. Allotments were provided to compensate for the loss of garden space. There were two main types of house, the 'kitchen' house and the 'parlour' house. The former had a kitchen/living room, plus scullery, with three bedrooms upstairs, the latter had an extra room — the parlour — downstairs and four bedrooms above. The dimensions of the rooms were around 14 feet by 12 feet and might seem rather cramped by today's standards. Indeed where houses have been sold, those buying have tended to be childless professionals and retired people. Only in the last twenty-five years was there a renovation programme on the estate which included the installation of bathrooms and central heating. Port Sunlight's importance in both housing and architectural terms was recognised in 1965 when the houses became Grade II listed, and the whole village became a conservation area in 1978 (Barker 1990).

Similar in form to Port Sunlight was Bournville, the Birmingham suburb which was the creation of the chocolate manufacturer George Cadbury. It was never the intention, however, that all the housing should be occupied by Cadbury employees; on the contrary the estate which was developed was open to working men and their families from all over Birmingham.

Initially, in 1879, sixteen cottages were built adjacent to the factory. These, like the later dwellings developed on the estate, were grouped in pairs or threes, set back from tree-lined roads and each with their own gardens. Behind each cottage was a vegetable garden with fruit trees. All houses had living room, three bedrooms, and either a kitchen or scullery, but some also had a parlour, and all had internal sanitation. The first houses were available for sale, with mortgages made available, but later, housing was built for rent. Almshouses were also built, and numerous communal facilities, including shops, churches and an Arts and Crafts Institute. By 1900, the settlement had changed from the Bournville Building Estate to a garden village and this was reflected in the setting up of the Bournville Village Trust to safeguard Cadbury's legacy (Henslowe 1984).

Finally the ideas which had been developed at Port Sunlight and Bournville by Lever and Cadbury were taken a stage further at New Earswick, a model village outside York developed by Joseph Rowntree. Once again, houses were grouped with gardens rather than being built in long straight terraces, but the layout was adapted by the architect, Raymond Unwin, to make sympathetic use of the site and to ensure that houses faced the sun. Thus, 'the traditional plan for narrow-fronted terrace houses was therefore abandoned in favour of wider frontages, which allowed a better organisation of space and took advantage of sun and light' (Burnett 1986, p183). Total floor area of the houses was just over 1000 square feet.

The turn of the century was thus characterised by new directions in housing design and an increasing recognition of the need to provide good quality working class housing, spacious internally and more imaginative in layout. There was still an order about these settlements and the anti-urban attitudes displayed in Port Sunlight and Bournville 'owed more to the picturesqueness of Kate Greenaway than to the urbanism of Dickens' (Higgins 1986). Nevertheless the work of Lever, Cadbury and Rowntree paved the way for the garden city idealists who were soon to arrive on the scene.

Ebenezer Howard and the Garden City Movement

The 'invention' of the garden city is usually ascribed to Ebenezer Howard, although Howard himself may have been influenced partly by contemporary ideas such as those proposed by Edward Bellamy regarding ideal communities and socialist societies and partly by the movement towards 'people's parks' within the city, such as Joseph Paxton's development in Birkenhead.

In 1898, Howard published a pamphlet entitled *Tomorrow: A Peaceful Path to Real Reform*. It was well received and in 1902 was republished as *Garden Cities of Tomorrow*. Howard began by discussing the problems of overcrowding and congestion which characterised the larger cities, particularly London. He accepted that such cities presented opportunities for employment and high wages but felt that such advantages were counterbalanced by the poor quality of the housing, the lack of sunlight and the pollution. Nevertheless, the cities provided an enormous magnet for people from the country and there was substantial movement away from rural areas. This in turn led to problems of depopulation and shortages of agricultural labour.

Howard's solution was to try and balance the advantages of both town and country in a series of new settlements. Although built as towns, they would contain sufficient open space and greenery to make them rural in character. They would be 'garden cities'. He illustrated his proposal in his now-famous diagram of three magnets with the 'Town–Country' magnet having the best of both worlds (Figure 1.5),

> Human Society and the beauty of nature are meant to be enjoyed together. The two magnets must be made one. As man and woman by their varied gifts and faculties supplement each other, so should town and country. The town is the symbol of society — of mutual help and friendly co-operation, of fatherhood, motherhood, brotherhood, sisterhood, ... of science, art, culture and religion .... The country is the symbol of God's love and care for man. All that we are and all that we have comes from it .... But its fullness of joy and wisdom has not revealed itself to man. Nor can it ever, so long as this unholy, unnatural separation of society and nature endures. Town and country **must be married**, and out of this joyous union will spring a new hope, a new life, a new civilisation.
>
> (Howard 1985 edition, p11)

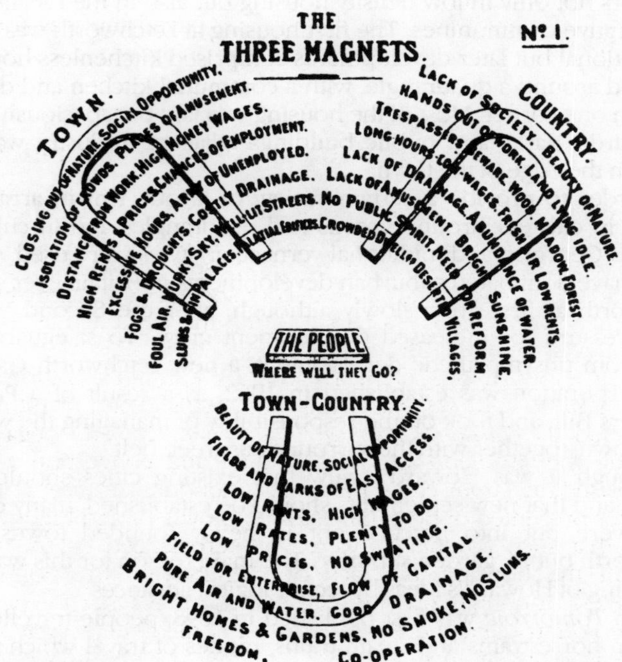

Figure 1.5 Howard's three-magnet diagram. Source: Howard (1989 edition)

Howard suggested that cities should grow not through the addition of suburbs but through the establishment of satellite settlements —'garden cities' — each with a population of around 30,000 and with its own industries, shops and community buildings. He suggested that such a city would cover 1,000 acres, could be circular in form and with grand boulevards leading from centre to circumference. Such a city would have 5,500 building plots, of an average size of 20 feet by 130 feet. This was around half the size of the average plots at Bournville.

Howard's ideas had a profound effect upon British town planning, and were first put into practice in 1903, five years after the publication of his book, with the founding of Letchworth Garden City. A new philanthropic company, First Garden City Limited, was set up, and the architects selected for the task of developing this new settlement were Raymond Unwin and Barry Parker.

Unwin and Parker had been responsible for the design of Rowntree's model village of New Earswick, near York. They were firm believers not only in low density housing but also in the idealism of co-operative communities. The first housing at Letchworth was fairly conventional but later developments comprised kitchenless housing grouped around a quadrangle, with a communal kitchen and dining room in one corner. Most of the housing was laid out spaciously with boulevards, parks and public buildings adjacent. Industry was located on the edge of the town.

In order to provide a certain variety of layout, Unwin arranged houses in clusters, around greens and quadrangles and in culs-de-sac. Neo-Georgian and traditional vernacular styles were used, styles which have dominated suburban developments in Britain ever since. Letchworth at first grew slowly although, after the Second World War, pressure for increased development grew. To safeguard the town from unsympathetic development, a new Letchworth Garden City Corporation was established in 1962, as a result of a Private Members Bill, and took on the responsibility of managing the whole of the town, together with the surrounding green belt.

Although it was Howard's view that existing cities should not expand and that new settlements should be established, many of his ideas were put into practice not in newly founded towns like Letchworth but in 'garden suburbs'. The main reason for this was the overtaking of Howard's ideas by technological advances.

When *Tomorrow* was first published in 1898, people travelled to work on horse trams and steam trains, modes of travel which were often slow, dirty and uncomfortable. Long distance commuting was only possible for a very few who could afford it and there was therefore a certain logic about self-contained satellite communities. But technology began to change.

> ... in 1890, the first of London's electric underground lines was opening, in 1888 Dunlop patented the pneumatic tyre and in 1887, Gottlieb Daimler ran his first car. These three devices (together with the electric traction which expanded greatly during the next ten years) invalidated Howard's technological premises. Electric traction and the motor vehicle made it possible for all but the poorest workers to have a house with a garden some miles from office or factory. Suburbia ceased to be the prerogative of the few ... and the garden suburb, not the garden city, became the typical housing pattern of the twentieth century.
>
> (Edwards 1981, pp83–4)

Perhaps the best known of these garden suburbs was Hampstead, designed like Letchworth by Unwin and Parker but in collaboration with architects such as Edwin Lutyens. The suburb was generously laid out, making full use of the hilly site, with its wooded areas on the edge of the heath. Generally though it was at higher densities than

Letchworth, because the area was smaller (240 acres); and the higher price of land necessitated the building of more houses. Dwellings were grouped around open squares and culs-de-sac, in the Letchworth fashion. Such garden suburbs were frequently promoted as co-partnership housing societies, with an emphasis on community life and co-operation. The movement was particularly widespread in the early years of the century, under the leadership of Henry Vivian MP, and garden suburbs were established in most large cities.

A good example of the garden suburb and the contrast which it provided to the bye-law housing of twenty years previously, is provided by Wavertree in Liverpool, where the Liverpool Garden City Association established a development in 1910. Figure 1.6 shows the layout of the first part of the suburb, built on a 20 acre site at 11 houses per acre, together with the layout which would have resulted, had the same area been laid out to meet bye-law requirements. The diagrams were used at the time to illustrate the spaciousness of the garden city approach. Interestingly, the street layout of Wavertree involved the use of culs-de-sac half way along one of the main roads, called Northway. This was because the relevant Liverpool bye-law prevented the construction of any new street longer than 150 yards (which Northway was) without at least one intersecting street. The bye-law, designed to prevent monotony in terraced houses, was therefore applied in quite different circumstances from those envisaged at the time of its introduction.

Before leaving the issue of garden cities, mention must be made of those settlements developed in relation to new military establishments, of which perhaps the best example is Rosyth on the Firth of Forth. The site was chosen for a new naval dockyard in 1903, and in 1913 Raymond Unwin was appointed by the Admiralty to prepare a plan for the new housing, based on garden city principles. Once again, the housing was of low density, around 10 houses per acre, and every house had a garden, something that was relatively uncommon in Scotland at that time. During the First World War, nearly 1,900 houses were completed by a new body, the Scottish National Housing Company, which later went through various changes to become the Scottish Special Housing Association (SSHA). A similar organisation in the north east of England, North Eastern Housing Association, subsequently became North Housing.

The importance of Rosyth lay in the fact that Unwin was, once again, able to test out his ideas about planning and design and this was one of the projects which he conceived immediately prior to the setting up of the Tudor–Walters Committee discussed in Chapter Two. 'Curiously, however, despite the pleasant architectural character of the houses, the trees, pretty front gardens and studious avoidance of straight streets, the houses at Rosyth were not at first

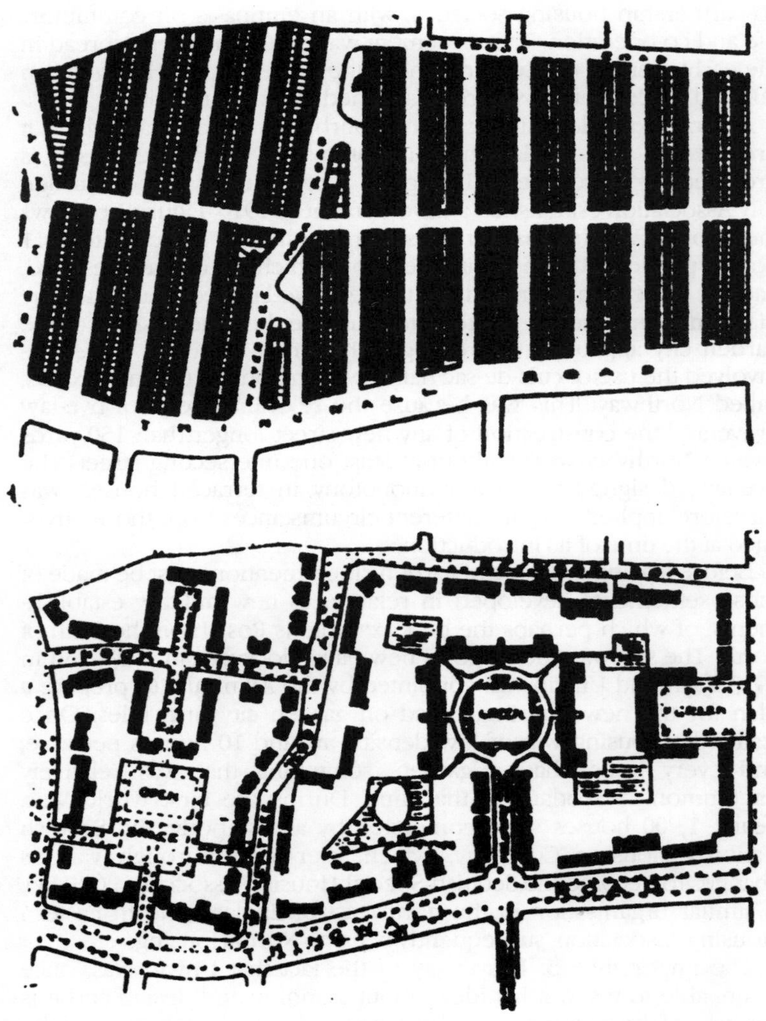

Figure 1.6 Conventional versus garden city layout: a 20-acre site in Liverpool (above) as it might have been, laid out to meet bye-law requirements, at 41 houses per acre; (below) as it was, laid out as a garden suburb at 11 houses per acre. Source: Swenarton (1981)

popular with the tenants who complained that the rooms were awkwardly shaped and that the terraced houses had no rear access' (Begg 1987, p48). Tastes change, of course, and today Rosyth is a conservation area with high levels of 'right-to-buy' sales.

Early Council Housing and the LCC

Eight years before Ebenezer Howard published *Tomorrow*, the Housing of the Working Classes Act of 1890 had given extended powers to local authorities to act in housing matters. The strongest parts of the Act related to London where the housing problem was deemed to be most critical. Local authorities there were empowered to buy land for improvement schemes and they were obliged to rehouse at least half of those displaced by demolition. Importantly, the Act could be made to work effectively because of the creation two years earlier of a new system of local government including the London County Council (LCC).

The LCC formed, in 1893, a new group within its Architects Department, called the Housing of the Working Classes Branch, which became extremely powerful. 'Excited by the Socialist philosophy of William Morris and its architectural expression in the buildings of Philip Webb and the teaching and writing of W.R. Lethaby they understood how radically the stock and terrible predicament of the poor in Victorian cities could be changed by architectural means.' (Beattie 1980, p9).

The first test of their idealism soon came in plans for the Boundary Street area in Bethnal Green, where proposals to clear the slums had been agreed in 1890. Originally, it had been intended that the replacement housing would be arranged in tenement blocks, similar to the Peabody and Waterlow estates elsewhere in the capital and that the streets would be laid out in a rectangular, gridiron fashion. But a new scheme was then put forward, to replan the area on a radial basis with housing arranged along tree-lined avenues radiating from a central circus (Figure 1.7). Quite apart from the improved environment which would be created, more housing could be built at a slightly reduced cost. The main approach road was 60 feet wide, the other six avenues fifty feet wide and secondary streets forty feet. Earth displaced from the foundations of the housing was used to build a raised garden in the circus. A bandstand was provided here to provide a focus for the community (Beattie 1980).

The flats ranged from one to four rooms, although half were of two rooms. They were therefore not large but the importance of Boundary Street was the attempt to raise standards of space, layout

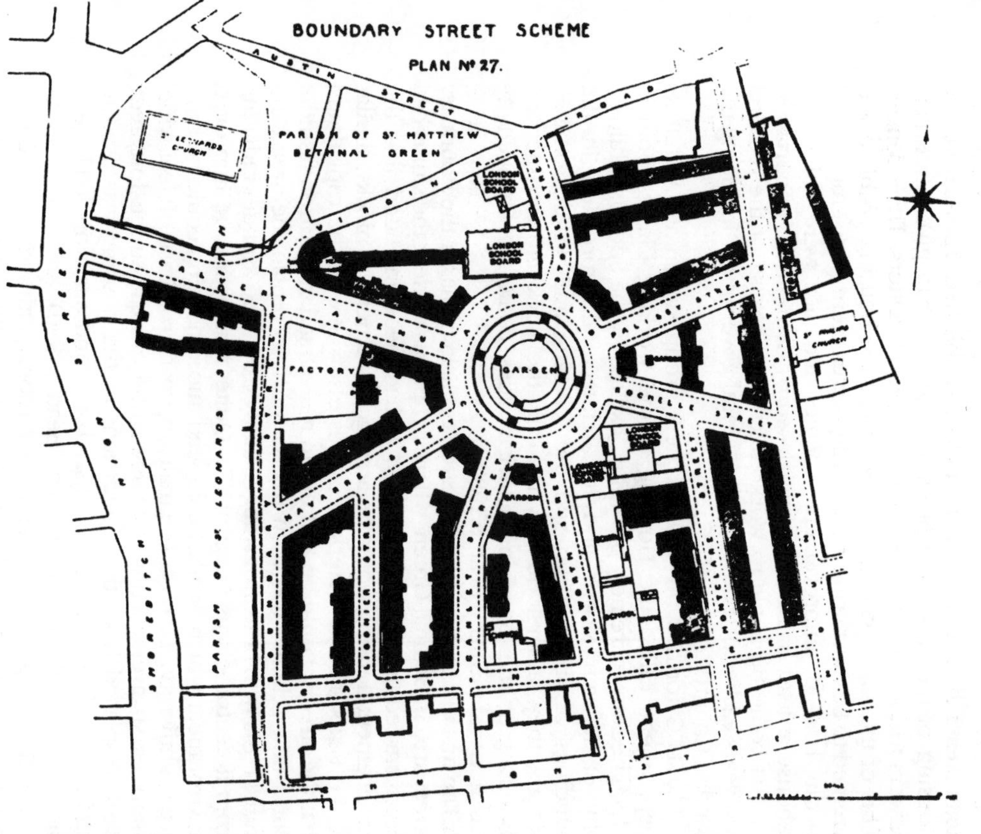

Figure 1.7 The Boundary Street Estate, Tower Hamlets. Source: Beattie (1980)

and amenity, to provide vistas and to get away as much as possible from the barrack-like appearance of early tenement blocks.

The LCC continued to experiment with similar housing in other inner city areas but in 1898 it took the decision that in future schemes it would attempt to rehouse all those displaced by demolition. Clearly this was impossible to achieve on the same site and it therefore pointed the way to the growth of suburban estates for those who were forced to move from the old slums.

LCC estates of this period were able to draw on the garden city ideas then being developed and some of the housing was copied directly from suburbs such as Hampstead. Nevertheless, tight financial controls restricted what could be achieved and while the density of housing in the early garden cities and suburbs was around 10 per acre, on the LCC estates, it was anything between 21 and 32.

> Yet, steering a middle course between their own well-tried and practical vernacular style and the picturesque conceits of the model villages, listening to the reforms preached by Ebenezer Howard and Raymond Unwin . . . [the LCC] created a modified form of garden city that introduced thousands of working class people to a new style of life and is no less remarkable a contribution to the movement for having gone largely unrecognised within it.
>
> (Beattie 1980, p89)

Early examples of LCC estates were Totterdown Fields, in Tooting, laid out in the early 1900s, and the White Hart Lane Estate in Tottenham, developed between 1904 and 1914. In the latter there was an increasing use of features recommended by Parker and Unwin including bay windows and projections to allow for variations to the frontage. The later part of the scheme was grouped around a miniature village green to create a community 'feel' to the area. Densities were around 25 to the acre, less than in Totterdown with 31.

The estate which is often seen as the pre-war culmination of the work of the LCC is the Old Oak Estate in Hammersmith. Work began around 1911, by which time the influence of garden suburbs like Hampstead could be clearly seen. Nevertheless, the size of the houses was limited to three or four rooms, partly because of cost constraints and partly in order to keep rents low for working families, and the estate had only a limited value in rehousing large overcrowded households.

The houses had gardens, and there was plenty of open space and greenery, but the internal layout was cramped. Living rooms were around 12 feet by 13 feet, the kitchen/scullery at the rear would be around 8 feet by 9 feet and there were two bedrooms of similar dimensions upstairs. The 'two up, two down' arrangement was, ironically enough, reminiscent of the older bye-law housing, on which these suburban estates were supposed to be an improvement. One great advancement, however, was in sanitation and the LCC had ensured that all houses possessed a toilet, although not all had a bathroom.

Conclusion

Despite the work of the health reformers and the influence of the garden city movement on housing design, the bulk of British housing was in a shocking state. What finally brought the problem home to central government was the introduction of conscription in 1916 and the poor health of many of the conscripts. By the last year of the First World War, four in ten conscripts were being deemed unfit for military service. There was, therefore, an increasing debate about the condition of the nation's housing stock and, more importantly, the type of new housing which should be built once hostilities had ceased.

A national housing policy was clearly needed and one of the first areas to be looked at was the question of housing density, a recognition of the health problems caused by overcrowding. A Select Committee was appointed under the Chairmanship of Sir John Tudor-Walters MP, and it reported in 1918. The Report and its influence are discussed in Chapter Two.

Chapter 2
The interwar period

Introduction

The recognition during the First World War, of the enormous housing problems which beset the nation, grew. Quite apart from the health issue and the unfitness of many working class people, there was a numerical shortage of houses. Secondly, those houses that existed were in appalling condition and there was a growing belief that the private sector had failed to match people's housing aspirations. When Lloyd George famously declared that he intended to build 'homes fit for heroes', it was to the public sector, after 1919, that he increasingly looked.

This chapter begins by examining the Tudor-Walters Report of 1918, which focused on housing design, and which led to the advice on new housing developments which was issued to local authorities after the 1919 Addison Act. There is discussion of different house types within the public sector and of the speculative private house building which led to the widespread development of the semi-detached house and the bungalow. The spread of European influence in the Modern Movement is also considered, and the chapter ends with reference to the problems of building shortage which occurred at the end of the period, with the outbreak of the Second World War.

The Tudor-Walters Report

In 1917, a Committee was set up 'to consider questions of building construction in connection with the provision of dwellings for the working classes in England, Wales and Scotland, and report upon methods of securing economy and despatch in the provision of such dwellings'. Sir John Tudor-Walters, a Liberal MP, was appointed Chairman and, importantly, one of the Committee members was Raymond Unwin, a leading architect who had been responsible for early garden city layouts such as Letchworth. The Report therefore drew on the experiences of model towns and garden cities and the ideas of Ebenezer Howard. It was published in the late autumn of 1918.

Although the Committee's brief had been to look at questions of building construction, it was interpreted extremely widely. They argued that the issue of housing supply could not be considered merely at a technical level but had to take account of the administrative framework for the housing programme. The Report recommended the establishment of a Housing Department within Whitehall, and a system of regional commissioners to stimulate and co-ordinate the work of local authorities. The Government should act immediately to stimulate production and give priority to housing in the use of the material available (Swenarton 1981).

The Report also focused in particular on the question of housing design. Perhaps this was unsurprising, given Unwin's membership of the Committee but it is significant that the two parts which were the second and third largest in terms of text length, as well as being the only two to contain illustrations, both dealt with design (Markus 1988). The central design concerns addressed in the Report related to the house plan and to the range of rooms to be provided within the house. Part IV of the Report examined the type of accommodation required by the working classes and raised the issue of whether a parlour should be provided in addition to a living room and scullery. It recognised the genuine desire by families to have a parlour or third room downstairs and the flexibility which could result:

> . . . witnesses state that the parlour is needed to enable the older members of the family to hold social intercourse with their friends without interruption from the children, that it is required in the case of sickness in the house . . . that it is needed for the youth of the family in order that they may meet their friends; that it is generally required for home lessons by the children of school-age, or for similar work or study, serious reading or writing on the part of any member of the family; that it is also needed for occasional visitors . . . .

This represented the first official recognition of the different needs which existed within a family and the ways in which those needs could be accommodated.

The inclusion of a parlour was also recommended by the Women's Housing Sub-Committee, set up in 1917 largely at the instigation of the Women's Labour League. They argued that women should have the use of a separate parlour which, although not always in daily use, did provide a separate space in which to relax (Wilson 1991).

Another key issue was the provision of kitchen accommodation, although the word 'kitchen' was not one that was generally used. There were three alternatives proposed. The first was the combined kitchen and living room, with a small scullery off, mainly intended for food storage. The second was the working scullery, adjacent to the living room, where most of the cooking would be done but with the retention of a large grate in the living room which could also be used. The third was the entirely separate scullery sometimes divided from the living room by a lobby.

> Thus, the established nineteenth century concerns with housework, the woman's role and space in the household, hygiene and privacy, are focused onto three house types, which vary in the arrangements for good preparation and cooking (eating is given a quite subsidiary role, and is assumed, from comments about extra tables, etc, to take place in the living space). Over the next half century, all future planning recommendations, and house types, focus onto the same issue, and move further and further in the direction of removing food preparation from the living space into a specialised, well-equipped workspace.
>
> (Markus 1988, p38)

The Tudor-Walters Report therefore recommended that there should be a variety of house types to suit different needs. The Report advocated wide frontages, averaging 22½ feet, and that there should be an emphasis on light and air. While parlours were a reasonable expectation, they would not be provided in every house; nevertheless where there was only one living room, it should be a 'through' room running from front to back of the house and therefore with windows at each end.

The space standards recommended were 855 sq ft for a three-bedroomed, non-parlour house and 1,055 sq ft for a parlour type, excluding coal shed, storage etc. Bedrooms were to be of a reasonable size for families, the main one being around 150 sq ft and the others of 100 sq ft and at least 65 sq ft respectively. These sizes may be compared with those in the early LCC cottage estates such as Old Oak where the total net floor area was less than 700 sq ft.

In terms of estate layout, Tudor-Walters recommended a density of development no greater than 12 houses to the acre and advocated the use of culs-de-sac for preventing through traffic. There were added economic advantages in culs-de-sac, which could provide frontage for as many houses as a through road but allowed for savings of up to 50 per cent in road construction costs. The Report advocated also the use of a variety of house types to prevent monotony and, instead of access to back gardens being achieved by a rear lane, it was recommended that in the case of semi-detached housing side access be used and in the case of terraces, a tunnel should be provided through the centre of the frontage. Tudor-Walters advocated plenty of garden space and praised the American open garden system. But, 'recognising the public's desire for private gardens, most council estates achieved uniformity by means of a continuous meeting clipped privet hedge. Public open spaces were, however, deliberately incorporated into most estates to emulate the greens of village communities' (Barrett and Phillips 1987, p127).

In order to achieve maximum daylight, especially in winter, Tudor-Walters recommended that there should be a minimum of 70 feet between opposite houses, although it was recognised that this width could be reduced slightly in certain circumstances such as the accommodation of the road layout. In fact, although the layouts which resulted from the application of these standards were undoubtedly airy and spacious, there was the danger of monotony, something Tudor-Walters had been attempting to avoid. The 70 feet rule, for example, 'made it impossible to create the dramatic contrasts of the medieval town', while it could be argued that the Report's logic was in any case, shaky. 'It implied that there would be sunshine at noon and in mid-winter (and this at a time when pea-soup fogs occurred frequently), that there would be no trees between the houses to obscure sunlight . . . and that 'considerations of architectural effect' were of less importance that the winter insolation of certain rooms' (Edwards 1981, p106). The low density in relation to building height was a clear recipe for suburban sprawl.

Most of the Tudor-Walters Committee's recommendations were accepted by the Local Government Board, the central government department responsible for housing at the time. In 1919, the Board issued its *Manual on the Preparation of State Aided Housing Schemes* which contained guidance for local authorities based on Tudor-Walters principles. Indeed, the Manual was even more generous in its recommended space standards than the original report, at 900 sq ft for three-bedroomed, non-parlour houses and 1,080 sq ft for those with a parlour. Every house was to have an internal toilet, and a bath either in a bathroom or in the scullery; hot water was to be provided to the sink and to the bath.

The Manual was surprisingly detailed. It suggested that the living room should have few doors, so as to minimise discomfort to 'those occupying the space about window and fire'. The parlour, where provided, should have a westerly aspect. The larder, on the other hand, would be best sited on the northerly side of the house to keep the food cool. Bedrooms should, as far as possible, be on the sunnier side of the house. There was thus a careful consideration of aspect, design and layout, and there was an emphasis, outside the house, on the development of vistas within the street pattern.

Finally, there was an emphasis on 'economy'. Partly this meant economy in building, with careful planning of services such as water, drainage, chimney flues etc, but partly it meant economy in maintenance and there was an emphasis on the use of good quality, durable materials which would last (Gaskell 1986).

The Development of Council Housing: the 1920s

The Manual was issued to coincide with the implementation of the 1919 Addison Act, whereby the principle of state-aided housing was accepted, for the first time. Because there were no special cash incentives for slum clearance, housing provision was not especially targeted at slum dwellers or, indeed, the most needy. Instead, the emphasis was on providing good quality housing for general needs, mostly on cottage style estates. There was a belief that 'well-built artisan housing would enable better-off workers to vacate the slums, allowing densely overcrowded families to spread out.' (Power 1987, p23).

Initially, there were difficulties in achieving the housing targets — immediate need in 1919 had been put at 500,000 houses — because of building shortages. Some authorities therefore began to experiment with new materials such as concrete blocks as an alternative to the more traditional brick, while timber-framed and steel houses were also built. In fact, the shortage of materials was resolved around 1923, and as costs of construction began to fall, authorities quickly reverted to brick construction (Morgan 1989). The lower prices also enabled councils to build to more modest standards, at rents which lower-income families could afford.

Although most local authorities drew up their own plans for housing schemes, using their own architects and engineers, the Government's Design Manual was highly influential (Figure 2.1). Indeed, many authorities built to even higher standards:

> It is clear that in respect of space, Tudor-Walters and the LGB Manual recommendations were interpreted very liberally and often exceeded, the first Ministry of Health Report showing that subsidies were being granted for three-bedroomed houses of not less than 950 sq ft and up to as much as 1,400 sq ft, a size comparable with many 'middle-class' detached houses and considerably larger than most speculative semi-detacheds.
>
> (Burnett 1986, p227)

CLASS B. PAIR, Southerly Aspect.

Ministry of Health, Plan No. 164.

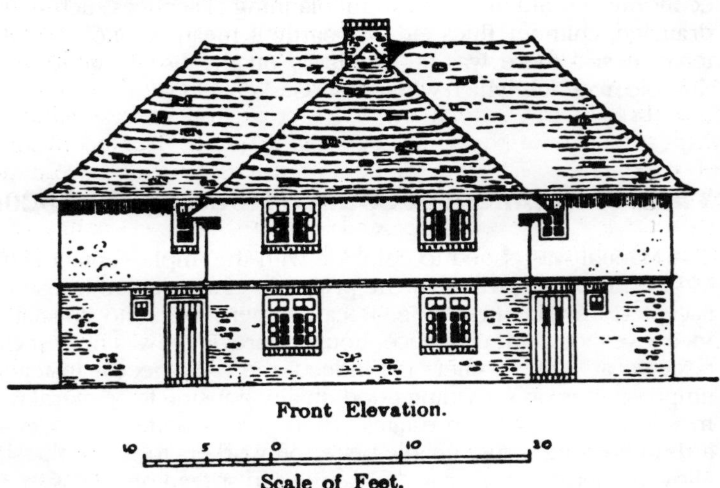

Front Elevation.

Scale of Feet.

12'·0" SCULLERY (80) PARLOUR (132) 10'·0" OPEN LOBBY LARDER COAL PRAM LIVING ROOM (174) FRONT ENT. 27'·8½" 20'·7½" 14'·6"

10'·0" 12'·0" BEDROOM Nº 3 (78) BEDROOM Nº 2 (132) BATH Rᴹ 6'·3" × 4'·6" WC BEDROOM Nº 1 (174) 11'·0" 14'·6"

Ground Floor Plan. First Floor Plan.

(Reproduced by permission of the Controller of H.M. Stationery Office.)

Figure 2.1 Tudor-Walters' influence. Parlour type three-bedroom semi-detached houses, designed by Ministry of Health c 1920 for local authorities. Source: Sayle (1928)

Most housing built was of three bedrooms with a fairly even split between parlour and non-parlour types. Despite the recommendations of both Tudor-Walters and the 1917 Women's Housing Sub-Committee that a parlour should be provided, greater encouragement was subsequently given by the Ministry to non-parlour housing, on the grounds that it was £100 per unit cheaper. Economies were also made in the positioning of the bathroom and in the hot water supply to the bath. Further economies resulted from the 1923 Chamberlain Act, particularly in regard to rear access which was dispensed with in houses smaller than 830 sq ft. 'The inconvenience of negotiating bicycles and perambulators from the front door, through the lobby and scullery to the back of the house must sometimes have been considerable, and the undesirability of carrying dustbins and coal from back to front even worse.' (Burnett 1986, p232).

In 1924, the Labour Party assumed power for the first time and John Wheatley became Minister of Health. He had long campaigned for good quality housing for the working classes (Wheatley 1913) and quickly piloted a new Housing Act through Parliament. The Act remained in force for nine years and produced over half a million houses but the designs of these houses were not vastly different from those built under the 1923 Act. Thus, although more houses were built and, because of the cheaper cost of materials, were within reach of poorer families, they were generally not of the standard achieved in 1919. In the main, they were still of a cottage style, although in parts of London, the County Council began to build flats once again.

Housing estates developed under the 1919, 1923 and 1924 Acts were laid out with a frequent use of crescents and culs-de-sac. Houses had their own front gardens while there was generally some public open space in the tree-lined verges between the pavements and the roads. Such verges served a dual function, partly to soften the lines of the buildings but also as a position in which to lay gas and water mains, telephone and electricity cable. The growth of motor transport also encouraged a generous road layout with roundabouts, rounded corners at road junctions and parking space, although there was little formal car parking provision. Although necessary, such developments brought management responsibilities to the local authority, in terms of the maintenance of such trees, grassed roundabouts and verges. What was missing was children's play space; there seemed to be a general assumption that children would play in their own (rather small) gardens and often no additional provision was made.

Good examples of such estates exist throughout Britain and they still have the power to impress, if only from their sheer scale and size. One of the best known is Becontree in north east London, begun in 1921, but there are others such as Wythenshaw in Manchester, Knightswood in Glasgow, Chesser in Edinburgh and Low Hill in Wolverhampton.

Council Housing in the 1930s

By the end of the 1920s, there was a belief that the council housing thus far provided had met the needs of those who could afford it. What was of increasing importance was to tackle the housing needs of those who still lived in the slums. National policy therefore switched from general needs housing to slum clearance and this was reflected in the Greenwood Act of 1930 and later in the 1933 Act. The 1930 legislation introduced a new Government subsidy based not on new dwellings built but on the number of people rehoused through slum clearance. The subsidy was higher when such rehousing was in flats over three storeys high on costly inner city sites. There was thus a direct incentive for local authorities to build upwards.

The encouragement of flats, after a decade in which cottage-style housing had generally been the norm, provoked a wide debate. Flats were still identified with the poor and conjured up images of Victorian tenements. They were totally resisted by Unwin and the other leaders of the Garden City movement. Some authorities sent deputations of members and officials to European cities where flats were more commonplace but many remained unconvinced. Some medical officers of health expressed reservations about flats because of the possible effects on health. The position was put particularly forcefully by the architect Maxwell Fry:

> The flat is logical only under the conditions imposed by the development of industry and transport and the absence of domestic service. Our present system of development is heaping up trouble for us in the future. Flat life as known in London fails to recognise the existence of children and denies the proper entry of sun and air. To live in boxes lifted off the ground and away from contract with the earth is not the life of a free man.
>
> (Quoted in McAlister and McAlister 1945, p126)

In fact, as noted earlier, the construction of new flats had already begun in the late 1920s, in London. Such flatted estates often followed continental models such as those in Vienna or Sweden, in retaining a concern for good brickwork and pitched roofs. This helped to set LCC housing apart from the earlier Peabody and Waterlow estates which were more barrack like in appearance. Some of the London estates were 'neo Georgian' in their use of small paned windows, cornices and cupolas and were built around small squares (Powers 1989).

Later estates were not so aesthetically appealing and the pressure to build large numbers of slum clearance dwellings led to experimentation with different forms of building construction. In Scotland, concrete blocks were increasingly used and a recognisable style of estate evolved, of three storey flats, grey in appearance (because of the concrete) and often devoid of facilities. They became a 'distinctive and second class brand of housing scheme' (Morgan 1989).

In other cities, the European influence was strong. One of the best documented examples of a flatted estate is Quarry Hill, in Leeds, begun in 1934. The Viennese estates served as a model while the construction used a system devised by the Frenchman Eugene Mopin for housing estates around Paris. This system depended on a light steel frame encased in pre-cast units and filled with poured concrete. The elimination of brickwork removed the need for skilled labour and it was seen as being a particularly economical system (Ravetz 1974). Quarry Hill was built in a series of crescents, of between six and eight storeys and with community facilities built into the estate. Although problems arose in the 1970s, particularly in relation to the fabric of the structure, at the time it was seen as being an important contribution to local authority housing provision.

In Liverpool, there was another fairly ambitious programme of housing development, in various inner city areas. Mostly the housing consisted of four and five storey tenement flats with balcony access, usually around large central open spaces. Many of them were christened 'Gardens', which may have reflected the fact that the architects who designed them saw themselves as still providing model housing in the Garden City tradition (Thomas 1990). In the event they were seen as being of poor quality; like the Glasgow estates, they too were 'second class', and it was unsurprising that such housing featured in films of Liverpool's gangland in the 1950s (Anson 1988).

Although the new housing represented a major advance, in terms of sanitation and general facilities, on the slum housing from which tenants had been cleared, space standards remained problematic. In 1934, a National Housing Committee was formed from professional interests, and addressed the issue of standards. They concluded that the minimum standard of decent housing accommodation should be a three-bedroomed non-parlour house with an area of 760 sq ft (Gaskell 1986). But such minima were frequently regarded as maxima in the depressed economic climate of the 1930s, and this space figure should be seen against the area of 1,000 sq ft, and more, usually achieved by local authorities after 1919. Within blocks of flats, dwellings were often of two bedrooms only and families were therefore rehoused into conditions which created immediate overcrowding. The principles of Tudor-Walters were constantly under threat.

Despite the design problems arising from the 1930s legislation, however, it is important to appreciate the advances made in rented housing provision between the Wars. Overall the stock expanded by 44 per cent while the proportion of council housing rose from 0.2 per cent in 1914 to 10 per cent in 1938 (Power 1987). Owner-occupation expanded too while the private rented sector began its inexorable decline.

Speculative Housebuilding and the Suburban Semi

Before the First World War, most people had lived in rented housing and only 10 per cent or so of all families were owner-occupiers. Investment in private rented property, however, became increasingly uneconomic after the War, not least because of the operation of the Rent Restriction Acts.

> Nevertheless, the slump in the British economy, particularly in the period after 1920, made housing — as opposed to houses — seem more attractive than stocks and shares to many investors. So, although private investment in rented houses declined, funds began increasingly to flow into the building societies which had largely financed the development of the pre-war rented suburbs. The societies had to adapt to these changed circumstances or go under: the financing of owner-occupation — which, after all, had been the original function of the early terminating societies of a century before — became once again their major concern.
>
> (Oliver, Davis and Bentley 1981, p71)

In the main, incomes of wage earners began to rise substantially and, by the 1930s, regular wages of £200 a year were regarded as adequate to service a mortgage. Building Societies expanded, doubling their advances during the interwar period and, by the end of the 1930s, they had reduced the level of deposit required on a house from around 25 per cent to 5 per cent. In addition the introduction of mortgage interest tax relief made house purchase relatively painless. There were increasingly seen to be psychological as well as financial advantages to having a 'home of your own' and the result was a huge expansion in housebuilding.

What made such an expansion possible were the technical advances in transport which had recently taken place. Many suburban railway lines, particularly in the London area but also in Liverpool, Tyneside and elsewhere, had been electrified. The Metropolitan Line, running into Middlesex, gave its name to the resultant suburban development which became known as 'Metroland'. In addition there was an expansion of bus services in the interwar period, providing a degree of flexibility in serving new housing estates which the tramcar could not match.

Suburban developments increasingly became based on bus routes and this led to substantial changes in the pattern of building:

> Trams and trains are inflexible devices. Their rails are expensive to lay and once set down can hardly be moved. Furthermore, trains are slow to accelerate and take time to come to a halt. Stations have therefore to be placed wide apart if the trains are to travel at maximum speed for any distance. Buses on the other hand, can change their routes at short notice, can stop where they will, and can wander wherever there may be a reasonable road. Rail transport resulted in clumps of housing based upon the stations; bus transport resulted in ribbons of housing which stretched from town to town . . . .
>
> (Edwards, 1981 p117)

The suburban sprawl which developed increasingly became a matter of concern, and highlighted the weaknesses of existing planning control. To some extent this was remedied in the 1935 Restriction of Ribbon Development Act but it was not until after the Second World War that comprehensive town planning legislation was introduced. Suburbia was deplored by conservationists and by those anxious about the destruction of the countryside. The poet John Betjeman, taking a particular dislike to the sprawl along the Great West Road out of London towards Slough, caught the mood:

> Come, friendly bombs, and fall on Slough
> It isn't fit for humans now
> There isn't grass to graze a cow
> Swarm over, Death!
>
> Mess up the mess they call a town
> A house for ninety-seven down
> And once a week a half-a-crown
> For twenty years
>
> (Betjeman 1937)

A contemporary author who also attacked the monotony of suburbia was George Orwell, in his novel *Coming up for Air* (1939):

> Do you know the road I live in — Ellesmere Road, West Bletchley? Even if you don't, you know fifty others exactly like it. You know how these streets fester all over the inner–outer suburbs. Always the same. Long, long rows of little semi-detached houses — the numbers in Ellesmere Road run to 212 and ours is 191 — as much alike as council houses and generally uglier. The stucco front, the creosoted gate, the privet hedge, the green front door. The Laurels, The Myrtles, The Hawthorns, Mon Abri, Mon Repos, Belle Vue. At perhaps one house in fifty, some anti-social type who'll probably end in the workhouse has painted his front door blue instead of green.
>
> (Orwell 1939)

Yet, despite the criticism, suburbia was popular and, thanks to the speculative builders, people got largely what they wanted. The basic house type was the semi-detached house, very much in line with the recommendations of Tudor-Walters. Such houses provided garden space, including a private back garden which was safe for children to play in, while access to the rear could be obtained along the side of the house, avoiding the need for a back lane or tunnel access, which would have resulted from a terraced style. Often, each pair of semis received a quite different architectural treatment from its neighbours, to emphasise variety and individuality.

In terms of size, semi-detached houses usually had a floor space of between 1,000 and 1,200 square feet. The front door led on to a hall and staircase and, downstairs, there were usually two main rooms to be used as sitting and dining rooms, the latter the equivalent of the Tudor-Walters 'parlour'. There was usually a separate kitchen to the rear. Upstairs the norm was three bedrooms, two fairly large and capable of taking double or twin beds and one a smaller single bedroom, often located over the front hall. There was a separate bathroom.

It has been suggested that the layout of bedrooms, enabling parents, sons and daughters to sleep apart, conformed to the recommendations of the Women's Housing Sub-Committee of 1917 (Quiney 1986). In fact, changes in household size were also important, with fewer children sharing the available space. The average number of children per household in 1931 was 2.2 and the birth rate was 15 per 1,000; this had fallen from 3.5 and 28 per 1,000 at the beginning of the century. There was also a greater expectation of longevity amongst old people, and the house size required for young families, elderly couples and the like was smaller than before. The suburban semi fitted these requirements.

Also evident amongst families in the 1930s was their increasing affluence, visible partly in the greater use of domestic appliances but most obviously in the purchase of the family car. It became increasingly common for semi-detached houses to include a garage, either attached to the side of the house or in some cases, integrated within the structure. A short driveway led from the garage, along the side of the garden, providing access to the street.

The layout of suburban estates increasingly reflected the greater use of the motor car. Roads became wider, some with dual carriageways and by-passes were built to cater for car-borne journeys to work. Within housing estates, gently curving roads were frequently christened 'Drives', 'Avenues' or 'Ways', to reflect a kind of rural image. But although suburbia, in this way, sought to build on the ideals of the garden city and the relationship between town and country developed by Ebenezer Howard, suburban housing had, in reality, little in common with such ideas. Suburbia was essentially just housing and contained little of the industrial, social and community life which Howard would have deemed necessary.

Despite the accusations of montony, the suburban semi was surprisingly varied in style. Roofs were generally of red tile but added interest was created by the inclusion of gables and overhanging eaves. Often the gable would sweep down towards the ground, thereby creating a porch over the front door, a technique which owed its origins to the work of the architect C F A Voysey. As well as the projecting porch, semi-detached houses usually had bay windows and sometimes oriel ones. There was also a liberal use of wood, particularly for the front door (often oak) and to provide a half-timbered mock-Elizabethan effect. Builders were also capable of adding leaded windows, inglenooks, false beams and wood panelling in an attempt to create a cottage vernacular style, often derided as 'Jacobethan'. The cartoonist Osbert Lancaster satirised these styles with his references to 'Stockbroker's Tudor', 'Wimbledon Transitional' and 'By-pass Variegated'. Later in the 1930s, more modern motifs were adopted, with 'Suntrap' houses having larger metal framed windows to admit more light and the half-timbering frequently being designed in a 'sunburst' pattern.

The variety of styles of the suburban semi was a reflection of its tenure and the desire of the new owner-occupiers to emphasise their individuality. There was thus a clear contrast with the local authority estate whose neo-Georgian terraces suggested a greater communality of living. Nowhere was this contrast more evident than in north Oxford where an area of private housing abutted the council estate of Cutteslowe. Claiming that links with the council housing lowered property values, in 1934 the builders of the private estate built seven foot high walls across the roads linking the two areas of housing. The walls were not finally demolished until 1959.

The Bungalow

Although suburbia is often seen as being synonymus with the semi-detached house type, other forms of housing were developed during the interwar period, with the bungalow being a particularly popular form. The name stems from the Indian word 'bangla' or 'of Bengal' and the bungalow was a relatively common house type in the India of the Raj, particularly in the country or the hill-station. On import into Britain, the association of bungalows with places of resort continued and the earliest developments were in seaside towns, in the years before the First World War.

The change in image of the bungalow is attributed to the influence of early Hollywood films which showed the luxurious bungalows of California with their associated lifestyle (Barrett and Phillips 1987). But in fact there were several excellent reasons for its increased popularity. Firstly, bungalows were smaller — and hence cheaper — than semi-detached houses and could therefore provide the cheapest entry into owner-occupation at the time. Secondly, the bungalow, unlike the semi, was often territorially separate, with its own gardens and this was an important symbol of private property. Thirdly, for the middle class who could afford it, the 'bungalow in the country' provided the perfect opportunity to emulate the style of a country-house owning elite (King 1984, p160).

The typical internal layout consisted of a central front door with the two main rooms leading off either side of a small hall. At the rear would be one or two more rooms, a kitchen and a bathroom; the number of rooms thus totalled three or four in contrast to the usual five in a semi. Although some criticised the design of bungalows with 'the four chimney stacks sticking up from the outside walls like the legs of an upturned table' (Hurd 1957), the bungalow was often as varied as the semi-detached.

As far as the common characteristics of a bungalow were concerned, there were few,

> . . . save a pitched roof and the fact that the building is usually single storey . . . . Their idiosyncratic details may well represent popular taste having a chance to express itself for the first time. As one might expect, it is expressed more clearly around the windows and the doors, of which there is the most astonishing variety . . . . There was no general pattern in plan form, considerable numbers of bungalows being semi-detached, a lot square, a lot rectangular, and a lot L-plan. They might or might not have bay windows, might or might not be symmetrical, and might or might not be entered from the side, the front or in the corner.
>
> (McKean 1987, pp158–9)

Bungalows were particularly popular in Scotland. Partly this may have been because they were smaller and Scottish house sizes have traditionally been smaller than those in England. But partly it was because Scotland, with its tenements, already possessed a housing tradition whereby a household lived on one level. A bungalow could be seen therefore as a flat with a garden. Builders such as Miller in Edinburgh and the Glasgow-based Mactaggart and Mickel developed large bungalow estates, such as Newton Mearns in the south west of Glasgow, some with Indian-style loggias. Some bungalows reflected a sort of Scottish vernacular style with turrets and towers, others were in a chalet style, with dormer windows and extra space in the roof area. As in England, there was a tendency for development to follow main roads, until the 1935 Restriction of Ribbon Development Act prevented this.

Like the semi-detached, the bungalow received its fair share of criticism from both the architectural lobby and the conservationists in the 1930s. Their universal appeal, however, was difficult to ignore and they have now become an accepted part of the interwar housing landscape.

The Mansion Block

The trend towards the building of flats by local authorities in the 1930s has already been identified; it would be surprising perhaps if such a trend made no impact at all on the private sector. Nevertheless, the flat as a dwelling for the middle classes did not gain widespread acceptance outwith parts of London and the south east, and Scotland.

Technical advances in construction made it easier to build blocks of flats, using concrete frames, with an outer layer of brick. Much attention was paid to access and lighting in order to ensure the maximum use of daylight, and large metal framed windows similar to those of the 'suntrap' houses were often used. Blocks of flats had lifts, the common areas were private, access from the street being strictly controlled, and there was usually a caretaker employed. Generally such flats were rented rather than owned and the rent was set at a level to cover the services provided.

In London a number of mansion blocks were built, in areas like Kensington and Chelsea, and many leading architects worked on them. But they tended to appeal to the single and the childless rather than to families. The image of the 'young upper-class twits and flappers', like P G Wodehouse's Bertie Wooster, is perhaps inseparable from the image of life in a mansion flat.

In Scotland, where there was still a tradition of flat dwelling, some mansion flats were built in all the major cities. The largest development was Kelvin Court in the west end of Glasgow, over 100 flats in two 11 storey blocks. Located on a main road adjacent to bus and tram routes and a suburban railway station, it proved popular. Internally the flats consisted of a sitting room, dining room and three bedrooms, plus kitchen, bathroom, entrance hall and cupboard space. The overall size was in the order of 1,000 square feet or more, comparable with a semi-detached house and relatively well-proportioned by earlier Scottish standards.

New Approaches to Design

The interwar period was one characterised by innovations in design, not merely in housing but in public buildings, and with due attention being paid to both interior and exterior. British designers, however, were influenced in a variety of different ways, and we have already explored the relationship between semi-detached suburbia and an older, rather rustic England, with liberal use of half-timbering and mock-Tudor styles. Bungalows were an imperial import with their origins in India. European architects were forging a quite different path for themselves and, unsurprisingly, many of their ideas were adopted in Britain, although it must be said, sometimes with limited acceptance by the public.

A key figure in European architecture after the First World War was Walter Gropius, director of the Bauhaus. This was a design school, established in Weimar in 1919 and with a stated aim of improving design and craftsmanship. Initially, the focus was on designing for industrial production but by the mid 1920s, members of the Bauhaus began to turn their attention to housing.

There was a serious European housing shortage after the First World War and, following the election of socialist administrations in a number of European cities, particularly in Holland and Germany, new forms of building for public housing were developed.

> Minimum standards were established for kitchens and bathrooms, the efficiency of the interior circulation of apartments was considered, careful studies were made of the relationship of building height to sunlight and open space, and the possibilities of mass-producing dwellings and of using standardised parts were examined.
>
> (Relph 1987, p109)

In many cases, the results were slab blocks, well equipped

internally for the time, but rather uniform in their external appearance.

Contemporary with the Bauhaus were a number of famous architects such as Le Corbusier, Mies van der Rohe and, in America, Frank Lloyd Wright. The first two are associated in particular with the development of high rise housing and their contribution will be discussed in Chapter Four. Wright's approach was radically different. He envisaged low-density, low-rise cities, occupying a kind of wide, democratic landscape, democratic because it was highly decentralised, with a mixture of dwellings, farms, and occasional large buildings. His vision is often regarded as the origin of the typical-sprawling American suburb with houses in large grounds, no real town centre and miles of freeways and open space.

The European architects set out their stall at a number of exhibitions. In 1927 a housing exhibition was held in Stuttgart and the leading architects designed buildings for it.

> These were all angular and unornamented. They were also light, airy, functional, and a serious attempt to find ways of improving urban living conditions, especially of the working classes. The hope was that any one of the buildings could serve as a prototype for mass production, for it was believed by the modernists that houses should, as Gropius put it, be as easily mass-produced as shoes.
>
> (Relph 1987, p109)

Three years later, there was a similar exhibition in Stockholm.

British architects began to embrace the ideas of the new Modern Movement, but apart from schemes like Quarry Hill, discussed earlier, and Highpoint One, the earliest British high rise block, built in Highgate (London) in 1935, most modern houses were in the private sector. Some were built for individuals, some were built speculatively. Characteristics of the houses included a generous use of glass, not just in terms of large windows, but also in the doors. Kitchens and bathrooms were well-equipped with up to date fitments in chrome, and living rooms and bedrooms were light, airy and decorated in an art deco style. Externally, such houses were characterised generally by, first, a flat roof, second by curved walls, sometimes involving a kind of drum-shaped tower, and third, by a white cement rendering to reflect the sunlight and emphasise the brightness of the dwelling. This whiteness, coupled with the use of rounded windows like portholes, led to house designs sometimes being referred to as in the 'ocean liner style'.

Although such housing is relatively common throughout Britain (although more so in the South), the Modern Movement was not universally accepted. The attitude of architects like Gropius has been criticised for its paternalism, with affluent socialists designing housing for the poor and imposing modernism upon them (Relph 1987). But ironically, it was perhaps the very design of the houses which made them unsuitable for the poor. Some of the designs, with their curving staircases and wide balconies, were very expensive to build, while the flat roofs were particularly suspect in the unpredictable British climate. Few local authorities could afford to experiment with such designs, and the architect-designed modern house became associated with the wealthier parts of suburbia.

Some local authorities did experiment with housing designs and there are examples of blocks in parts of London which were constructed in an art deco or art nouveau style. Generally, however, authorities turned their attentions to experimentation with building materials. Reference has already been made to the shortages of such materials after the First World War and the increasing use of concrete blocks rather than brick or stone. In areas like Scotland where the housing shortage was at its most acute, local authorities turned to steel-framed and timber-framed houses. Some houses, like the 'Atholl' steel type, were built by Beardmore's, the Glasgow steelmakers, as a means of keeping production going at a time when shipbuilding was in recession. The Scottish National Housing Company, forerunner of the Scottish Special Housing Association, was in the forefront of experimental building methods and during the Second World War, built a complete development of experimental houses in Edinburgh (see Chapter Three). Such designs, although successful at the time, had implications for renewal policy in later years, with many types being designated under the 1984 Housing Defects Act.

Conclusions

The interwar period was important in two key respects, firstly in the expansion of local authority housing after 1919 and secondly in the expansion of owner-occupation, funded by a building society movement, which had become increasingly successful in drawing in funds and then making them available to aspiring home owners. The private rented sector, increasingly squeezed, began its inexorable decline into a residual form of tenure.

In design terms, the impact of the Tudor-Walters report was highly significant in influencing the earliest council housing, as well, to an extent, as owner-occupied suburbia. The world recession and the cuts in local government expenditure in the 1930s led the designers to the building of flats and a cheaper form of housing provision. The period was characterised by new approaches to house design from the expanding planning and architecture professions. The impact of the Modern Movement began to be felt, a process which continued after the Second World War as planners, following the teachings of Le Corbusier, began to look upwards. Elsewhere in the private sector, the development of bungalows and mansion blocks added to a variety of new designs.

But criticisms may be made. The smaller size of council houses in the 1930s and the move back to flats laid the foundations for problems — particularly in housing management — in the postwar era. In areas of private housing, the burgeoning expanses of suburbia, while relatively pleasant in themselves, did not provide a wholly satisfactory housing environment. The absence of amenities in such areas was therefore a subject which was examined by the Dudley Committee, set up during the war.

Finally, of course, the Second World War itself provided the country with an opportunity to plan afresh for the peace. The foundations of the Welfare State were laid, while a series of planning reports made recommendations about population distribution, rural areas, and compensation and betterment. As far as housing was concerned, the Dudley Report of 1944 pointed the way to postwar reconstruction and new considerations in housing design, and these are discussed further in Chapter Three.

Chapter 3
The postwar years

Introduction

The outbreak of war in September 1939 led to an immediate cessation of building activity. This, together with bomb damage, led to a serious housing shortage in the immediate postwar years. Out of a total of 11.5 million homes, 0.75 million were either demolished by bombing or seriously damaged (Power 1987). As a result of this, immense public interest was generated in how reconstruction could be effected at the end of hostilities, and town planning became a popular theme for discussion.

The war years saw the publication of a remarkable series of government reports which began to lay the foundations for reconstruction. The Barlow Report of 1940 was the first of these, containing a detailed analysis of the advantages and disadvantages of large cities, in particular London, and the imbalance which had been created in British population distribution. The report recommended the redevelopment of congested urban areas and the dispersal of both industry and people, to garden cities, satellite towns or other regional centres. The report was praised by supporters of the garden city ideal, now formed into the Town and Country Planning Association, and after the war, the Barlow Report became part of the justification for the extensive British New Towns programme.

Two years after Barlow, the Uthwatt Committee on Compensation and Betterment considered the issue of land costs and whether individuals had the right to be compensated for a refusal to allow development or, indeed to gain from a development without being taxed. The Report recommended a separation of planning control from the issue of land value and Government accepted that a central planning authority be set up to control development. A Ministry of Works and Planning was set up in February 1942, occupied initially by Lord Reith, but soon after by Lord Portal. In 1943, the Ministry was renamed the Ministry of Town and Country Planning, the first such Minister being W S Morrison. The Ministry began to pilot through Parliament the necessary legislation for postwar reconstruction, beginning with the 1944 Town and Country Planning Act, which gave strong new powers of land acquisition for the comprehensive redevelopment of war-damaged areas.

In the replanning of Britain, one name which stood out in particular was that of Patrick Abercrombie, Professor of Town Planning at University College, London. He undertook the task of preparing a long overdue plan for London which, to the disappointment of the Garden City movement, did not opt for total dispersal but instead for retaining the old structure — and making it work. Its weakness, however, lay in the fact that it was confined to the administrative County of London, whereas it was important to set London's planning problems in a wider regional context; Abercrombie therefore embarked on a Greater London Plan to address these wider issues (Cherry 1988). Abercrombie was also responsible for plans for the Clyde Valley, the West Midlands, Plymouth, Hull and Edinburgh and had a major impact on the shape of British cities in the period of postwar reconstruction.

Another key element in this reconstruction was the 1942 Beveridge Report, widely seen as having laid the foundations for the postwar Welfare State. Housing was an essential part of this concept and it was accepted that this would be planned not only to deal with individual need but also with a view to a more general improvement of postwar society. The government had in mind a programme of between three and four million houses to be built in the ten years or so after the war, a doubling of the interwar rate of house completions.

What made the need so great, quite apart from war damage, was demographic change. During the war, an estimated two million marriages had taken place and, from 1941, the birth rate began to rise, reaching a peak in 1947 of 20.7 births per thousand. Household size expanded briefly and exacerbated the existing housing shortage. Some families were reduced to squatting, in the absence of more permanent accommodation, and the problem was particularly acute in London.

The 1945 Labour government took office determined to make decent housing available to all, a change from the 1930s when council housing had increasingly become targeted only at the poorest and those affected by slum clearance. Local authorities were seen as having the key role while, later, New Towns were launched to aid the postwar housing drive.

There was an overwhelming belief in planning but, in addition there was an increasing recognition that houses should be well designed. This had arisen in two ways. Firstly, during the 1930s, there had been a growing appreciation of good quality housing and in particular of the various labour-saving domestic fittings which were being introduced. Secondly, the experience of women during the war, in hostels and factories, had shown them that higher standards of services and equipment could be achieved, and made them less tolerant of inferior conditions at home (Gaskell 1986).

> In the same way, both men and women had become conscious during the war of the practicalities of modern scientific developments and expected to enjoy the benefits of these discoveries at home. The broad extension of public services between the wars, in terms of piped water, electricity and gas, had brought changes in domestic habits, particularly with regard to appliances for cooking and the consequent nature and design of the room in which cooking was undertaken. These developments reinforced the view that the most important question in designing and equipping dwellings was that of how a house was run and the use made of the various rooms.
> (Gaskell 1986, p159)

As a result, design became an important element of postwar housing provision and local authorities were therefore expected to make use of trained architects in the design and planning of housing estates. Central government, for their part, were to prepare manuals of plans for the use of authorities and their architects. Such manuals took as their source the recommendations of the 1944 Dudley Report into the Design of Dwellings, a report which, like Tudor-Walters after 1919, had immense impact on postwar rebuilding.

The Dudley and Westwood Reports

In 1942, the Minister of Health had appointed a sub-committee of the Central Housing Advisory Committee to make recommendations on the design, planning and layout of dwellings, and this sub-comittee named after its chairman, Lord Dudley, took as its starting point the failures which had occurred in interwar housing planning.

At a general level, it was recognised that mistakes had been made. Private and public housing had been too rigidly separated, leading to the tensions, of which the Cuttleslowe wall incident is the best example (p39). Secondly, many 1930s housing estates lacked social and community facilities such as churches, shops and other amenities. Thirdly, the spread of suburbia had resulted in the development of a major separation between home and place of work with the result that the journey to work was becoming of major significance in transport planning.

As far as the dwellings themselves were concerned, the Dudley Report recognised further defects. There was a lack of variety in the type of dwelling which had been provided; the living rooms were too cramped — a particular problem as house sizes had contracted in the 1930s; equipment and storage space was inadequate, given the improvements made in domestic appliances, labour-saving devices and the like; and the outbuildings, garages etc which had been provided were poorly planned and set out.

These problems were identified in a study by Kirby (1971) of interwar council dwellings in the north east of England, in which the lack of space for family activities was clearly identified. In the kitchen and bathroom areas, it was also clear that there were major deficiencies.

> ... based on the housewife's subjective judgement, the interwar dwelling would appear to fall below the standard with regard to the provision for heating, natural lighting, power points, hot water and a satisfactory cooking facility .... Moreover, though the interwar council dwelling may possess certain of the required basic facilities, these may not be as efficient or attractive as their modern counterparts.
>
> (Kirby 1971, p261)

The Dudley report recommended that local authorities should continue in general to concentrate on providing three-bedroomed family housing, although it was recognised that need would vary from place to place. Houses should have two large rooms on the ground floor, one of which could possibly be a working kitchen, large enough to accommodate the family for meals, as well as for cooking. Laundry and similar household work should be done not in the kitchen but in a separate utility room. An alternative proposal was for a smaller kitchen with the living room enlarged to allow for a dining recess. In both cases, the floorspace of the ground floor rooms would amount to 310 square feet. The Report dismissed the use of the word 'parlour' which it felt was old-fashioned, and suggested that it did not matter what the rooms were called, so long as they were used to the best advantage.

Upstairs, the Dudley Report suggested that the bedroom sizes of interwar houses as proposed by Tudor-Walters, of 150, 100 and 65 square feet respectively were adequate, although the two smaller bedrooms might be increased slightly to allow for the provision of built-in wardrobes. The Report also recommended that the bathroom should always be upstairs, whereas in interwar housing it had frequently been located downstairs. Overall, the total minimum floor area recommended by Dudley was 900 sq ft, with slight variations to be dependent on aspect and siting. This was not too dissimilar to

Tudor-Walters but significantly higher than the sizes of houses actually being built in the public sector in the late 1930s.

The Dudley Report also looked in some detail at domestic fittings and appliances. It recommended improved heating systems, particularly some form of central heating and of improvements to windows to reduce heat loss. It also urged the use of new materials on floors and other surfaces, which could be easily cleaned and maintained.

> The model for the postwar house thus incorporated a general raising of the level of services and equipment. This was particularly evident in the kitchen, with its fitted cupboards, sink, draining-boards and work surfaces, and in the bathroom, with the availability of constant hot water, lagged plumbing and more efficient sanitary fittings. More connections for light and power made the use of electricity and gas a normal expectation.
>
> (Gaskell 1986, p113)

Outside the dwelling, the Dudley Report considered issues of housing layout. It suggested that the large interwar housing estate had been insufficiently planned with appropriate facilities and recommended the 'neighbourhood' as being the most desirable social unit. Such an area would have a population between 5,000 and 10,000 with sufficient community provision to aid the development of community life. Dudley suggested that densities could vary, but in only a very few cases, in the inner city, should it be necessary to rebuild at 120 persons per acre. In outer areas 30–40 persons per acre was more sensible.

The Dudley Committee's remit extended only to England and Wales; in Scotland a parallel committee — the Westwood Committee — was operating. Appointed like Dudley in 1942, the Westwood Committee did not, however, report until 1948. Unlike Dudley, Westwood accepted that flats could be a perfectly adequate form of housing (very much in the Scottish tradition); but did recommend that cottage style houses were preferred and that the largest proportion of houses to be built after the war should be of this type.

In terms of house size, Westwood recommended that a three-bedroomed house should have a living room of 190 sq ft while the bedrooms themselves should be 150–160, 120 and 120 sq ft while there should be a utility room of at least 40 sq ft. Thus, although the arrangements of rooms suggested were similar to those in the Dudley Report, the recommended room sizes were slightly larger, perhaps a reaction to the enormous overcrowding which was a feature of Scottish housing at this time.

In other respects, such as the provision of better heating, domestic equipment and house layout, the Westwood Report was similar in its recommendations to its English counterpart. It did, however, pay particular attention to the building of the traditional Scottish tenement which, in the past, had been erected in enclosed hollow squares with back courts behind the blocks. In future, it recommended that flatted developments be built in such a way as to allow better daylighting, with blocks in parallel and the spaces between properly planted and with adequate playing and clothes-drying areas.

The Government Housing Manuals

The first Housing Manual to be issued by the Ministry of Health for local government guidance was in 1944. At that time it was still assumed that the most urgent task after the war would be the provision of homes for families, and great emphasis was laid on the provision of three-bedroom, two storey houses. Flats were largely ignored and the provision of new services such as central heating was also given scant attention. The Manual was really issued too quickly for the recommendations of the Dudley Committee to have been incorporated.

Much more detailed advice was therefore issued in the 1949 Housing Manual. Firstly, there was a greater recognition that the long term postwar housing problem would not be solely confined to families and that there was a need for a greater variety of house types to be built 'in order to meet in a balanced way the varying requirements of the population as a whole'. Secondly, the Manual covered the revised standards for local authority housing which had been designated by the Ministry of Health, particularly in the area of heating.

While recognising the need for different house types, the Manual still focused on the three-bedroomed house as the standard design, using a standard of 900–500 sq ft, an increase from the 1944 Manual's 800–900 sq ft, reflecting acceptance of Dudley's recommendations. Within this overall framework, there could clearly be different layouts but architects were urged to have regard to efficiency in the use and the heating of the space provided (see Figure 3.1).

> It is not possible to anticipate how each family will elect to use the accommodation provided, but housing authorities and their architects, in deciding which plan arrangement to adopt, must have a clear idea of the way in which the accommodation can most conveniently be occupied.
> The planning of a house is largely determined by the arrangements for cooking, serving and eating meals, and the way of living in the house will be dictated by these factors and by the efficiency and

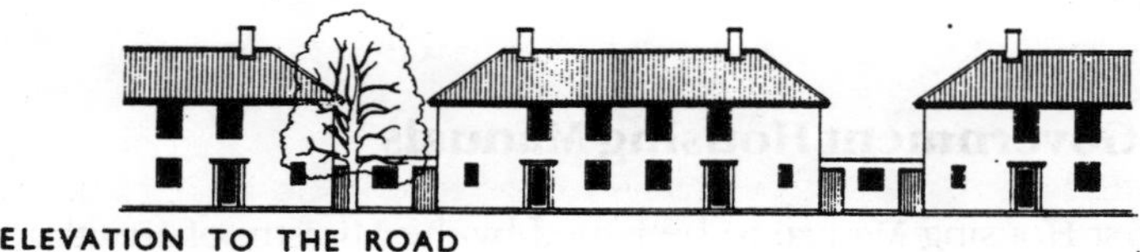

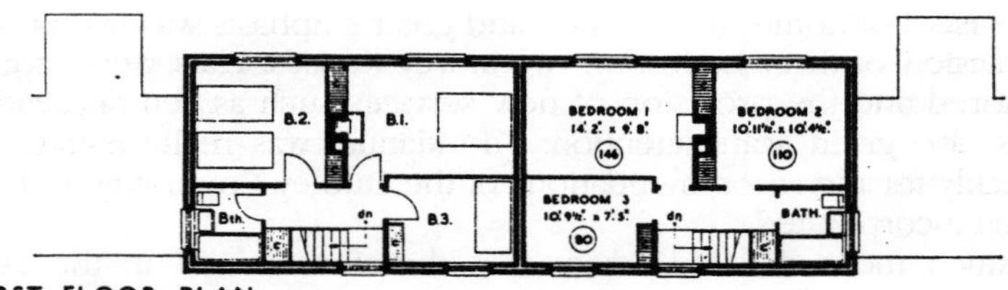

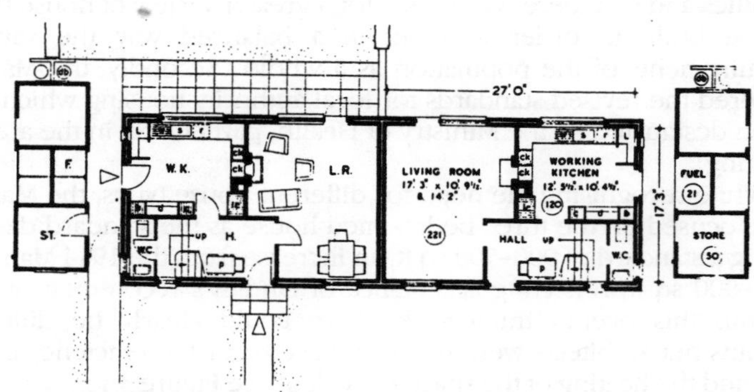

URBAN SEMI-DETACHED HOUSE **East or West aspect**

Five person. Floor area: House 931 sq. ft.; outbuildings 72 sq. ft.

Figure 3.1 Dudley influence. Semi-detached houses designed for the post-Blitz rebuilding. Source: Ministry of Health (1949)

planning of the space heating appliances. Space will be wasted unless it can be cheaply and efficiently heated and the choice of fuels and suitable appliances will have an increasing influence on the plan of the future.

(Ministry of Health 1949, p41)

Heating was an important issue and the Manual considered district heating systems for flats as well as central heating systems for individual houses. Reference was made to the progress being made in developing such systems, which were clearly a major advance on pre-war standards.

Finally, the Manual stressed the importance of designing housing which was sympathetic to its surroundings. This was true, not only in urban areas where redevelopment on bombed sites was taking place but also in rural villages where small-scale infill development was needed. The Manual contained numerous illustrations of what it regarded as good practice in different parts of the country, using a wide variety of styles and local building materials. There was therefore no attempt to impose a 'Whitehall view' on to the different local authorities.

The Housing Shortage and Non-Traditional Building

Although the advice given to local authorities in the Dudley Report recommendations and in the various Housing Manuals was sound, in practice it proved difficult to implement. The extreme shortage of houses at the end of the war, coupled with a depleted labour force in the building industry and a lack of traditional building materials, led to a search for new solutions. In England, the Ministry of Works under Lord Portal announced that a policy of introducing temporary prefabricated houses would be adopted and that up to half a million such houses would be produced. Special legislation, in the form of the Housing (Temporary Accommodation) Act 1944, was passed which allowed local authorities to ignore bye-laws governing building standards, although in the event ony 157,000 prefabs were actually built.

Prefabrication, using aluminium, was started in five former aircraft factories after the war, producing the Aluminium Bungalow. Other similar designs included the Arcon, the Uni-Seco and the Tarran. The houses were small, of around 650 square feet (only two thirds of Dudley's recommended house size) and consisted of a living room, two bedrooms, hall, kitchen and bathroom. After manufacture, they were placed on site on concrete slabs. Although designed to last only ten years, some are still in use today and remain popular with tenants. Housing shortages were particularly acute in Scotland and a second major programme of non-traditional houses was conceived in 1942 when the Government set up a Committee on House Construction under the chairmanship of Sir George Burt. The Burt Committee reported in 1944 after reviewing a range of non-traditional house types then in existence. The Scottish Special Housing Association was encouraged to experiment with demonstration house types and an experimental site was developed at Sighthill in Edinburgh, including no-fines concrete houses, 'foamed-slag' houses, 'Gyproc' houses, steel framed houses and timber houses (Begg 1987; Scottish Office 1987). In all, between 1945 and 1954, approximately 204,000 new public sector houses were built in Scotland, almost half of these being of non-traditional construction.

In England, the Minister of Health, Aneurin Bevan, encouraged the development of non-traditional designs, as a means of speeding up the postwar programme. In the Spring of 1946, he settled on two main types, the British Steel House and the Airey House, of precast concrete. Later a further ten non-traditional types were approved and altogether around 180,000 such houses were built by the end of the programme in the mid-1950s.

Interpreting the Design Standards: the Labour government

Because of the housing pressures, little permanent housing was built at the immediate end of the war. In 1945, only 3,000 permanent dwellings were completed, in comparison with the average rate between 1934 and 1939 of 350,000 per year, although within two years, the figure had risen to 147,000 (Scoffham 1984).

The man responsible for the postwar housing programme was the Minister of Health, Aneurin Bevan, and he enlisted the active support of the local authorities. Low interest loans from the Public Works Loans Board were introduced, thereby ensuring that authorities had the resources to get on with the job. Under the 1949 Housing Act, local authorities were given responsibilities for all the housing needs in their area, the implication being that council housing was for everyone and not just the working classes. Bevan was alarmed at the division which had developed between public and private housing in the 1930s and saw as his ideal a social mixed estate, built on garden city principles. He believed that it was essential for the full life of a citizen 'to see the living tapestry of a mixed community'.

Bevan's priorities can most clearly be seen in his attitude to the recommendations on house size in the Dudley Report. Bevan accepted the Dudley formula while at the same time encouraging authorities to do better. He was attacked on the grounds that a cut in standards, in room size, in the provision of a separate WC, could allow more houses to be built for the same amount of money. But he regarded that as the coward's way out.

> It would be 'a cruel thing to do. After all, people will have to live in and among these houses for many years. Enough damage has already been done to the face of England by irresponsible people. If we have to wait a little longer, that will be far better than doing ugly things now and regretting them for the rest of our lives'.
>
> (Foot 1973, p78)

Bevan also embraced the recommendations of the 1949 Manual regarding local variations in housing design and spoke against the domination of the three-bedroomed semi-detached house. He encouraged variety because 'while we shall be judged for a year or two by the number of houses we build, we shall be judged in ten years time by the type of houses we build' (Foot 1973). But numbers remained a problem and the failure to achieve their house completion targets led in part to Labour's defeat in 1951.

It is instructive to examine a couple of examples to illustrate the problems which Bevan's policies created for local authorities. In Newcastle the postwar housing programme had been slow to start because of extended negotiations over land purchase, and by the end of 1946, only 28 houses had been completed. Despite public spending cuts in 1947, Bevan's unwillingness to sacrifice standards meant that Newcastle was allowed to build less than 4,500 houses between 1946 and 1949. In 1949 Labour lost control of Newcastle and the new Conservative administration began to plan cheaper flatted dwellings to deal with the housing shortage although, initially these had to be outside the city boundary at Longbenton (Benwell 1978). In Dundee, the City Council had only built 2,851 houses between 1947 and 1951, despite the fact that nearly 14,000 families were said to be in urgent need of housing and squatting was beginning to take place. The Housing Convenor stated that the city was not even keeping pace with the number of weddings which were taking place, which had averaged 1,678 a year for the previous four years (Edgar, Rowbotham and Stanforth 1992).

Where houses had been built in large numbers, the pressures for completion had led to a lack of design work on the estates which were being created. Semi-detached houses continued to dominate, changed little from the 1930s, but there was little consideration for site or context, and the standard of architecture was poor. In 1953, the term 'prairie planning' was coined to describe the result (Cullen 1953).

By the time that Labour left office in 1951, around 900,000 council houses had been completed out of a total of well over 1 million completions nationally. In itself this was an impressive number, almost as great as the total number of completions during the interwar period. But the shortages remained and the 1951 Census showed the same deficit of houses to households as had existed twenty years earlier. Local authorities were finding it difficult to cope, particularly in the face of shortages of land and materials.

> The Labour policy of providing for general needs was difficult to sustain .... There was such scarcity that demand was too great to be met by public effort only; in any case private landlords still owned nearly 90 per cent of homes after the war and there were strong political differences over the desirability of mass council housing .... But shortages continued with a further million homes needed urgently .... The urban land shortage reinforced the trend towards flat-building which seemed the only answer to city problems.
>
> (Power 1987, pp41–2)

Interpreting the Design Standards: The Conservatives

Housing was a key issue in the 1951 General Election and the Conservatives pledged a target of 300,000 houses a year to tackle the shortage. After their victory, it fell to their new Housing Minister, Harold Macmillan, to see that these targets were met.

Macmillan advocated the adoption of a 'People's House' which would be of no more than 900 sq ft for a three-bedroomed house, with only the bare essentials in terms of storage and circulation space. In this way, he argued, more houses could be built for the same money, a complete reversal of Bevan's position. Macmillan's impact can be seen in the supplement to the 1949 Housing Manual, published in 1952 (MHLG 1952). The report argued that while the design of houses was of prime importance, there was a need to balance essential housing standards with a need to reduce capital costs and rents:

> ... further savings may be possible in housing layouts, the construction of roads and services, and the use of terraced forms of development instead of semi-detached houses. The architect must play his full part by designing economically ....
>
> (MHLG 1952, p1)

The advocacy of the terraced house was one of the main ways in which savings could be achieved although such designs presented problems of access from front to back of the house. Separate tunnel access was no longer advocated and so dustbins were to be located in a special compartment beside the front door. Where this was deemed inappropriate, the Manual pointed out that a secondary means of access would be necessary — a return to some kind of back lane (Figure 3.2).

In order to effect space savings within the house, the 1952 Manual recommended larger living and dining areas with, in some cases, the staircase rising from the dining space. These 'dining hall' or 'large living room' houses were said to be an adaptation of American and Canadian house designs which, it was felt, would appeal particularly to the younger generation. The Manual stated that 'the whole house can be used by the children for play or study', a shift from the Dudley committee's position which had recognised the value of separate quiet rooms for study, reading etc.

In 1953, a further supplement to the Housing Manual was issued by the Ministry of Housing and Local Government (MHLG 1953a). This publication referred to the savings of £150 a house in construction costs which had been achieved through the adoption of the 1952 Manual Supplement, but took a new theme:

> The purchase of land, the construction of roads and sewers, and the building of houses, are three distinct operations carried out at different times. As a result the cost of each item is often considered in isolation. But the total cost of all three largely determines rents. Therefore, it follows that economy in the use of land, in the construction of roads and services, and in the cost of houses must constantly be kept in mind from the start.
>
> (MHLG 1953a, p1)

The document went on to point out that every penny saved on the cost per square foot of a 900 sq ft house would save almost a penny a week in rent and reduce the cost of Macmillan's 300,000 annual housing target by over £1 million.

The plans provided in the Manual were again largely terraced, designed to save space in their frontage. There was particular attention paid to corner sites which, it was clearly felt, had been underused in the past, and the Manual advocated the use of small two storey blocks of flats to 'increase densities and economise in the

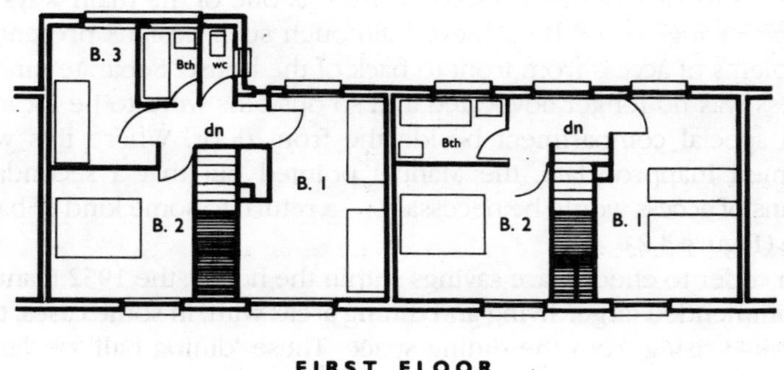

FIRST FLOOR

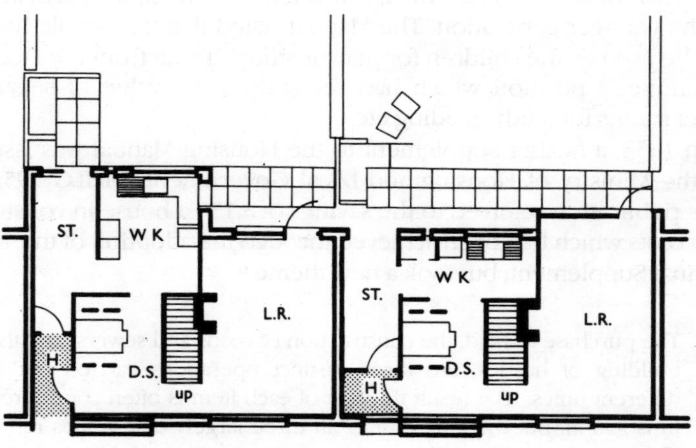

GROUND FLOOR

			Fig. 16 5 Persons sq. ft.	Fig. 17 4 Persons sq. ft.
Gross House Area *(including Outside Fuel)*			897	784
Fuel	12	12		
Store	59	50		
			71	62
Net House Area			826	722
Aggregate Ground Floor Living Area			325	292

Figure 3.2 Macmillan influence. Four- and five-person terrace houses without parlour. **Source: MHLG (1952)**

use of road frontage'. Indeed, there were a number of recommended plans for three-storey blocks of flats, which could be of two main alternative designs. One would combine maisonettes with flats, with the staircase serving flats on the top floor, over two-storey maisonettes for larger families; a block of this type which had recently been developed in Lansbury (Poplar) was used as an illustration. An alternative would involve the construction of a much larger block with four flats on each floor, still served by only one staircase. The amount of external walling in relation to the floor area was reduced and this would result in savings of 5 per cent. There was thus a shift towards the provision of more and more flats and eventually in 1956 a subsidy was introduced which increased with storey height. This is dealt with more fully in Chapter Four.

Macmillan's reductions in standards and increases in densities began to have an effect, and in 1953 he achieved his target of more than 300,000 house completions in a year. In 1954, a record 348,000 houses were completed. From 1953 onwards, however, the proportion of council dwellings fell, and Macmillan encouraged private developers through the removal of building licences in 1954. Two years later, the subsidy to local authorities to provide housing for general needs was abolished, except in the case of one-bedroomed dwellings. By the late 1950s, the worst of the housing shortage had been overcome, partly through new building but partly also because of the end of the postwar 'baby boom' and a decline in the overall growth of the population. As a result, attention began to focus once again on slum clearance.

Inevitably perhaps, the early slum clearance solutions were seen as being blocks of flats, although their construction in poor quality inner city environments stored up problems for the future. In Newcastle, the Conservative/Progressive administration concentrated on building blocks of flats throughout the city, up to a height of five storeys. The mix of flats and maisonettes, however, led to problems of high child density, inadequate refuse disposal systems and overuse of stairs and circulation areas. One of the most problematic schemes was in Noble Street in the city's west end, dubbed a slum while it was still on the drawing board (Benwell CDP 1978). Such developments were a side effect of the push for new housing but helped to develop the argument for qualitative as well as quantitative improvements in housing provision.

The shift towards flats in the Macmillan era was less of an issue in Scotland where flats were a traditional form of housing. In Glasgow, where the greatest shortages were occurring, the Housing Department was keen to experiment with multi-storeyed construction. The Scottish Office agreed that a prototype should be built, and an eight-storey block for single women was erected in 1949–52. A much larger development at Moss Heights in the south west of the city was completed in 1954. But the bulk of the postwar rehousing programme consisted of the construction of three and four storey walk-up tenement blocks, of two and three-bedroomed flats, built in roughcast or terrazzo-faced brick or blockwork (Horsey 1990). What was perhaps surprising was the fact that these houses, some 40,000 or so in all, were almost all built in estates round the city's periphery, as it is questionable whether such high densities were appropriate for such suburban locations. Their construction, however, represented a determination by Glasgow to build within its own boundaries, rather than enter into overspill agreements with the New Towns.

Other Scottish authorities also adopted tenement styles with slight variations. In Dundee, for example, the Department of Health for Scotland refused the city permission to build a scheme in the Douglas area because of its high cost. As a result, the Housing Committee decided to build dwellings of a reduced size. Floorspace and celing heights were reduced and the new scheme consisted of 4-storey blocks containing maisonettes, served by outside stairs at each end and a covered balcony giving access to individual doors. In some respects they were an early example of deck access (Edgar, Rowbotham and Stanforth 1992).

Generally speaking, although standards of space had been reduced in Scotland, as in England, the recommendations were slightly more generous. In 1956, the Department of Health for Scotland issued a manual of house design, revised from a 1950 edition, which contained recommendations on house size. A three-bedroomed, two storey house should have 960 sq ft, some 60 sq ft more than the standard being applied in England. The manual suggested a similar size for maisonettes, while housing for elderly couples could have up to 560 sq ft (Department of Health for Scotland 1956). These rather more generous recommendations mirror the differences in the 1940s between the Dudley and Westwood Reports.

Design in the New Towns

Reference has already been made to the 1940 Barlow Report and the issue of decentralisation of population and industry from the congested metropolitan areas, which it addressed. Such decentralisation was not willingly accepted by many cities who saw it as a weakening of their role and a blow to civic pride. The enthusiasm with which Glasgow sought to build within its own boundaries rather than support overspill (mentioned above) is an example of this. But it had already become clear that housing conditions in inner areas could only be improved through tackling overcrowding, and this could only be done through decentralisation. The Abercrombie Plan for the postwar redevelopment of London, therefore, took decentralisation as a key theme.

After Labour's election victory in 1945, Lord Reith was appointed to head a committee comprised of eminent planners, to examine the issue of establishing satellite settlements in the garden city tradition. The committee reported early the following year and later in 1946 the New Towns Act reached the statute book. By 1950 fourteen 'Phase One' New Towns had been designated, eight around London, beginning with Stevenage in 1946, two in north east England, two in Scotland, one (Corby) in the East Midlands and one (Cwmbran) in South Wales.

The first New Towns were influenced by the garden city planners, although they also borrowed the concept of neighbourhood units from America. Towns were supposed to be self-contained, with populations of around 50,000, and with their own industries, shopping centres, social and community facilities. Much of the initial criticism they attracted centred on the low densities commonly adopted of 12 houses per acre. Housing tended to be very largely in the form of two-storey dwellings, often terraced, and this led to a degree of monotony. Nor was there any variety of land uses because of the strict controls exercised by the planners; the result was the creation of large areas of housing, unrelieved by anything other than open space.

To some extent the monotony was perhaps inevitable given that the new towns were created fairly quickly, in contrast to the slow evolution, and resultant variety of older settlements. But,

> this might have mattered less if the scale of the housing had been large. Terraces four-storeys high posses a certain intrinsic dignity, and when suitably designed they can be given an urban character. But the atmosphere of the new towns' housing was cosy rather than dignified, while the pattern of their layouts and the architecture of their two-storied dwellings derived from rural, not urban, prototypes. The new towns are less like towns that vast overgrown villages.
> (Edwards 1981, p165)

The low densities and the lack of non-housing uses led to social problems and many of the new tenants began to feel isolated. The carefully planned neighbourhoods did not quickly develop a community spirit.

The first changes in the density of new Town housing came with the designation of Cumbernauld in 1955, the only New Town designated during the 1950s. The site was a hilly one and partly because of this, partly because of the Scottish climate and partly because of a recognition of the value of compact urban development, densities were much higher. In the first two estates, densities of 80–90 persons per acre were achieved using two, three and four-storey blocks. Terraces were used to create closer groupings of dwellings than in other New Towns, and enclosed garden areas, parking areas and narrow lanes were created. The high densities and the absence of large gardens were contrary to many of the garden city principles which had informed early New Town design but instead derived from the Scottish urban tradition; as a result Cumbernauld contained a large number of flats. Such low rise, high density schemes helped to influence architects who began to experiment with various forms of courtyard housing, and as renewal of inner city areas became more significant in the late 1950s and early 1960s, such forms of housing were seen as highly appropriate for inner city areas.

The Parker Morris Report

The issues of density, first addressed in Cumbernauld, surfaced again in the Parker Morris Report published in 1961. The committee, chaired by Sir Parker Morris, was appointed by the Central Housing Advisory Committee 'to consider the standards of design and equipment applicable to family dwellings and other forms of residential accommodation, whether provided by public authorities or private enterprise, and to make recommendations'. The Committee interpreted its task in terms of considering standards of internal design, although it also looked at the relationship between the dwelling and its site, at issues affecting layout, at play space and at car parking.

The social context within which the committee worked was a very different one from the wartime years of the Dudley Committee. There had been a huge increase in the number of families with washing machines, fridges and televisions, one in three households possessed a car, and personal wealth had increased. The pattern of living had therefore undergone substantial change.

> Housewives now increasingly look to machinery to lighten their household tasks: ... so that she has more free time to live a life of her own .... Teenagers wanting to listen to records; someone else wanting to watch the television; someone going in for do-it-yourself; all these and homework too mean that the individual members of the family are more and more wanting to be free to move away from the fireside to somewhere else in the home .... These changes in

the way people want to live . . . make it timely to re-examine the kinds of homes that we ought to be building . . . .

(MHLG 1961, p21)

Parker Morris was a significant report therefore because it tried to examine the changing needs of all members of the household and the spaces which they would use. They suggested that open planning (such as in Macmillan's 'large living room' houses) was unpopular because of noise and lack of privacy and that there should be living space provided which allowed both for the family to be together (eg for meals) and for individual members to carry on their own separate pursuits.

Within the house therefore, a number of changes were proposed. The Report recommended a working kitchen large enough for family dining or, in larger homes, a separate dining room. Upstairs, bedroom space should be improved, particularly for children who would tend to use the rooms rather like bedsits, for a range of study or leisure activities. There needed to be room for a desk, chair and bookcase, as well as the bed, wardrobe and bedside table.

Storage was particularly important, not least because of the tendency towards hoarding which, as Parker Morris recognised, is common to many families. As well as general storage, there was a need for space for garden equipment, bicycles, and, in family houses, for prams, and the Report recommended that the general storage area in the local authority house for four or more persons should be 50 sq ft, excluding bin stores and access ways.

Heating was another important area, because of a higher expectation of comfort levels. As the Report stated, 'whether the design of homes takes radically new directions or not, the person moving into a new home increasingly expects to be **warm**'. The practice at the time in many local authorities was for the installation of a back boiler which, apart from water heating, could service at best two or three radiators. These tended to be placed in the living space, and the bedrooms and bathroom were rarely heated. Parker Morris recommended that the minimum standard for new houses should be an installation capable of heating the living areas to 65°F (18.5°C) and the kitchen and circulation areas like the hall to 55°F (13°C). In practice, however, it was felt to be better value for money in the long term, if heating systems could be installed capable of heating the bedroom to 65°F as well.

The increasing use of domestic appliances was recognised, and the Report considered not only kitchen layout where this was particularly important but also the question of electric sockets. The practice at the time was to instal the minimum of around six sockets.

This was deemed to be totally inadequate and the Report recommended 20, with 15 as a minimum.

In terms of the overall floorspace of the house, the Report recognised that the average five person house then being built by local authorities was of around 900 sq ft, including storage. Parker Morris recommended a minimum of 910 sq ft, plus storage space of 50 sq ft, an increase overall of 60 sq ft, or 6.7 per cent (Figure 3.3).

Outwith the dwelling the increased affluence of families was recognised and the Report contained a discussion on increasing car ownership and the need to provide car parking close to the home. As far as gardens were concerned, they were being used almost exclusively for recreational use rather than for the growing of food and vegetables. Many of the gardens being provided, however, were rather small for families to use to play in and this suggested a need for proper provision of children's playspace. In all gardens, there should be adequate privacy for families to sit out and have meals outside, another recognition of lifestyle changes.

Unlike the Tudor-Walters and Dudley Reports, Parker Morris was not followed by government housing manuals with plans of recommended house types. Instead, a series of Design Bulletins began to appear examining space in the home, safety, layout of children's play spaces etc. Nevertheless, Parker Morris standards became mandatory for public sector housing in 1967 and resulted in some high quality residential buildings.

The typical house design of this period, although often still semi-detached, was frequently in the form of two- or three-storey terraces. Many had garages and, as central heating became increasingly common, houses often had no chimneys. Bay windows vanished completely, to be replaced by large 'picture windows', and there was a considerable amount of uniformity in the simple lines of the modern house. Some architects began to react against such uniformity and it was not uncommon for brick, tile or timber cladding to be added to relieve the monotony.

As the 1960s progressed, the differences in style between public and private sectors all but disappeared. Indeed, many private houses were smaller than their local authority equivalents and less well equipped.

> What had actually happened was that the all important symbols of status had shifted away from the house on to moveable objects, particularly gadgets . . . washing machines became status-enhancing possessions and mass car-ownership and package holidays abroad meant that one's new standing could be expressed in new ways . . .'
>
> (Barrett and Phillips 1987, p137)

Although the average size of council houses rose during the 1960s,

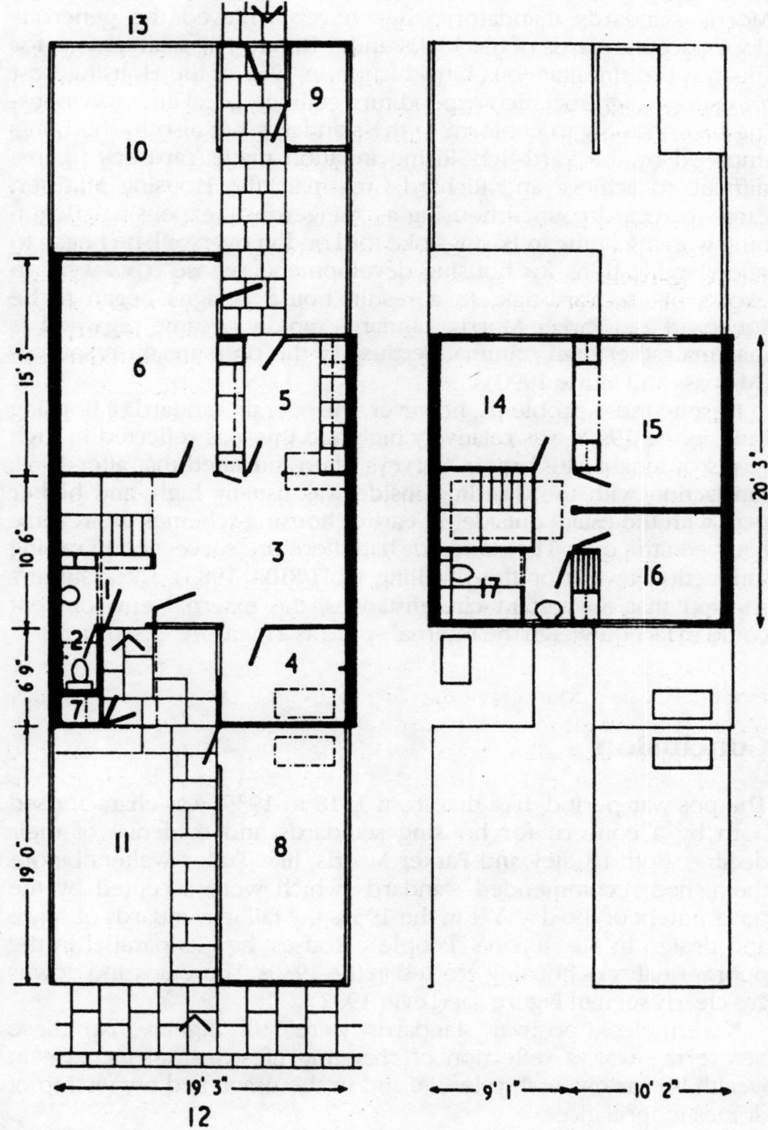

Figure 3.3 Parker Morris five-person house published by Ministry of Housing and Local Government, 1963. Source: Burnett (1986)

particularly after the 1967 Housing Subsidies Act which made Parker Morris standards mandatory, they never achieved the generous floorspace standards of the 1940s under Bevan. The main reason for this was the simultaneous introduction in 1967 of the Housing Cost Yardstick which specified expenditure ceilings. Local authority housing had not only to conform to the standards but also to the limits imposed by the Yardstick. Rising inflation made Yardstick figures difficult to achieve and Richard Crossman, the Housing Minister, came to regard council housing as 'dangerously expensive'. Beginning with a scheme in Basingstoke for London overspill, he began to reject applications for housing developments whose costs were in excess of the Yardstick. As a result, house designs began to be squeezed and Parker Morris standards rapidly became regarded as maxima rather than minima, because of the pressure on resources (Malpass and Murie 1990).

Despite these problems, however, the overall standard of housing built in the 1960s was relatively high and this was reflected in high levels of tenant satisfaction. Surveys often indicated that after 1967, satisfaction with the dwelling inside was usually high, and higher than with the estate outside. In earlier housing schemes the reverse had been the case. The standards had therefore succeeded in raising satisfaction levels for the dwelling (IoH/RIBA 1983). Later surveys showed that, in certain circumstances, the external environment could in fact outweigh the internal space as a measure of satisfaction.

Conclusion

The postwar period, like that from 1918 to 1939, was characterised both by a concern for housing standards and evidence of their decline. Both Dudley and Parker Morris, like Tudor Walters before them, had recommended standards which were accepted by the government of the day. Yet in the 1950s the fall in standards of space and design in Macmillan's 'People's Houses' had its parallel in the poorer quality of housing erected in the 1930s. These ups and downs are clearly seen in Figure 3.4 (Levitt 1982).

Nevertheless, postwar standards were still higher than those before the war, a reflection of changing lifestyles, an increase in wealth, in car-ownership levels, and in the usage and ownership of domestic appliances.

As in so many areas of public policy, it was the state of the British economy which had a key effect. Just as the financial crisis of the late 1940s prevented Bevan from building on the scale which he desired, so the rising inflation of the 1960s, coupled with the introduction of

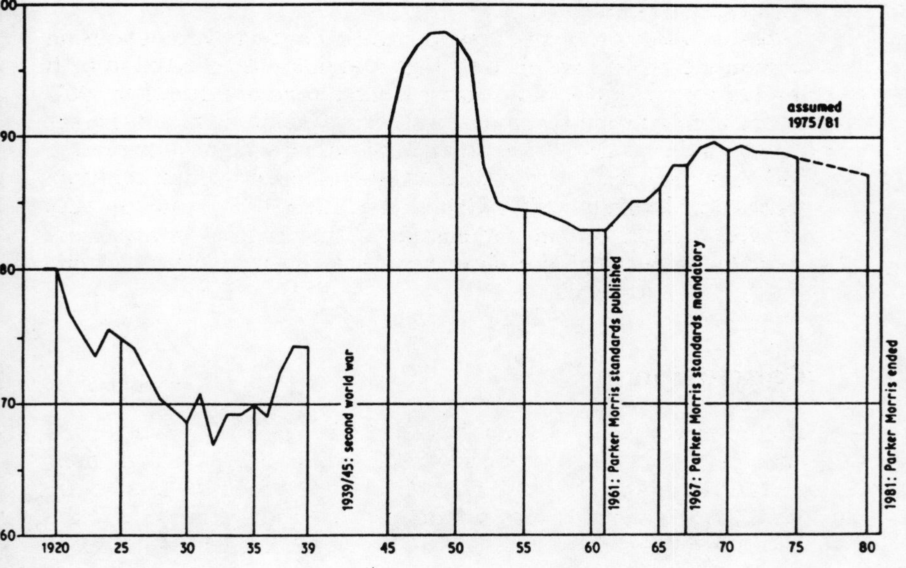

Figure 3.4 Changing space standards in the average five-bedspace house in England and Wales, 1919–80. Source: Levitt (1982)

the Housing Cost Yardstick in 1967, led to problems with the implementation of the Parker Morris standards. The solution, adopted extensively in the postwar period, was to build more houses more cheaply and on less land. Flats became increasingly common as the postwar period progressed, and this approach to the housing shortage is discussed in Chapter Four.

Chapter 4
High rise solutions

Introduction

It became clear in Chapter Three that, during the postwar period, there was an increasing encouragement of high rise housing. In the main, this was because of the continuing quantitative shortage of housing in the 1950s as authorities struggled to cope with families swollen in size by the late 1940s 'baby boom'; the development of flatted estates appeared to offer a way of building large numbers of houses, relatively cheaply, while saving on the costs of land. The process was assisted by, first, the developments in architectural thinking during the 1930s and 1940s which stressed the benefits and advantages of multi-storey construction and, second, by technical advances made in the 1950s in building systems which simplified and speeded up the building of high rise flats.

This chapter begins by examining the architectural trends of the 1930s, and the early high rise developments which then took place, before moving on to discuss the widespread high rise building in the public sector after the war. The chapter spends some time examining public disenchantment with such housing before discussing some of the initiatives currently under way to try and tackle both technical and management problems which have occurred.

The origins of high rise

The building of public sector flats on a large scale can be dated back to the 1930 Housing Act which provided local authorities with extra subsidy for the provision of flatted estates for slum clearance families. Further legislation in 1933, 1935 and 1938 consolidated the position, with subsidies for flats to relieve overcrowding made available as of right while similar subsidies for houses were available only at a lower rate and at the discretion of the Minister concerned (Ash 1980).

Technical advances at the time, particularly in steel-framed construction, made possible the building of modern working class flats on a large scale and the example of Quarry Hill, in Leeds, has already been quoted (Chapter Two). The development of mansion blocks in the private sector also dates from this period.

Although there was thus considerable development of flatted housing, their appearance sparked a fierce debate. For some, the building of flats offered an opportunity to build a new and better form of life for working class people, while for many architects and planners, flatted schemes which could be integrated into the existing urban fabric were infinitely preferable to the suburban sprawl which was increasingly occurring on the urban fringes. For others, however, flats presented an image of nineteenth century philanthropy and represented little advancement from the days of Peabody. The Garden City movement, now in the form of the Town and Country Planning Association, deplored the lack of vision being demonstrated, when alternative decentralised new settlements could have been built.

The debate was increasingly influenced by developments in Europe and by the proponents of the Modern Movement. The Bauhaus School and architects such as Walter Gropius and Mies van der Rohe advocated clear angular lines for buildings, and the use of materials like glass, steel and concrete, all of which could assist in the building of large scale housing projects. But it was the work of the Swiss architect Le Corbusier which influenced a whole generation of architects and led to the more widespread acceptance of multi-storey development.

Born Charles-Edouard Jeanneret, he took the pseudonym of Le Corbusier at an early age and it is by this that he is universally known. In 1927, his great work *Vers une Architecture* was first published in English translation, followed two years later by *La Ville Radieuse*. Le Corbusier believed in five basic essentials for his new architecture. First, buildings should be raised on stilts ('pilotis') to allow access underneath; second, buildings should have terraces and roof gardens; third, because concrete construction removed the need for central load-bearing walls within the building, an open floor plan should be adopted; fourth, horizontal windows should run the length of the building; and fifth, facades should be treated sculpturally, taking advantage of concrete building techniques (Relph 1987). Le Corbusier envisaged vertical cities of towers, serviced by modern roads and with open space provided between the tower blocks. The blocks themselves would be 'machines for living in', containing shops, schools, and all kinds of social and community facilities. His Unité d'Habitation, an 18-storey block of 337 flats, constructed in Marseilles between 1946 and 1952, was designed on these principles, as well as containing 'streets in the air', served by lifts, off which the individual dwellings opened. The Unité had, within it, a creche, a kindergarten, a rooftop swimming pool, play area, gymnasium and running track while adjacent were a garage, and sports ground.

It is important therefore to stress that Le Corbusier himself, although postulating both high building and high population densities, was concerned to provide plenty of open space, with the buildings standing in open parkland. He referred to buildings being 'bathed in light and air' to illustrate his point. He was unhappy therefore with multi-storey blocks which were built too close together without adequate open space between, as was the case in many American cities. He spoke of finding the New York skyscrapers too small, before going on to explain that they should be taller and fewer.

> The skyscraper is not a plume rising from the face of the city. It has been made that, and wrongly . . . . The skyscraper is an instrument . . . for the concentration of population, for getting rid of land congestion, for classification, for internal efficiency . . . . But the skyscraper as plume multiplied over the area of Manhattan, has disregarded experience . . . . The skyscrapers of New York are too small and there are too many of them.
>
> (Le Corbusier 1947, pp51–2, 55)

Le Corbusier is frequently blamed for some of the failings of multi-storey building in the postwar period but it is important to realise that such failings stemmed in many cases from poor implementation of the ideas rather than the ideas themselves.

Although many flatted dwellings had been built in Britain prior to the Second World War, only one specifically high rise development was completed. This was Highpoint One, designed in 1936 by Berthold Lubetkin in the Highgate area of London, with white rendered facade, horizontal windows, and roof garden and surrounded by open space. Two years later, Highpoint Two was completed on an adjacent site. The blocks shared a number of facilities including garden, swimming pool, tennis courts and tea room. Le Corbusier himself praised the development, referring to Highgate as the 'seed of vertical garden-city as opposed to the horizontal extension' (Le Corbusier 1936).

The influences of European ideas and the Modern Movement could also be seen in some of the early estates built by the London County Council. In 1936, they constructed Kensal House in Ladbroke Grove, a slab block of 5–6 storeys with horizontal lines, balconies and flat roof, and other blocks in areas like Lambeth followed. Some of the first postwar schemes were of similar construction, with block heights increasing to eight or nine storeys as lift access was introduced; staircase rather than balcony access became more common. One of the most famous of these early schemes was Churchill Gardens, designed in 1946 for Westminster City Council, on a bomb-damaged site in Pimlico. The scheme consisted of tall slab blocks at right angles to the river with smaller four-storey blocks between them. In the courts thus created were gardens, trees and play areas. The development was a high density one to fit with the proposals set out by Abercrombie in his plan for postwar London and, an original feature at the time, the scheme was designed to use waste heat from Battersea Power Station.

These earliest flats appeared to be relatively popular. Many were in inner city locations close to facilities and the airiness and the views were a complete contrast to the congested housing from which families had moved. There was, too, a certain novelty about living in a modern flat, which was caught admirably by the humorist Heath Robinson:

> Of recent years, it has become increasingly apparent that the House has had its day, and that the dwelling-place of the future is the Flat — so called because it usually is, and to distinguish it from the maisonette, which isn't .... Reduced to its lowest terms, ... a flat is simply a portion of a house that has been converted but not entirely convinced. Since the primary purpose of flats is to enable at least five families to live where only one hung out before, thereby quintupling the landlord's income, they are apt to lack that spaciousness which characterises the Grand Central Terminal, New York. From the keen cat-swinger's point of view this is regrettable ...
>
> (Robinson and Browne 1936, p5)

Clearly then, the architectural mood was one of encouragement towards the building of flats, although, as explained in Chapter Three, the Labour government of the time was less convinced. The combination of the postwar shortage of building materials, the need to build more houses quickly and the coming to power of the Conservatives in 1951 changed things dramatically, however, and there was an increasing encouragement of high rise council housing.

High Rise Council Housing

Reference was made in Chapter Three to the 1953 Housing Manual which contained, for the first time, detailed plans of three-storey flats, together with designs for corner sites which could also incorporate small flatted dwellings. This encouragement towards flatted estates was given added impetus when, in 1956, the Government passed the Housing Subsidies Act whereby subsidy increased with storey height, but in the long term these subsidies became problematic. The intention had been to remove barriers to council building where it was most needed but, in the event, it encouraged local authorities to build in locations and at densities which later became extremely problematic.

To some extent, there was a logic in the Government's position. The demand for houses in the 1950s clearly needed to be met but, at the same time, there were increased concerns at the loss of agricultural land, particularly in the wake of a war when food production had been of crucial importance. New Towns were being encouraged, as was overspill, and this received an added boost with the Town Development Act of 1952 whereby established towns were assisted in the reception of families from the conurbations. But there was still a presumption against suburban sprawl and there were formal proposals in the early 1950s to establish a Green Belt around London. Building upwards appeared to be the only alternative.

Generally speaking, the maximum density for two-storey family housing was about 14 houses (or 45 persons) to the acre, but flats could be built quite acceptably at densities of 40 flats (133 persons) to the acre, because of the absence of individual garden space. The effect of this can be illustrated in Table 4.1, where it is clear that for the highest densities, of over 100 persons per acre, to be achieved, an estate consisting almost entirely of flats would need to be built.

Table 4.1: Densities of houses and flats

Combined Density (persons per acre)	Houses (at 45 persons per acre) %	Flats (at 120 persons per acre) %
45	100	—
50	84	16
60	61	39
75	36	64
100	12	88
120+	—	100

Source: Osborn and Whittick (1969)

In 1958, the Ministry of Housing and Local Government issued a further design guide and the title, 'Flats and Houses' suggested clearly the shift in emphasis. The then Minister, Henry Brooke did, however, suggest in his foreword that he did not wish to encourage the use of multi-storeys where they were not really necessary and spoke of the need to intermingle houses with maisonettes and flats (MHLG 1958). The Manual took as a layout study a site in Birmingham, and demonstrated a variety of different layouts and housing mixes which could be achieved on the site. Although the preferred strategy seemed to be for a mix of styles, the tone was unmistakably in favour of flats. In one particular plan, it was shown that if larger families were to be accommodated in houses with gardens, 'so much extra land is required for the extra houses that the designer has to use another 13-storey slab block to provide the dwellings which there is no longer the space to accommodate in low blocks' (MHLG 1958, p16). The need for cost effectiveness for all designs was a strong emphasis and, for this reason, the focus tended to be on high densities for each type of building. Little use was made in the designs of blocks of eight or nine storeys; 'it is usually better, from the aspect of overall cost, to go higher'.

Because flats had no internal stairs and hence reduced circulation space, the floor space tended to be much smaller than two-storey houses. In the Manual, plans for four-person (two-bedroomed) flats showed an overall floorspace of 700–800 sq ft., while five-person (three-bedroomed) flats were likely to have around 900 sq ft or more. In a sense then, they were comparable with the Macmillan 'People's House', although lacking the privacy which an individual garden could provide.

Although flats had no private outdoor space, the Manual emphasised strongly the need for adequate garaging and car parking, playspace and landscaped areas. There was also detailed consideration of communal facilities such as refuse disposal and laundry rooms, as well as storage space.

Good quality flat design was also a major consideration of the Parker Morris Committee in 1961. The Committee felt that, as with houses, floorspace standards could be improved, and drew attention in particular to problems of insufficient cupboard and storage space. Further problems were being created with the postwar rise in living standards and the increased use of washing machines and tumble driers; as well as having to find extra space within kitchens, families would in consequence make much less use of communal laundry rooms, which might no longer be needed in future flatted estates. The Parker Morris Report also paid particular attention to the problems of refuse disposal, exacerbated by the increased packaging of food, and of sound insulation and the problem of noise transmission within flats. Their aims were fairly clear:

> The human problem for the future in the design of flats and maisonettes is to provide for people who live in them an environment which is as workable, and as satisfactory, as for people who live in houses. Often most of the needs are met in mixed developments of flats, maisonettes and houses, which provide the opportunity for larger families to live at ground level or near it. For other households, sometimes including families with children, the problems of living at a distance from the ground remain. Ways of meeting the need for outdoor space may come to be found in newer forms of access to the dwellings associated with covered space in the open air at the level of the home, and providing some of the virtues of the back yard and the pedestrian street
>
> (MHLG 1961, p28)

As far as floorspace was concerned, the Parker Morris Committee recommended a net floor area plus storage of 785 sq ft for a four-person flat, rising to 965 sq ft for six people.

The effects of government subsidy and of exhortations to build upwards can be seen in the increasing proportion of council housing which was built in flatted form. Table 4.2 illustrates the changes between 1951 and 1980, with the peak period for flat building coming at the end of the 1960s. Subsidy was undoubtedly crucial for, as Power (1987) points out, the cost of building high rise flats was 50 per cent greater than building houses. Yet the subsidy at the beginning of the 1960s for a high rise flat was three times greater than a house. This later reduced to double and by 1968, the subsidy was abolished altogether following the Housing Subsidies Act, 1967.

Table 4.2: Local authority flats and houses built 1951–1980

Year	Houses		Flats and Maisonettes	
	No (000s)	%	No (000s)	%
1951–55	680	78.2	190	21.8
1856–60	385	65.2	205	34.8
1961–65	285	52.3	260	47.7
1966–70	360	49.3	370	50.7
1971–75	260	51.0	250	49.0
1976–80	275	55.3	222	44.7

Source: DoE — *Housing and Construction Statistics*

There is no doubt that the earlier multi-storey developments were of an extremely high standard. One of the most famous schemes was the London County Council estate at Roehampton, started in 1952, where 1,850 dwellings were built in a mixture of 11-storey slab blocks, 12-storey point blocks and low-rise maisonettes. The estate also included schools, shops, a library and elderly persons' housing but the most important feature was the landscaping. Set on the edge of the rolling parkland of Richmond Park, the estate seemed to be a perfect embodiment of Le Corbusier's ideals. Other LCC estates of the 1950s, of similar design although in less verdant surroundings, were the Loughborough estate, constructed between 1954 and 1958 in Brixton, and the Bentham Road estate in Hackney. In Corbusian style, the blocks were raised, but this was usually to allow for car parking and play space, rather than for landscaping. Still, the estates proved popular and sociological studies at the time suggested that the overwhelming majority of the families living on the upper floors of flats preferred living there to moving to a house at a lower level (Esher 1981). The difficulties which arose with some of the later estates had their origins in the subsidy arrangements. Hence,

> when local authorities were counselled by MHLG to be sparing in the use of high rise and were simultaneously offered considerable financial bonus for building high rise, they took the cash and let the cackle go. Some local authorities were able to build high rise under the officially estimated cost and could make a net 'profit' on the subsidy.
>
> (Ash 1980, p103)

The temptation to build multi-storey housing in congested inner areas, without the open space which might accompany it, stemmed also from weak regional planning. Although the large cities were faced with massive housing problems in the 1950s and a need for new development, it was not always possible to build in sufficient numbers within urban boundaries. Cities such as Manchester were therefore forced into protracted wrangles with adjacent semi-rural counties like Cheshire over the issue of building land and overspill. In some cases, new estates were built completely outwith the city boundary, as happened with Liverpool's Kirkby and Huyton estates.

Other authorities welcomed high rise as presenting an opportunity to rehouse families within the urban boundary and prevent a loss of rateable value. There is an interesting contrast between Manchester, which looked to adjacent green belt areas for building land, and Salford which did the opposite:

> Of the 8,462 dwellings built there between 1945 and 31 August 1968, 3,972 were in forty-seven blocks of flats. This drive for flats has been

> explained as a response to losses of population and rateable value so great as to threaten Salford's existence as an independent local authority
>
> (Cooney 1974, p161)

A similar situation pertained in Glasgow, where the City Council was opposed to overspill for many years, preferring to rehouse families within the city boundaries rather than lose rateable and rental income. In the event the city was forced to accept overspill because of the sheer scale of the housing problem, and although high rise redevelopment of the inner city was at 165 persons per acre, a greater density than suggested in Table 4.1, this was still only one-third of existing slum density. Glasgow's adoption of high rise was accompanied by a belief that blocks should be designed to an exceptionally high standard, to make a forceful statement about the city's commitment to slum clearance. Accordingly, the architect Basil Spence was commissioned to design some 20-storey slab blocks in the Gorbals, with inset communal balconies; in the long run the blocks presented structural and dampness problems but, at the time, they were significant milestones in the city's rebuilding (Horsey 1990).

In the early 1950s, the building industry had had little experience of high rise housing for local authorities, although it was, of course, perfectly capable of constructing tall office blocks. Early housing blocks used similar construction methods — a steel or reinforced concrete frame — but increasingly attention became focused on industrial building, using uniform components which could be factory-produced. The Government set up the National Building Agency in 1963 to advise on building methods and the following year, the incoming Labour government set a new target of 500,000 houses a year by 1970; in fact the maximum achieved was 426,000 in 1968 (Ash 1980). Clearly such targets could not be achieved by traditional (and slower) building methods and the NBA combined with the Ministry of Housing and Local Government to promote industrialised building, with many local authorities being encouraged into contracts with system builders for large scale multi-storey housing schemes. The Minister at the time, Richard Crossman, was particularly instrumental in these developments:

> In conversation, I asked why it was only 750 houses they were building at Oldham; why not rebuild the whole thing? Wouldn't that help Laing, the builders? 'Of course it would', said Oliver, 'and it would help Oldham too'. 'Well, why don't we do it?' 'It depends on the Minister.' And Whitfield-Lewis, the Chief Architect smiled, and I said 'Why shouldn't we? Why shouldn't we assume that instead of doing one little bit of the centre of Oldham, we should use the

> whole 300 acres and have a real demonstration that our system-building can work and really reduce costs? Let's see that one piece of central redevelopment is really finished by us.
>
> (Crossman 1975, p81)

Later, Crossman refers to a new method of building pioneered by Costain and the need for the builders to use it extensively in order to make it cost-effctive:

> [It] had cost Costain a lot of money because they couldn't get a continuous run by repeating it anywhere else, and I began to see the difficulties of system-building when you have hundreds of local authorities which all want to make each building just a little different and claim credit for it.
>
> (Crossman 1975, p82)

For the Ministry, the use of system-building was felt to be advantageous because the use of standard designs could release professional time to concentrate on improving layouts. In fact this rarely happened and the fact that most of these later multi-storey blocks were located in the inner city meant that there was seldom the opportunity for spacious layouts with adequate open space. Frequently such space was provided underneath the blocks but because of a lack of surveillance and the general darkness and dinginess of these spaces, they quickly became 'no-go' areas for residents.

Table 4.3: High rise by storey height

	6–9 storeys		10–19 storeys		20+ storeys		Total	
Area	No	%	No	%	No	%	No	%
West Midlands	528	69	216	27	21	3	765	100
Greater Manchester/ Merseyside	52	13	312	81	24	6	388	100
Strathclyde	12	3	168	46	183	51	363	100
Tyne and Wear	31	21	107	73	8	6	146	100
South and West Yorkshire	37	13	222	79	24	8	283	100
Greater London North	425	54	305	38	64	8	794	100
Greater London South	565	56	341	34	99	10	1005	100
All authorities	1837	40	2141	47	453	10	4570	

Sources: Anderson, Bulos and Walker (1985, p6); Bulos and Walker (1987, p8)

By the end of the 1960s and the end of the high rise council building programme, around 10 per cent of council stock was in the form of high rise development. The bulk of these blocks were concentrated in inner London and the big metropolitan centres, with eleven authorities having more than 100 high rise blocks. Table 4.3 shows the geographical distribution of high rise blocks, and the variation in block height is interesting. Glasgow has the largest number of very high flats while the Birmingham area has most of its stock in flats 6–9 storeys high.

Deck Access Housing

While many local authorities used the Government's advice and subsidy to build point and slab blocks, others adopted a deck access approach, with entry to the flats being achieved from decks or walkways — the 'streets in the air' of Le Corbusier. These principles of Le Corbusier were taken up by a new group of architects in the immediate postwar era; calling themselves Team Ten, they included Ralph Erskine, later to design Byker in Newcastle (see Chapter Eight), and Alison and Peter Smithson who helped to develop the concept of deck access blocks. This concept saw perhaps its greatest expression in Sheffield with the building of the Park Hill complex, from 1957 onwards.

Park Hill, and the later and adjacent scheme of Hyde Park were built on a 50 acre, sloping and hilly site immediately above the city's Midland railway station. Designed by Lewis Womersley, it consisted of 995 dwellings, of which around half were flats and half maisonettes. The scheme also contained over 30 shops, four pubs, a laundry, 74 lock-up garages and 100 parking spaces. Because of the slope of the ground it was possible to enter the walkways at ground level at one end of the site and arrive at an upper storey at the other end, where lifts carried families back to the shops at ground level. The walkways or 'decks' were 10 feet (3m) wide and, as well as a means of access, were also intended for social interaction, but generally this failed to happen:

> The first occupant at Park Hill was a 'trained social worker' who was detailed to provide feedback to the designers on tenant reaction. The intended social relationships based on the existence of 'streets in the air' failed to materialise — only four per cent of inhabitants 'remembered that (the decks) made it possible to stand and talk to people', while 70 per cent of them complained about the external appearance of the development.
>
> (Pawley 1971, p94)

Sheffield went on to build a second phase of deck access housing at Hyde Park, immediately north east of Park Hill, larger and higher than the original scheme.

The deck access idea gained ground in the 1960s because the notion of 'streets in the air' allowed families with children to live at a distance from the ground, the decks being easily used by bicycles, prams and shopping trolleys. Large numbers of such developments were therefore built although frequently the deck access blocks were incorporated into a mixed style development and most housing schemes did not present such a unified appearance as Park Hill. The introduction of industrialised building, however, led to the building of straight street decks of a rather brutal appearance and without much variety of design. As a result, deck access housing began to appear much less attractive.

Good examples of industrialised deck access housing are provided by the developments of the Yorkshire Development Group (YDG) which built its first such industrialised scheme in Leek Street in Leeds in 1966, with others following in Hull, Sheffield and Nottingham. The Sheffield scheme, at Broomhall, consisted of 653 flats, built of pre-cast concrete panels and, despite its leafy site, of a rather drab appearance. The flats were designed to be above Parker Morris floorspace standards but were inadequately heated and insulated, possessing an expensive underfloor heating system and suffering, from the beginning, from dampness (Goodchild 1987). These problems, shared by other YDG flats, led to the scheme being abandoned in 1984, after a life of less than twenty years.

In many respects, therefore, the problems of deck access housing derived not so much from the original concept of 'streets in the air' but particularly from the way that concept was realised. The shift to industrialised building methods and dampness were very much to blame. A similar situation to that in Sheffield arose in the Gorbals area of Glasgow with the development of the Hutchesontown 'E' scheme, opened by the Queen in 1968. The 'Tracoba' system of construction had been used successfully in European and African countries but was ultimately defeated by the Scottish climate. After years of suffering from irremediable dampness, they were demolished in 1987. In London, the Taylor Woodrow Anglian system was used for the 1,000 flat development of Broadwater Farm and, although not suffering excessively from water penetration or condensation, leaking roofs had to be replaced in the late 1970s.

Increasingly, during the 1980s, deck access schemes grew in their unpopularity, and the design faults led to serious problems of management, particularly in regard to allocations. Estates were increasingly used for lets to the homeless as void rates increased. The American author Tom Wolfe suggested that part of the problem stemmed from the lack of private space in such developments:

> On each floor, there were covered walkways, in keeping with Corbusier's idea of 'streets in the air'. Since there was no other place in the project in which to sin in public, whatever might ordinarily have taken place in bars, brothels, social clubs, pool halls, amusement arcades, general stores, corncribs, rutabaga patches, hayricks, barn stalls, now took place in the streets in the air. Corbusier's boulevards made Hogarth's Gin Lane look like the oceanside street of dreams. Respectable folk pulled out, even if it meant living in cracks in the sidewalks
>
> (Wolfe 1981, p81)

In some schemes, the decks became used for motor-cycling races, while the links from one block to the next enabled vandals and housebreakers to make an easy getaway. Certainly the lack of an involvement in the design by tenants may have been significant, explaining why they so conspicuously failed to use the decks for their intended purpose. One of the worst examples of this is provided by Hulme in Manchester. When the terraced slums were cleared in the 1960s, the deck access scheme which replaced them was the product of the architects and planners. Designed in a series of crescents, the estate was intended to replicate Georgian Bath and the blocks were therefore given names like John Nash Crescent, Charles Barry Crescent and Robert Adam Crescent. For the tenants however, faced with problems of dampness and a lack of amenities, the comparison with Bath was rather lost on them.

What went wrong?

Some of the problems of high rise housing have already been alluded to and during the 1970s and 1980s, there was an increasing disenchantment with this particular house type. But the most significant demonstration of the inherent problems dates back to the 16 May 1968, when the occupant of a flat on the 18th floor of Ronan Point, a 21-storey block in Newham, East London, attempted to light her gas cooker to make breakfast. The resulting explosion not only blew out the kitchen wall panel and ceiling but led to a progressive collapse of the entire south east corner of the building; five people were killed. The structural failure of Ronan Point had widespread consequences and the Tribunal of Inquiry, established following the disaster, concluded that there were inherent defects in the design. The Government subsequently recommended that owners of tall blocks built by industrialised or 'system' methods should survey and, if necessary, strengthen them. A particular issue was the way in which innovations in building design had been assimilated into the Building Regulations without all the consequences being recognised.

Another issue was the poor workmanship revealed by the collapse. Sixteen years later, shortly before the rebuilt Ronan Point was finally demolished, Newham Council conducted a full-scale fire test to investigate how safe the building actually was; it had to be stopped after just twelve minutes because of the warping and splitting of the precast panels. In 1986, as the block was being knocked down, it became clear that the main joints contained less than half the specified mortar and were packed with rubbish swept from floor slabs during construction (Hutchinson 1989).

In the wake of the Ronan Point collapse, over £100 million was spent strengthening tower blocks although, in some cases, demolition was recommended. Over 10,000 dwellings, built after 1970, were demolished within 15 years because of inherent building defects (Knevitt 1985). The problem was also an international one with similar issues being faced in North America. In 1972, the award-winning Pruitt-Igoe housing scheme in St Louis, Missouri, consisting of a series of deck access blocks, was simply blown up.

The decline in high rise building had, to an extent, already started before Ronan Point, with the abolition of extra subsidy in 1967. Ronan Point simply speeded up the process, not merely by highlighting the structural problems but also leading to widespread tenant reaction against that particular house type.

The social problems of living in high rise blocks were already being recognised in the early 1960s, particularly for families with children. Social work concerns in London led to an inquiry as early as 1961, entitled *Two to Five in High Flats* (Maizels 1961) and there was evidence that children's play was being restricted, with consequences for later development. Later work by Jephcott in Glasgow confirmed this:

> Practically no-one disputes that this form of home is unsatisfactory for the family with small children. It is a strain on the mother and an over-restricted environment, physical and social, for the child. There are problems even for families whose children are of school age since the children's world is so cut off from that of adults. And the trim orderly setting of the multi-storey estate requires unusually imaginative provision for play if the children themselves are not to be thwarted.
>
> (Jephcott 1971, p130)

Partly the problem was the limited play space within the home or within the landings and corridors of the blocks, partly the fact that if children played on the ground, they were too far away for parental supervision which, in a conventional house, could be exercised by means of a glance through the window. In Glasgow, the poet Adam McNaughtan drew attention to the inability of parents to hand out snacks to their children:

> I'm a skyscraper wean; I live on the nineteenth flair,
> An' I'm no' gaun oot tae play ony mair,
> 'Cause since we moved tae Castlemilk, I'm wastin' away,
> 'Cause I'm gettin' wan less meal ev'ry day.
>
> Oh, ye cannae fling pieces oot a twenty-storey flat,
> Seven hundred hungry weans'll testify tae that,
> If it's butter, cheese or jeely, if the breid is plain or pan,
> The odds against it reachin' earth is ninety-nine tae wan
>
> (McNaughtan 1967)

Many women, with or without children, found the excessively self-contained existence of flat life profoundly depressing. Jephcott points out that flats have none of those areas such as yards, gardens or doorsteps which help to encourage social interaction, and the blocks therefore become eventless places, short of 'those goings-on of life'. Roberts (1991) goes further and points out that the architects of many high rise developments positively discouraged women from doing simple things like hanging out washing as this would detract from the clean, simple lines of the building.

Although high rise flats may have been unpopular with many tenants, campaigning against them did not begin in earnest until after Ronan Point and indeed the 1970s, by which time new blocks were rarely being built. The issues for tenants were not wholly social, however, but were increasingly concerned about structural defects and, importantly, about dampness. The Hutchesontown 'E' development in Glasgow, demolished because of dampness, was the target of a sustained campaign in the mid-1970s (Bryant 1979). More recently, there was an important legal challenge in Birmingham in 1986 over dampness and mould within the city's tower blocks. Tenants served summonses on the local authority under the 1936 Public Health Act and the courts imposed a duty on the council to make improvements, including new heating systems, new extractor fans and double glazing.

Although Birmingham subsequently won an appeal against the verdict, it was largely on the technicality that only 16 tenants had brought the case and these individual cases did not necessarily mean the whole block was defective. To an extent, the appeal was academic as the repairs had already been carried out before it was heard but the case illustrates the very unsatisfactory living conditions facing many tenants.

The reaction by many professionals in these circumstances was to blame tenants for not heating their homes adequately. To an extent this was true but it failed to recognise the inability of tenants to afford the high running costs of the heating systems which had been installed. New initiatives have therefore focused on the need to provide adequate heating of the buildings but at prices which tenants can afford, and some authorities such as Glasgow and Liverpool are collaborating with local electricity boards to produce cheaper heating solutions.

A partial cause of the problem has been found to be the impact of tower blocks on wind patterns. The presence of high rise housing causes a down draught of cold air and this causes cooling of the outside walls. Gerry and Harvey (1983) suggested that adjacent low-rise developments are also affected and as a result require three or four times as much heating as similar buildings elsewhere. Many tenants would find it impossible to meet the costs of this extra heating.

While high rise housing may present many problems for tenants, there are also other issues. As noted earlier, they proved expensive to construct and, although the costs did not increase proportionately with height as originally suggested by the subsidy legislation, the heftier foundations which were required and the extra services such as lifts, combined to increase costs.

High rise housing was also extravagant in its use of land. Partly this was encouraged by the architects, on the Corbusian model, but partly it was due to the amount of open space and car parking required around the development. Thus, high rise solutions were not necessarily more satisfactory in this regard than conventional housing.

> It is also questionable whether the land freed by building high — the large, open expanses of grass, concrete and tarmac which are the normal setting for towers and slabs — has much intrinsic value for the flats' own population or the community at large. It is difficult to given such places visual interest . . . .
>
> (Jephcott 1971, p129)

The realisation of the high cost, in terms of finance and land, of high rise building proved another factor in swinging the mood against them.

At the height of the high rise boom, seven national companies dominated the market, namely Wimpey, Concrete, Laing, Wates, Taylor Woodrow, Camus and Crudens. Such firms exercised enormous influence on central government and developed similarly close relationships with local authorities, relationships which, in some cases, were subsequently found to have been corrupt, as the Poulson scandal demonstrated. After 1972, the switch away from industrialised methods and high rise building was seen as an attempt by both local authorities and designers to regain control from contractors and suggested a 'degree of reluctance with which some authorities adopted industrialised methods in the first place' (Dunleavy 1981, p123).

In essence, the difficulties with high rise solutions were two-fold. Firstly, there were the structural problems which, in turn, led to dampness, mould growth, and difficulties in maintaining heating levels, quite apart from the possible dangers inherent in the structure itself. Secondly, there were the social problems, which are fairly well documented, and which represent a failure to recognise the links between the development of a house type and its future management. High rise housing was, from the first, architect- and designer-led and, while it could satisfy the need for extra units — the 'numbers game' as it came to be called — it did not necessarily meet the needs of the local authority to cater for all the households on its waiting list. Authorities were therefore faced with allocating to families in need a type of housing which was not necessasrily the most appropriate for them, and many of the housing management problems which have dogged high rise estates are rooted in this basic contradiction. It is unsurprising therefore that the search for solutions to the problems of high rise housing has focused on management initiatives as much as on technical ones.

Some current initiatives

Despite the poor image of high rise housing, it is important to stress that many blocks are sound and popular and represent an important resource for housing authorities. Nevertheless, the problems which do exist have led to a series of initiatives during the 1980s in an attempt to deal with some of the worst difficulties. For some authorities, high rise housing is simply not satisfactory any longer and decisions to demolish have been taken; there are examples around the country, from Birkenhead to Glasgow to Rochester in Kent. One of the strongest critics of high rise housing in recent years was Liverpool City Council whose Urban Regeneration Strategy, adopted in 1983, focused on demolition and height reduction of flatted blocks and the construction of semi-detached and terraced house types (Mars 1987). Although the Strategy had its critics who argued it was too rigid and deterministic, it has had a profound effect on the Liverpool skyline. More recently, the City Council has pursued the setting up of a Housing Action Trust to deal with the remaining blocks, the first time that a Trust has been established on the basis not of a geographical area but of a house type.

Most authorities, however, have pursued the idea of rehabilitation and refurbishment of high rise housing, while introducing concomitant changes in estate management. Following the principles laid down by the Department of the Environment's Estate Action programme, authorities have set up local management offices, local repairs teams, better tenant consultation, improved lighting and security, and caretaking and concierge systems. In many cases, there has been a significant reduction in voids and turnover, and in vandalism.

In some cases, management changes have been taken a stage further. In Wandsworth, a seven-storey block is now managed by All Saints Tenants Co-operative, while similar management co-operatives exist in Glasgow, at Kennishead in the south-west of the City and Springwell, just north of the city centre. In Motherwell, the Garrion People's Housing Co-operative has taken over ownership as well as management of system-built, deck access housing. In all cases, the introduction of local management is seen as crucial in building up the sense of community which is often lacking in high rise estates.

Elsewhere, there have been transfers to the private sector, notably in Wandsworth, while in Sheffield, the Hyde Park development, whose origins were described earlier in the chapter, has been refurbished by the Northern Counties Housing Association, in partnership with the City Council. Initially intended for accommodation for athletes during the 1991 World Student Games, it then provided assured tenancy rented housing, only five minutes from the city centre.

At the same time as changes in the overall ownership and management of the housing are taking place, authorities have often taken the opportunity to review allocation systems for high rise estates, recognising their inappropriateness as family housing. In this, authorities have been helped by demographic changes in the population. At the time that most blocks were built, the greatest need was for family accommodation, but in recent years the ageing of the population, coupled with larger numbers of young people leaving home and an increased rate of separation and divorce, have resulted in pressure for housing for single people and the elderly. As such households are childless, they can be accommodated fairly successfully in high rise estates.

In some cases, a simple change of allocation policy has led to single people being offered high rise housing, but some authorities have instigated major conversion work. One of the first was Glasgow whose Red Road flats are reputedly the highest in Europe. In 1981, the Council rehabilitated one block with the result that floors 1–3 were then occupied by group and shared tenancies (ex-hospital patients and ex-offenders) floors 4–13 were let to mainstream tenants, floors 14–27 were let, furnished, to students and 28–30 were let as furnished executive flats. The 23rd floor was completely communal, for the use of all residents. The initiative appears to have been successful and a second block was refurbished and let to the YMCA.

As far as the elderly are concerned, high rise housing can be most suitable so long as security is good and lifts work. The old Scottish Special Housing Association introduced a number of conversions for elderly persons' housing into its multi-storey schemes, while there are other examples in Dudley, in Delyn (Boneham nd) and Wirral (Hellman 1988). Generally renovation work includes supplementary heating, new lifts and alarm call systems, as well as renewal of fittings and alterations to layout.

Finally, in most cases, the question of energy efficiency has been addressed, in order to improve heat retention and prevent dampness. Properly designed energy packages can ensure that tenants have the means to achieve warmth, involving insulation, proper ventilation and affordability. Surveys suggest that a very small proportion of high rise blocks have so far been insulated yet with internal dry lining, draught-proofing and the use of heating systems such as off-peak storage heaters, tenants can save up to 27 per cent on their bills while local authority management problems can be eased (Ward nd).

Conclusions

The move towards high rise housing has its origins in architectural thinking between the wars and in particular the work of Le Corbusier. His vision of blocks of flats surrounded by parkland was, however, rarely achieved and with the pressure for increased output after 1945, many of his recommendations were forgotten. The housing which was built, through the use of untried system-building methods and through lack of thought about future management, was not wholly satisfactory. Many blocks have now been demolished while others are the subject of technical and management initiatives.

While it is important to remember that much high rise housing is of good quality, there are nevertheless lessons to be learnt, of which the key one is the need to ensure that development and management issues are considered together. While there is no doubt that many of the new estates were architecturally exciting, tenants did not react or behave in the way that designers had anticipated. The finding of social workers that residents in Park Hill, Sheffield, did not know how to 'use' the walkways is a particularly damning indictment. More than anything, this points to the need for users to be involved in the design of their dwellings, and this is a theme to which we will return, firstly in Chapter Six, which examines the debate surrounding the notion of security and 'defensible space' and secondly in Chapter Eight, which looks at the rise of community architecture and increased levels of participation in housing design.

Chapter 5
Design outside the dwelling

Introduction

So far, our main focus has been the design of the dwelling itself, although it is already clear that the external environment — the layout of the estate, the road pattern and the provision of open space — have all been closely linked. People live outdoors as well as within the home and therefore the outdoor environment needs to be as pleasant as possible, requiring careful thought and planning. In this chapter, we will examine the attempts to achieve this through the creation of neighbourhoods, the separation of vehicular and pedestrian traffic, and the provision of landscaped spaces and play areas, and we will discuss the reaction of residents to such moves. Finally, we will examine the specific areas which must be considered if a successful housing layout is to be achieved.

The Idea of Neighbourhood

The neighbourhood idea has its origins in the work of the Garden City Movement in the early years of the century and in the plans developed for new settlements like Letchworth by Parker and Unwin (see Chapter One). The Movement's influence was felt in America as well as in Britain and it was in Chicago that the term 'neighbourhood unit' first appears to have been used, in connection with a planning competition. The term also owes its origins to the work of Clarence Perry, who wrote about the relationship between school and the community, in part with a view to making schools more accessible to local people by using them for community activities. Perry developed these ideas during the 1920s and in 1929 contributed them to the New York Regional Plan.

His argument was also based on the increase in car traffic which was beginning already to cut cities into cellular blocks, between the main traffic arteries. Neighbourhood units were excellent ways of tackling this problem and Perry identified six principles which he argued should be followed:

(a) The size of a neighbourhood unit should be determined by the amount of housing required to support an elementary (primary) school. In practice, each school would serve an overall population of about 5,000;
(b) The arterial roads would form the boundaries of the unit and through traffic would not therefore enter the neighbourhood;
(c) About 10 per cent of the area should be in the form of open space;
(d) The school and other community facilities should be at the centre or most accessible point;
(e) There should be local shops at the edges of the unit, in particular at the intersection of arterial roads (and hence units) where business opportunities were greater;
(f) The internal road layout of the unit should be varied with road widths being adequate only for local traffic (Perry 1929). The diagram which Perry used in the New York Regional Plan to illustrate his concept is shown at Figure 5.1.

Perry's ideas have been enormously influential and his argument that the neighbourhood unit could be applied to existing as well as new districts has been accepted in many redevelopment and renewal schemes. The concept has not, however, been without its problems, not least the fact that it tends to create:

> urban islands, cut off by busy arterial roads, which may meet most domestic needs but which offer few employment opportunities. The assumption that residents would turn their attention inward has not been clearly validated .... Even more fundamentally, shifts in the age structure of populations have sometimes made it necessary to close the schools, thereby undermining the essential logic for neighbourhood units.
>
> (Relph 1987, pp64–5)

A development of the neighbourhood unit concept linked also to the increasing problems of car traffic was the Radburn principle. Radburn was a new town in the Garden City tradition which was developed in New Jersey at the end of the 1920s. It was planned by Clarence Stein and Henry Wright in a form which made great use of neighbourhood units and which broke away from the traditional grid street pattern so characteristic of American towns and cities.

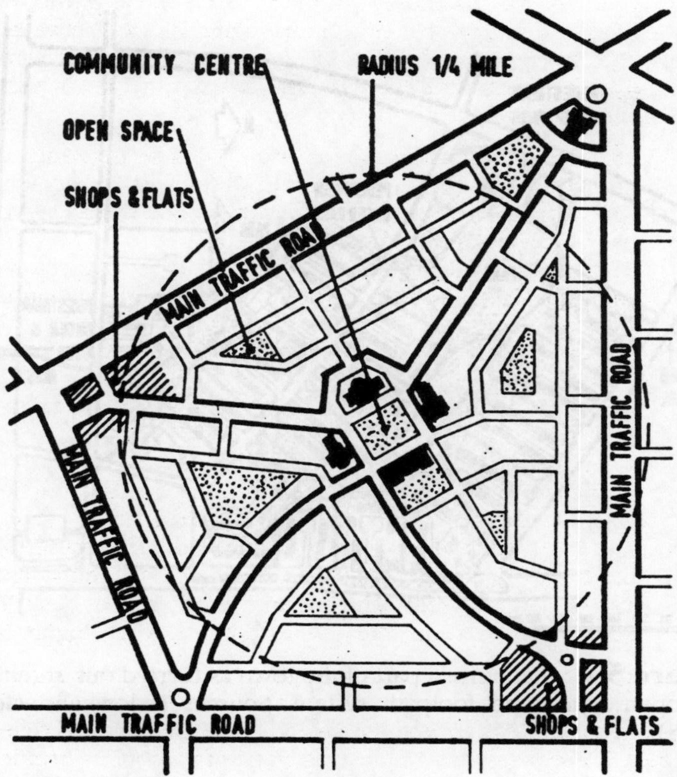

Figure 5.1 The neighbourhood unit as proposed by Clarence Perry in 1929. Source: Tetlow and Goss (1965)

The school formed the nucleus of the neighbourhood, which would have a population of between 7,500 and 10,000. There was open space and playground areas, and through traffic was channelled onto main arterial roads, as proposed by Perry. What was particularly revolutionary was that the houses faced parkland which ran through the whole town, and through this ran a series of footpaths. Where the footpaths met an arterial road, underpasses and footbridges were constructed, thereby achieving complete vehicular and pedestrian separation for the first time (Figure 5.2). Although Radburn was never completed in this form because of the Depression of the 1930s, and did not attract industry as expected, it gave its name to a system of road layout which was used extensively in later years.

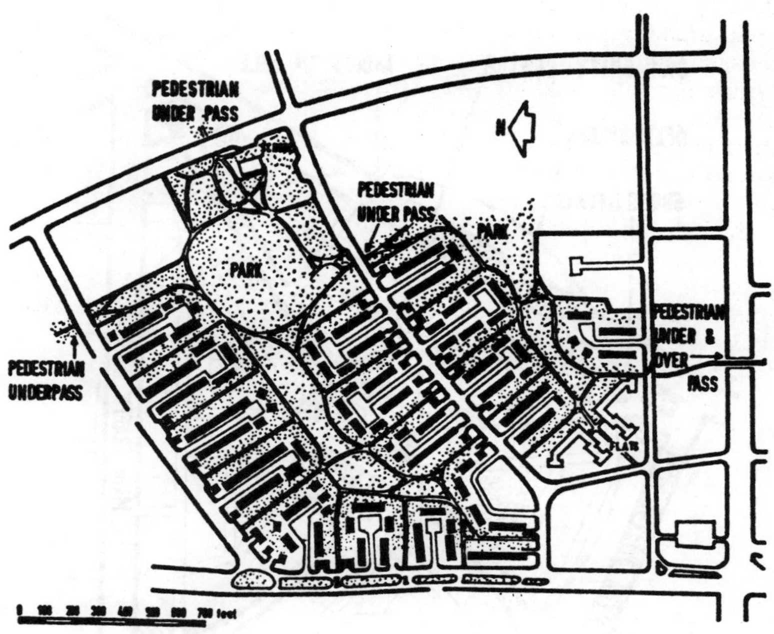

Figure 5.2 Radburn: a part of the town as carried out, showing the open space and footpath system. Source: Tetlow and Goss (1965)

The issue of separating out local and through vehicular traffic from pedestrian traffic and, indeed, dealing with the overall growth in car usage, was a theme which ran through much of the planning of the 1930s and 1940s. Some planning pioneers saw the solution as a horizontal separation, with neighbourhoods separated one from another; some, like Le Corbusier, argued for a vertical separation with road and rail systems serving the multi-storey blocks in his 'Radiant City'. Although Le Corbusier's ideas were embraced by the planners, as explained in Chapter Four, they were hardly ever implemented in the form recommended by him and Corbusian neighbourhoods were almost unknown.

Instead, British planners focused on horizontal separation of traffic and neighbourhoods and one of the most significant contributors was Sir Alker Tripp, then Assistant Commissioner of the Metropolitan Police, who argued for a system of 'precinct planning'. Shortly before the Second World War, he suggested a hierarchy of roads, namely arterial, sub-arterial, and local, and in 1942 he developed these ideas in an attempt to secure greater vehicular–pedestrian segregation. His argument was that road traffic had grown to such an extent that the idea of an all-purpose highway was obsolete; roads could no longer be main through routes while also providing access to the houses, shops and other buildings along their frontage. A hierarchy of roads would create areas, within the arterials, which would be served only by local roads and which could be residential, commercial or industrial in character.

Such areas, similar to Perry's neighbourhoods, were called 'precincts' by Tripp and are illustrated in Figure 5.3. As is clear from the diagram no part of the precinct was to be more than a quarter of a mile from an arterial or sub-arterial road and, hence, a bus service, and each princinct would have its own life and activity. Access to major roads would be limited, to prevent traffic congestion.

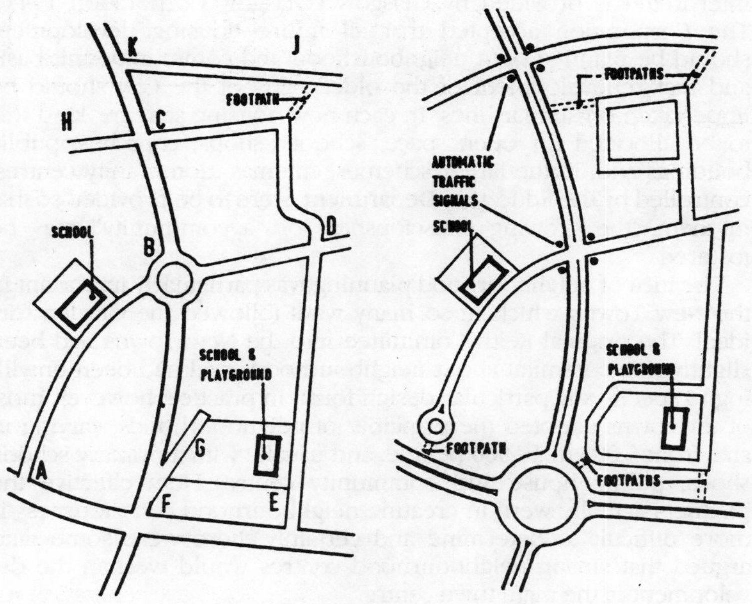

Figure 5.3 Alker Tripp's 'precinct': on the left, a typical street pattern with many dangerous traffic intersections; on the right, the 'precinct' principle has been applied to the same district. Source: Tetlow and Goss (1965)

> This was, of course, no more than an English version of the Radburn superblock, evolved by a traffic expert looking at the problems produced by the motor vehicle from his own specialised point of view. But it was a most important contribution; it is remarkable that the differing functions of roads are only now beginning to be studied seriously.
>
> (Tetlow and Goss 1965, pp54–5)

These contributions led to changes in official thinking about planning and design, first evident in the Dudley Report of 1944 (Ministry of Health 1944). The neighbourhood was seen as being the most desirable unit to plan for, with a population of between 5,000 and 10,000. Such a size was necessary to ensure that adequate social and community facilities could be developed, while the boundaries of neighbourhood units could be 'natural' barriers such as railway lines and main roads. The report also stressed the need for such neighbourhoods to have a mix of income and population groups, to avoid creating one-class communities.

A good example of the way in which this neighbourhood ideal was interpreted is provided by Glasgow (Glasgow Corporation 1947). The Corporation accepted that all future housing development should be planned on a neighbourhood and community unit basis and that redevelopment of the older parts of the City should be undertaken on similar lines. In each new housing scheme, land was to be allocated for open space, schools, shops, churches, public buildings and, in the larger schemes, cinemas. Community centres, controlled by the Education Department, were to be provided so that in them, 'the growing consciousness of "a community" may be fostered'.

The idea of neighbourhood planning was particularly important in the New Towns which in so many ways followed the Garden City ideal. The original Reith Committee into the New Towns had been slightly non-commital about neighbourhoods and had been unwilling to specify any particular design form. In practice, however, most of the towns adopted the principle of neighbourhoods, varying in size from 5,000 to 10,000 people, and usually with a primary school, shops, public house and community centre. How effective the planners actually were in creating neighbourhood consciousness is more difficult to determine and certainly there were some who argued that strong neighbourhood centres would weaken the development of the main town centre.

Many New Towns also adopted the Radburn principle of separating pedestrian and vehicular traffic, and the issue of traffic and its impact on the environment and on housing planning continued to be important. One of the most significant studies of the problem was the Buchanan Report on Traffic in Towns, published in 1964

(Ministry of Transport 1964). Buchanan broadly accepted the views expressed by Alker Tripp in the 1940s that areas within towns should be created where vehicles had only a limited penetration. These would be called 'environmental areas'. The only difference with Tripp was that Buchanan suggested that the main distributary system could be underground, passing below, as well as around the environmental area; this was the concept of grade-separation.

Although the neighbourhood idea was therefore a major theme within planning and housing design for many decades, it has, to an extent, lost some of its appeal. From a planning viewpoint, dissatisfaction was expressed at the way in which the neighbourhood centres had frequently been developed, 'isolated from the housing in a grassy or muddy sward, open to vandals in the evenings and bearing little or no relationship to the community they serve' (Forsyth 1983, p20). Forsyth went on to suggest that a scatter of small shops and other facilities was preferable to concentration in one centre, as this would encourage residents to know their area, besides using up gap sites within a housing estate.

From a sociological viewpoint also, the concept of neighbourhood began to lose its appeal, as it was realised that propinquity did not necessarily mean that community life would develop. In low density New Towns, the loneliness and the boredom of those confined to the home all day increasingly became apparent. As a result, in later New Towns, beginning with Cumbernauld and continuing through to Milton Keynes, greater housing densities were planned with neighbourhoods being served by more than one school or group of shops, while recognition was made of the need for identity and community at all levels. As Scoffham (1984, p31) put it, 'the neighbourhood became a framework for the town rather than a formula for its organisation'.

Radburn and Road Layouts

The Radburn principle of pedestrian and vehicular traffic separation has already been referred to and, like the neighbourhood idea, it was one which influenced design for many years. It was, however, some time after the development of the original Radburn that the principles were adopted in the UK, with the first example being the Queens Park housing estate in Wrexham, developed between 1950 and 1952. There were later examples in Northampton, Sheffield and Coventry, as well as in the New Towns.

Official sanction had been given to Radburn in the Ministry of Housing and Local Government's 1953 Housing Manual, where it was referred to as a 'service cul-de-sac layout'. Houses would have their back gardens overlooking the cul-de-sac, while the fronts of the houses would be accessed from the footpath system within the open space. Because the culs-de-sac would be used for road access only, there could be a saving on the provision of pavements, while the safety of the common paths and front gardens for children was stressed. The only drawback appeared to be a lack of privacy in the back gardens but this was discounted in view of the limited amount of traffic using the culs-de-sac. Figure 5.4 shows a suggested 'service cul-de-sac' layout from the Manual.

The potential for attractive landscaping within Radburn layouts was further explored by a related Government publication entitled *Design in Town and Village* (MHLG 1953b). Recognising that pedestrian routes would be significantly divergent from the roads, it suggested the delineation of specific 'pedestrian ways'. Such ways should not develop into a complicated system of landscaped walks but could nevertheless make use of natural features such as tree belts.

One of the earliest examples of a Radburn layout was the Willenhall Wood scheme in Coventry, with generous provision of parking and garages and a comprehensive footpath system. But other problems soon emerged, not least the monotonous, rather dreary rear access to the dwellings. In addition, the provision of blocks of garages at the rear of the dwelling groups denied privacy to the back gardens.

For many British housing developments, the difficulty in achieving a satisfactory Radburn layout was related to the high housing densities being demanded. In Basildon, for example, one of the earlier New Towns and with a density of around 14 or 15 houses per acre, a partial adaptation of Radburn was used, not least because, although early New Town densities were fairly low, they were nowhere near as low as the 6 to 9 houses per acre of Radburn itself. As densities increased, as at Cumbernauld New Town, the Radburn principle was completely reversed with the private (usually the back) garden linked to the pedestrian routes and with the front door accessed in the more usual way.

There is no doubt that some of the early Radburn layouts were less than popular. With vehicular access being to the back door, this was confusing to visitors, while the communal nature of the front garden made it difficult for families to use them in traditional ways:

> It is not easy to incorporate such things as washing-lines, green-houses or motorcycle sheds in a tidy garden, and a Radburn layout can lead to their suppression. Anything which limits the active use of leisure is surely to be deplored, and a Radburn layout can have this effect. This is perhaps its most serious disadvantage.
>
> (Edwards 1981, p170)

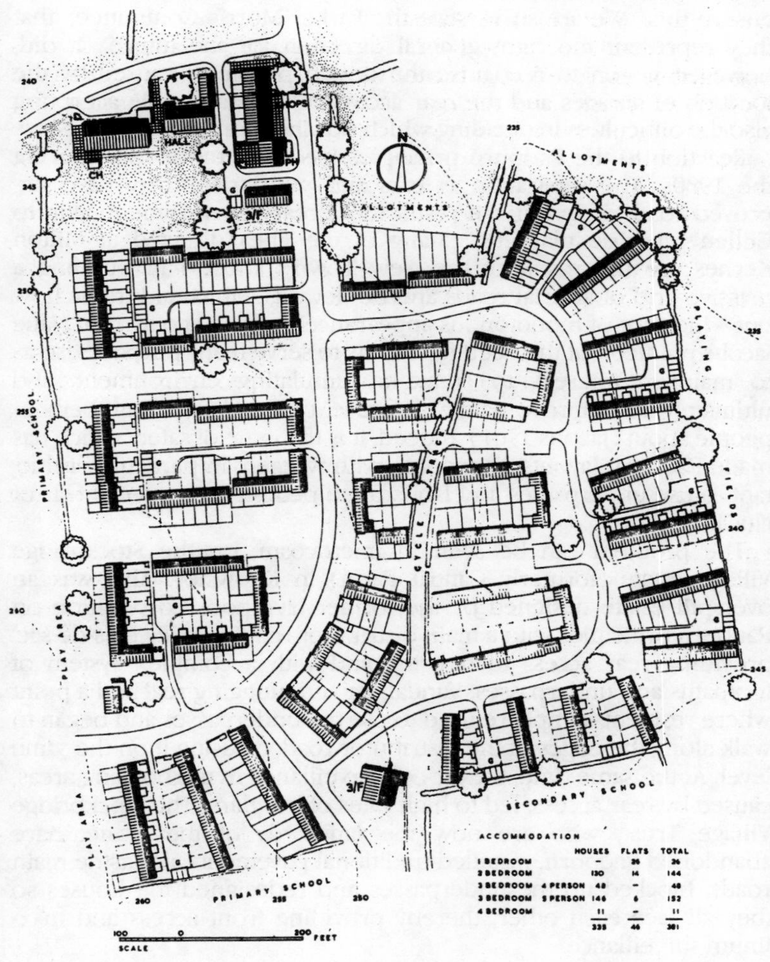

Figure 5.4 Serviced culs-de-sac. Source: MHLG (1953a)

The conflicts thus engendered by the Radburn principles were clearly identified in the Parker Morris Report of 1971. The Report, like many of its predecessors, addressed the question of increasing car ownership which needed to be planned for. Nevertheless, the over-riding concern in designing with the car in mind was to design for the pedestrian to stay alive. This implied segregation of pedestrian footpaths and cycleways from roads carrying motor vehicles, and the Report identified the Radburn layout as the one which would ensure this. 'We are sure', state the Parker Morris Committee, 'that they represent the right general direction for the future'. It did, however, go on to recognise the design problems caused by the location of garages and the rear access culs-de-sac, while accepting also the difficulties in deciding which was the 'front' door.

Reaction to the Radburn principles has been more vocal during the 1980s. The separation of cars and pedestrians may have improved road safety but can result in a dreary environment, akin to Cullen's 'prairie planning'. Many of the jibes directed at Milton Keynes are the result of the New Town's success in building a massive grid of arterial roads and boulevards, which aid traffic flow but which are of monotonous appearance. As long ago as 1961, Jane Jacobs pointed out the need for streets to serve many purposes, so as to maintain interest, to create a stimulating environment, and ultimately to improve safety, because of the larger numbers of people about (Jacobs 1961). Indeed, it is the issue of safety which has made Radburn layouts unpopular, with women, in particular, reluctant to use underpasses and landscaped pedestrian ways, for fear of attack.

The problem can be seen in microcosm, on the Stockbridge Village estate (formerly Cantril Farm) in Knowsley. This was an overspill estate designed by the former Liverpool Corporation on Radburn principles with a main distributor road, 'service culs-de-sac' providing rear access to housing and with a complex system of footpaths and underpasses. Vandalism and mugging reached a point where residents simply refused to use the underpasses and began to walk along the edges of the distributor road, crossing it on the same level. At the same time, the lack of surveillance in the housing areas, caused by rear access, led to high rates of burglary. The Stockbridge Village Trust, who are now the landlords of the estate, have abandoned Radburn, installed traditional pavements alongside main roads, blocked up the underpasses and redesigned the houses so they all face each other, thereby providing front access and maximum surveillance.

Similar reversals of Radburn layouts have occurred elsewhere. In Hull, the Orchard Park estate has been redesigned to create better defensible space, while Estate Action is now funding a number of such adaptations throughout the country. In the Rawnsley estate in Cannock, for example, houses have had their internal layouts turned round, so that the former back door became the front door. Incurtilage parking has now been provided in what was formerly the back garden, providing better security and surveillance. The former pedestrian routes have been incorporated into individual gardens, to reduce the level of communal open space.

During the 1980s, therefore, the emphasis has been less on traffic segregation and, instead, on traffic calming, enabling all forms of traffic to share a common space. The main aims of traffic calming have been identified as (a) to reduce accidents; (b) to reduce the space given over to vehicular traffic and the barriers this can cause to pedestrian movement; (c) to promote greater feelings of security amongst pedestrians and cyclists; and (d) to create environmental improvements which may in turn stimulate local economic activity (Pharoah and Russell 1989).

Such traffic calming measures have been pursued more vigorously in European countries than in Britain and the best known example is probably the Dutch 'woonerf'. Within a 'woonerf', pedestrians and cyclists have priority and cars must be driven at walking pace and parking is restricted; this sometimes causes problems in relation to residents' parking. By 1985, the Dutch had established 4,000 'woonerven', covering 7,400 streets (Sherlock 1991), sometimes involving the resurfacing of streets to give motorists the impression that they were driving on the pavement.

In Britain, the part that shared surface roads could play in creating both formal and informal settings was recognised but Government Design Bulletins advised caution until appraisals could take place. The current Department of Environment/Department of Transport *Design Bulletin* now refers to such studies and the results have been encouraging. Firstly, the intimate scale and landscaping were appreciated by residents and the roads were found to be safe and convenient for both pedestrians and motorists. Secondly, the majority of residents did not consider safety for pedestrians to be a problem and thirdly, a study of accident records found that no accidents at all had been reported on shared surface roads. Clearly, both drivers and pedestrians, by sharing the same surface, had had to be more aware of each other, and extra care had been taken (DoE/DoT 1992).

The Bulletin goes on to provide detailed design on such roads, as well as on other traffic calming measures. A variety of devices may now be seen in new housing estates, including chicanes or road narrowing, with accompanied tree planting, 'rumble strips' (a change of road surface or texture) and sleeping policemen. Narrow entrances to culs-de-sac, small turning radii, reduced visibility, and a heavily textured road surface such as cobbles, all help to reduce traffic speeds and emphasise to the driver that s/he is entering an area where the vehicle does not necessarily have priority.

There is a certain irony in the fact that, after years of encouraging pedestrian and vehicular segregation, official thinking should now be to welcome designs and layouts which do precisely the opposite. As in so many areas of design, the wheel of fashion has come full circle.

Gardens and Open Space

At the end of the First World War, the private garden was a rarity, enjoyed only by the wealthier classes; working class children played either in public parks or in the street. Yet the value of open space had been recognised by the Garden City movement and the 1919 Housing Act, for the first time, enabled local authority housing to be built with gardens attached. Housing estates built under this and its successor, the 1924 Wheatley Act, are still deservedly popular, not least because houses had front and back doors, with front and back gardens to match. Cuts in public expenditure in the 1930s and the shift back towards the construction of flatted dwellings, however, slowed the movement towards the provision of individual garden space.

Gardens and play areas had been seen by the Garden City pioneers as essential contributors towards increasing public health and standards of living, although in practice, little research appears to have been carried out on how families actually used their gardens. For some, of course, they were areas to be cultivated, a practice which became widespread during the Second World War. Indeed, 'with the end of hostilities, the evidence that crop yields were higher from gardens than from farm land was advanced as an argument for keeping the densities of new housing development low' (Cook 1968, p27).

The 1944 Dudley Report and the subsequent Housing Manuals did not explicitly discuss the provision of gardens although, as the most common house type was assumed to be the semi-detached house, gardens would normally have been provided. There was some thought given to landscaping and in the 1949 Manual, the introduction of wedges of local open space connected to the countryside was recommended, so as to provide the town dweller with 'the visual relaxation that can be given by the sight of grass and trees' (Ministry of Health 1949, p35).

In Scotland, with a tradition of flat-dwelling, private gardens were less common, and Government reports did not always see them as necessary. The Westwood Committee, in fact, felt that the housing designers had been over-generous:

> In many cases we have found that the rigid application of density formulae has involved the allocation of extensive areas of garden ground ... it is a mistake to provide larger gardens than are really required or than can be maintained by the tenant without the excessive expenditure of time and energy.
>
> (Department of Health for Scotland 1948, p59)

The Committee went on to suggest that garden size should be a factor in allocating houses to tenants, in accordance with expressed preferences.

Although flatted dwellings could not normally have individual gardens, the land which surrounded blocks of flats was important for children's play space. Despite the difficulties of supervising children at ground level from an upper flat, referred to in Chapter Four, the provision of play areas was clearly one of the first calls on the space available in multi-storey developments. Government advice recognised the different demands of older children and toddlers and recommended that the approach to the provision of play facilities should be a generous one. Ominously, however, it added that large play spaces might only be obtainable at the expense of reducing the number of low-rise dwellings with gardens in the same estate (MHLG 1958). Given the pressures in the 1950s to build quickly to relieve the housing shortage, it was inevitable perhaps that, faced with a choice, the designers of new estates frequently sacrified the play area.

There was thus relatively little recognition of the intrinsic value of gardens and play areas and they were seen as being relatively expendable. The Parker Morris Committee dealt with gardens in only two paragraphs and it is unsurprising therefore that the bulletin issued by the Ministry of Housing following their report paid little heed to garden provision. There was an increasing emphasis on low-rise, high-density development, as first demonstrated at Cumbernauld New Town, and gardens as a result were 'modest'. Evidence gathered in the late 1960s suggested that the average area of private garden in these schemes was 680 sq ft (63 sq m).

That this was rather too small for many families was demonstrated in Cook's (1968) study of garden usage on housing estates. He found that those with gardens of less than 800 sq ft (74 sq m) made relatively little use of them, with half the householders expressing the view that they were simply too small. This was particularly true where the households concerned had children. Cook went on:

> Few respondents with gardens up to 800 sq ft can find room for the play generated by three or more children and many smaller families feel a lack of space. Thus the extent of any reduction in garden size would probably be limited by the desire to ensure a reasonable level of satisfaction on this score. If other means were developed of satisfying the demand for play space near homes such as semi-private enclosed areas associated with small groups of dwelling, the small private garden might well be adequate for most current needs.
> (Cook 1968, p232)

Children's play was not the only issue, however, and Cook drew attention to changing social habits with many families increasingly using the garden, or patio within it, as a place to sit, eat and socialise.

The desirability of small, local play provision for children, to compensate for reduction in garden size, has been echoed by other research. More recent work on children's play suggests that well-stocked, imaginatively-designed play areas should be provided all around housing estates, and that the existence of playgrounds in the wider neighbourhood is no substitute for this very local provision (NACRO 1988). One of the major advantages of such local provision is surveillance and the ability of parents to supervise their children's play; surveillance is a theme to which we will return in Chapter Six.

The importance of play space and gardens is now generally recognised, with an enclosed private garden providing 'not only privacy and security but an area which residents can mould and fashion to their own personal needs and preference' (IOH/RIBA 1983, p42). This publication by the two professional institutes suggested that gardens should have a minimum area of around 50 sq m (540 sq ft), but this may be too small for many families, and provision of local open space and play areas would be needed to compensate.

The Residents' Perspective

Reference is made above to the varied ways in which residents use their homes and their gardens and this theme, a reflection of the varied nature of domestic households, is one which has been of some concern to housing planners over the years. As discussed in Chapter Three, the Parker Morris Committee was particularly important in drawing attention to the changing requirements of households and the need for housing to be adaptable, as circumstances and the family life cycles change. As children grow up into teenagers and adults and as parents return to work or retire, the use made of housing space changes and Parker Morris took the view that research

1. Middle class housing from the late eighteenth and early nineteenth centuries. Lansdowne Crescent Bath.

2. Late Victorian terraced housing for the newly-rich merchant classes. Princes Road, Liverpool.

3. Bye-law terraced housing with small backyards and rear access lane. Most yards have now been used for house extensions.

4. Typical Scottish four-storey tenements in Govan, Glasgow. These have been rehabilitated by the local housing association.

5. In the Newcastle area, the nineteenth century house type was the Tyneside flat. In each

6. In Sunderland, single storey terraced housing was built. In recent years, many have been extended through the use of loft conversions with dormer windows.

7. Early London County Council housing. The Kennington Park estate in Lambeth.

8. Early twentieth century public sector housing. Bevington Street, Liverpool.

9. Interwar semi-detached houses. The tree-lined road and variety of house styles are typical of virtually all English cities. Note the original 'sunburst' gates, centre right.

10. The move back to flat building after 1930. Council tenements at St Andrews Gardens, Liverpool.

11. The flat roofs and curved lines of the 1930s Bauhaus style. Near Walton-on-Thames.

12. Interwar mansion blocks in West London.

13. The housing shortage after the Second World War led to a variety of non-traditional designs and to prefabricated building methods. Surviving prefabs in Glasgow.

14. Non-traditional housing. Levitt-Cartwright houses in Leeds.

15. A typical 1950s council estate. Plenty of open space but a little bleak and no provision for car parking or individual garages.

16. The postwar New Town. High density housing design with generous landscaping, at Cumbernauld.

17. The high rise council estate. At its worst it could look incredibly forbidding. Red Road, Glasgow, possibly the tallest blocks in Europe.

18. Sheffield's Park Hill estate, a pioneering deck access design.

19. Many deck access and high rise schemes failed because the external appearance, coupled with a maze of steps and walkways, produced an environment with which it was difficult to identify. This is Portsdown Park estate, Portsmouth.

20. Demolition of a failed deck access estate at Hebburn, Tyneside.

21. The perceived need for defensible space has led to changes in design, particularly in the private sector. Many estates, like this in Knowsley, use cul-de-sacs, to prevent through traffic while the unfenced garden areas provide maximum surveillance.

22. Changing road layouts outside the dwellings. Many 1970s estates used shared surfaces for cars and pedestrians like this example in Stirling.

23. Widely regarded as one of the first and most successful examples of user participation in design. The Byker Wall, Newcastle.

24. The ultimate form of user participation. Self builders in Lewisham, London.

25. The move back to low rise housing with private gardens. Liverpool's Urban Regeneration Strategy has resulted in large numbers of houses like this in the city.

26. Although flats have traditionally been less popular than houses in England, they are acceptable in inner city and waterside locations. Development near Tower Bridge in London.

27. An example of energy efficient housing design which has been developed at Milton Keynes.

into the development of adaptable and flexible housing was socially and economically necessary.

These social and economic changes also influence the use of the estate outside the dwelling and reference has already been made to usage of play areas and gardens. But much of the attention of housing designers in the postwar period was focused on internal housing layout, often to the detriment of the external environment. The Parker Morris Committee therefore recorded their concern that, while some housing estates were well-designed, others had been built in a very unimaginative fashion. The onus to achieve good design lay with the developer, be he private firm or local authority, and professional expertise was an essential ingredient:

> Good layout and landscaping, together with the use of good and well-chosen external materials and colours throughout an estate, go nine-tenths of the way towards creating beauty instead of ugliness, and it is in these broad and not necessarily costly ways, rather than in the laboured detailing of the individual dwelling, that housing developments can be made pleasing and attractive to the eye.
>
> (MHLG 1961, p37)

During the late 1960s and 1970s, the Government commissioned research to try and ascertain the attitudes of residents to newly constructed housing estates, in part to establish whether the adoption of Parker Morris standards had led to general improvements in the housing environment. The first study, carried out in 1967, examined estates in London and Sheffield, to test how different types of household reacted to various building forms and other aspects of layout. Surprisingly (for the authors), satisfaction with the estate was not determined by such factors as density, building form, living on or off the ground or with children's play provision, but was most closely related to the appearance of the estate and the quality of its maintenance (DoE 1972).

It had been thought that the building form would have been the major determinant of satisfaction and, indeed, the estates surveyed were chosen to reflect a variety of housing types (houses, deck-access, multi-storey point blocks etc). In fact, no house type emerged as being generally more or less satisfactory than any other, although very high blocks suffered problems of access related to lift failure while low (3–5 storey) blocks suffered from noise and lack of privacy. The attitudes of housewives (who formed the majority of respondents and who were in the estates all day) were strongly influenced by the appearance of the estates and important factors included colour and size of buildings, landscaping, spaciousness of surroundings, variety of buildings and the maintenance of the estate.

Trees, grass and flowers were seen as being vastly superior to large areas of grey paving and concrete finishes.

The issue of maintenance was an important one, with a quarter of housewives feeling that the estates were badly maintained and that more staff were needed. Greater supervision would reduce the amount of vandalism. The survey showed therefore for the first time the value which residents placed on their surroundings. The findings suggested that, in many cases, improvements needed to be made to the estate outside, but not at the expense of, the dwellings.

These findings were echoed by a second survey carried out for the Department of the Environment in 1979, which sought to compare the attitudes of tenants in estates built to Parker Morris standards with those built in circumstances where standards had been relaxed or those, built by the private sector, which had been acquired by the local authority (DOE 1981). A total of 3,000 tenants were interviewed, on fifty-five estates.

In fact, there was little difference in responses between the two groups of estates, although the results may have been affected by differing proportions of elderly and family households. What was of particular interest, however, was the fact that, once again, tenants seemed to be less sensitive to the particular arrangement of the house or flat and more sensitive to the arrangement, appearance and location of the estate:

> Statistical analysis showed that whether or not households were satisfied with their house or flat was more closely related to their opinion of the environment outside than to the internal characteristics of the dwelling. Opinions about the appearance of the estate, the approach to the dwelling and its outlook, were found to be more closely related to dwelling satisfaction than opinions about such things as the size of the kitchen or living room, the arrangement of the rooms, the amount of storage space or the heating provided.
>
> (DOE 1981, pp5–6)

In contrast to the earlier (1972) report, this second study did find some differences in attitudes relating to house type. The majority of local authority built housing was at relatively high density while houses bought in from private developers tended to be detached and semi-detached in suburban locations. While accepting that the two were not strictly comparable, the study did suggest that detached and semi-detached housing, with individual gardens, was more likely to provide satisfactory housing for families, from the tenant's point of view. This conclusion links to the general mood of the later 1970s which had swung against the provision of flatted dwellings, as discussed in the previous chapter.

What Constitutes Good Layout?

It is clear from the preceding section that thinking on estate layout has changed significantly in the postwar years. At the same time it is evident that, for residents, the extenal environment and the layout and design of an estate are much more important than the internal arrangements of the house. From this it follows that, for estates to be popular and to satisfy the aspirations of residents, it is vitally important for housing designers to produce a satisfactory scheme, and to do this, we need to have some understanding of what it is that makes a 'good' layout and design.

The first area of concern is aspect, since the studies carried out for the Department of the Environment make it clear that, for many tenants, the outlook and orientation of the house are most important. On high density estates it may not be possible to give all residents a view but, where possible, houses can be oriented to face south or away from blank walls and towards gardens and open space. For elderly people, this is particularly important so that a view of activities on the estate and other people passing by can lessen feelings of social isolation.

There are obviously dangers in this, in that the opening up of houses to a view may lead to a loss of privacy, with passers-by able to look in on residents. The need for privacy is a most important factor, and houses should be designed for maximum surveillance of garden areas, car parking space etc. This relates to the debate concerning 'defensible space' which will be dealt with in Chapter Six.

The orientation of housing should also be such as to reduce the impact of noise or pollution and designers of new build sites should be aware of micro-climatic factors. Prevailing wind can be significant, in the carriage of pollution, while wind speeds may themselves be affect by building form. As noted in Chapter Four, tall buildings can create their own turbulence at ground level and render gardens, play areas or balconies much less usable.

Finally, the local character of an area is also of importance, since no building site can be regarded as self-contained. The character of local buildings should have an influence on design, as should be materials used, and new house forms should ideally be on a scale to match the surroundings. The role of planning departments in producing design guides for developers is an important one here and will be discussed later.

The second area of consideration is access, covering the question of road layout, parking and pedestrian movement. It is already clear that thinking on road layouts has changed significantly, with shared surfaces and traffic calming measures becoming more important and allowing for more imaginative designs than the traditional 5-metre road plus pavement. On the other hand, it is essential to provide for access for large vehicles such as delivery vans and bin lorries, and turning circles, curves and gradients must take account of this.

Parking is a particularly problematic area since large numbers of parked cars can represent a considerable visual intrusion. It is clear, however, that the grouped garage and parking areas favoured in past decades have been unpopular, leaving cars susceptible to vandalism because of the impossibility of surveillance by the owner. As indicated by IoH/RIBA (1983), cars are now in such regular use that it is probably necessary for them to be within easy reach of the dwelling, either through the provision of parking bays adjacent to the housing, or through the construction of hardstanding within the curtilage. The latter may be the most satisfactory from the resident's point of view, allowing for later construction of a garage, but such provision may be at the expense of the garden, reducing what may have been already an area of modest size to the proportion of a pocket handkerchief.

Pedestrian access is ultimately more important than vehicular access, simply because on many estates large numbers of residents will not own cars. Pedestrian routes should, however, be planned together with road systems to ensure that conflict between the two is minimised. It is important that they are safe, well-lit and overlooked and that they are wide enough to take prams, children's bicycles and wheelchairs:

> Traffic routes should run as directly as possible along natural desire lines. They should be wide enough to bear their anticipated traffic and should allow people to stop and talk to one another without causing an obstruction. They should preferably offer some variety of spatial experience, and their course should be defined by enclosure, change of level or changes in paving material or pattern.
>
> (Scottish Development Department 1977, para.5.11.1)

Where such routes meet major service roads, the question of underpasses and footbridges arises. The experience of the Radburn layouts discussed earlier suggests that underpasses may appear particularly claustrophobic and offer opportunities for ambush and assault; in such circumstances footbridges may be more appropriate.

The third and final area for consideration is that of open space, including children's play space and landscaping. All too often in the past, open space was simply land which had not been built on and was distributed in an almost accidental pattern; cynics referred to it as SLOAP or 'spaces left over after planning'. But it is important that each area of open space should be located, designed and equipped for a particular use, be it as garden space, playing fields, bowling greens, recreation grounds or children's play areas.

Such space needs to be local, particularly play space, and be easily accessible by residents, but too many small areas should be avoided as they can be wasteful in land terms as well as leading to disproportionately high maintenance costs.

The style of landscaping and choice of trees and shrubs will play a vital part in developing the character of an area. The use of evergreen plants can create interest on a year-round basis while, in the long term, dense planting can produce a greater impact and be more vandal-resistant than sparsely planted species. Safety should not, however, be compromised and landscaping should never be so dense as to allow for the possibility of ambush and attack.

The Institute of Housing and the RIBA (IOH/RIBA 1983) recommend that an expenditure of about 2 per cent of the total scheme for soft landscaping represents a cost-effective outlay for most projects. Long term maintenance should also be decided at the outset as there are few more depressing sights in a housing scheme than landscaping gone wild, because initial design and future maintenance were not decided together.

In new build schemes, another issue is the retention of trees on the development site. Because the UK has such a temperate climate, tree growth is slow and it may take years before a newly planted tree can make its impact on the landscape. Retaining trees is therefore important in providing ready-matured elements of the landscape and helping to increase the amenity value of an estate (La Dell 1986). Such retention must be viable but it should not be difficult to design a layout which incorporates existing planting and, besides, the retention of trees may help secure planning approval by demonstrating a sympathetic treatment of the site.

As far as play areas are concerned there is a hierarchy of provision ranging from the toddlers' play areas which should generally be provided at one per 25 family houses up to equipped play areas for older children which are recommended at the rate of 0.2 Ha (0.5 acres) per thousand population. For teenagers, kick-about pitches may be provided at the rate of 0.12 Ha (0.3 acres) per thousand population.

Conclusions

The layout of housing estates has changed significantly in the post-1919 period. Ideas about neighbourhood have developed and been particularly influential in the postwar period, especially in the New Towns. Ideas about road layout have moved full circle as we have shifted from complete pedestrian and vehicular segregation towards shared surfaces and traffic calming. Perhaps this is a coming to terms with the motor car, instead of seeing it as something to be kept away from pedestrians at all costs. Our ideas about open space too have changed as we have begun to examine exactly how people use garden space and to have a better appreciation of the importance of children's play.

One other important change in recent years has been the shift away from large scale public sector housing development and towards smaller infill schemes, usually by housing associations. This means that the concept of the grand design so essential to interwar estates has now gone, and infill developments are more likely to take their design cues from adjacent buildings rather than to contribute themselves to the townscape.

One of the lessons which can be learned from these changes is the importance of linking initial design to continuing maintenance, as all too often the estate management implications are not fully understood by the designers. Landscaping will look attractive and play areas will be used only so long as they are well maintained. The aversion to Radburn road layouts sprang, in particular, from the dingy, depressing underpasses which residents were reluctant to use. But adequate lighting and a local presence on housing estates can go an enormous way towards enhancing security and safety and helping residents to feel that there are no parts of their estate which are 'no-go' areas. These lessons are only now beginning to be learned but the developments which are under way on some estates augur well for the future.

Another lesson which emerges from this chapter is the need for 'surveillance' so that residents can see their children playing and know that they are safe and, allied to this, the need for 'defensible space' so that intruders may be identified. This is a debate which has grown particularliy fierce in recent years and is the subject of the next chapter.

Chapter 6 The Defensible Space debate

Introduction

Reference was made in Chapter Five to issues of security and surveillance and the provision of private garden space for the sole use of one particular household. Such private space is frequently termed 'defensible space', a phrase first coined by the American Oscar Newman in 1972, and the first part of this chapter discusses the importance of his work. That the phrase has entered current usage is due in large part to the more recent, British-based research of Alice Coleman, and the chapter goes on to describe her enormously influential work, together with some of the criticisms which have been levelled against her.

Coleman's findings appeared at a time when crime — or fear of crime — was increasing and her ideas have been embraced enthusiastically by central government as contributing to the fight against it. There have therefore been a number of experiments in design adaptations in different housing estates across the country, often under the banner of a 'design against crime initiative'. There is not universal acceptance that this is the way forward, and more intensive housing management is seen by many as offering an equal chance of success in improving unpopular and rundown estates. The chapter ends by discussing this debate.

The Work of Oscar Newman

Newman's work was a comprehensive study of crime within public housing in New York City, using detailed statistics on physical design, tenant populations and crime, collected by the New York City Housing Authority. He began by looking at the types of housing estates which seemed to suffer from high crime rates, and identified five or six physical characteristics which reinforced criminal behaviour. The estates, or projects, were firstly very large, housing over 1,000 families and consisting of high rise apartment blocks over seven storeys in height. The sites of these projects were usually an assembly of four to six separate street blocks amalgamated and closed to through traffic. The areas between the blocks were completely public and open to surrounding streets and there was seldom any attempt to differentiate the grounds so as to make portions relate to a particular building.

The buildings themselves were generally slab blocks or cruciform towers, each housing anything from 150 to 500 families. Most had a single entrance and each floor would consist of a long central corridor with apartments lining both sides. In order to satisfy fire regulations, up to four sets of stairwells might lead off this main corridor, leading in turn to different exits at the base of the building.

Perhaps inevitably, such a building form leads to anonymity and a complete lack of community life and this in turn can provide the opportunity for petty crime and muggings, unobserved by other residents. Newman referred to the apartment tower as the 'villain of the piece', particularly in view of his finding that the crime rate increased almost proportionately with building height.

Newman's basic hypothesis, therefore, was that there was a positive correlation between building height and crime, although:

> recognising the fact that height alone was not the reason for such a connection, we took into account the various other factors that usually attend high buildings: a larger number of apartment units and people using a single lobby, entry and elevators, with resulting anonymity; more interior public space hidden from view and so on.
> (Newman 1972, p27)

Nevertheless, the apparent effect of building height on crime was quite evident, with the size of the housing estate or project being much less significant. The evidence seemed to suggest that, in a large project, the existence of low buildings helped to offset what might have been thought to be a factor conducive to high crime rates. Newman collated data on felonies for a period of one year and when these were analysed, by building heights, there was a dramatic increase in felonies per thousand population from a mean of 8.8 for three-storey buildings to 20.2 for buildings sixteen storeys and over. When the locations of these crimes were studied, a remarkable 79 per cent of them had occurred within the buildings proper, suggesting that the buildings themselves rather than the grounds were unsafe. Almost half the felonies took place in unsurveyed public areas such as lifts, landings, halls and lobbies.

Newman examined in detail two housing projects within New York city to illustrate his findings. One, Van Dyke, consisted exclusively of high rise towers while the other, Brownsville, had lower blocks of three to six storeys with a greater element of defensible space; interestingly the projects were adjacent to each other within Brooklyn. The tenant profiles of the two projects were similar and both suffered from crime and vandalism but Van Dyke homes had 50 per cent more total crime incidents, with over three and a half times the robberies and 64 per cent more felonies and other misdemeanours than Brownsville.

From his work in New York, Newman went on to identify four major, inter-related characteristics of defensible space. First, there was the capacity of the physical environment to create perceived zones of territorial influence, whereby residents could assume territorial attitudes and prerogatives. In the case of detached family housing, this was simple since the house possessed its own grounds or garden, fenced from the street or from its neighbours but, as one moved to denser building styles, such as terraced or 'row' houses, walk-up flats and high rise apartments, this became more difficult. Sub-divisions of buildings could, however, help residents to adopt a more proprietorial attitude towards parts of the building with which they could identify.

The second characteristic of defensible space was the capacity of the physical design to provide opportunities for surveillance. This allowed residents to observe public areas and to be aware of 'intruders' or strangers to those areas. Hence, 'if there is any modicum of morality and accompanying social pressures in a community, opening up all activity in public spaces to natural supervision proves a very powerful deterrent to criminal acts' (Newman 1972, p100). Once again, the sub-division of housing projects could assist in this process.

Third, Newman identified the capacity of design to influence the perception of a project's uniqueness, isolation and stigma. Many projects had a poor image and their design often helped them to stand out as public sector housing which could be a vulnerable target of criminal activity.

Finally, there was the geographical juxtaposition of housing areas with adjacent areas which might be seen as 'safe' — certain streets or other public space. The positioning of parks, play areas etc which would be relatively well used could have an impact on the crime rates of the houses nearby.

Newman's thesis has not been without its critics and Bottoms (1974), for example, suggested that Newman's period of study was too short. In the case of his Brownsville–Van Dyke comparison, there was no information about the early years of the projects which would have enabled a picture to be constructed of how the different reputations of the projects came to be established. Further, Bottoms suggested that Newman used crime statistics in an uncritical fashion and, while the relationship between poor design and crime may exist, the case had not been proven.

In fact, Newman was careful to emphasis that poor design was not the only factor in the development of crime:

> We are concerned that some might read into our work the implication that architectural design can have a direct causal effect on social interactions. Architecture operates more in the area of 'influence' than control. It can create a setting conducive to realising the potential of mutual concern. It does not and cannot manipulate people toward these feelings, but rather allows mutually benefiting attitudes to surface.
>
> (Newman 1972, p207)

Newman's work aroused a great deal of interest in the 1970s, not least because it coincided with a period (in Britain) when high rise building was coming to an end and those blocks already built were beginning to develop problems. On the other hand, levels of crime on British housing estates are simply not comparable to the high crime rates in New York, making it difficult to establish firm relationships between crime and defensible space.

One study which did attempt to look at the relationship between design and vandalism — which had a much higher incidence than other forms of crime — was that carried out by Wilson in 1974 (Wilson 1980). Her work examined rates of vandalism in 285 blocks of dwellings on 38 inner London housing estates, attempting to relate these to physical characteristics such as defensible space, landscaping and open space as well as management issues of maintenance, caretaking and concentrations of children. The study found that the principal factor related to levels of vandalism was actually child density, although it did give some limited support to Newman's theory. Certainly, areas which were not surveyed by local residents and which could be regarded as impersonal suffered from the greatest levels of vandalism and Wilson used these findings to suggest that, in future, housing estates should incorporate precepts of defensible space, to increase feelings of territoriality and to maximise surveillance opportunities.

Newman himself later came to accept that design on its own was not perhaps as significant as he had once thought, and began to emphasise the role of management. Where a bad physical environment existed, mere modification would be insufficient and it would be more effective to attempt to change the resident population, perhaps through reducing numbers of children. Where high rise housing existed, both physical and social modifications would be necessary (Heck 1987). This relationship between design and management will be discussed further, later in the chapter.

Alice Coleman: 'Utopia on Trial'

Taking her cue from Oscar Newman, Alice Coleman's work represents another, significant, contribution to the defensible space debate although, like Newman, she has not been without her critics. Assembling a 'Design Disadvantagement Team' at Kings College, London, Coleman set out to advance Newman's theories in the following ways:

(a) by exploring if there were additional features which could be seen to be disadvantaging;
(b) by investigating whether these features were associated with forms of social malaise other than crime which had already been studied by Newman;
(c) by comparing design features of the periods before and after 1948 and the introduction of town planning legislation;
(d) by examining non-design issues as poverty and unemployment to assess their influence;
(e) by making recommendations for design improvements.

The study focused on the two inner London boroughs of Tower Hamlets and Southwark, together with the Blackbird Leys estate in Oxford; between them, these areas had 4,099 blocks (Coleman 1985).

The team studied each of these blocks, mapping and recording examples of litter, excrement, graffiti, and vandalism, and then measured these against certain design variables which were felt to be 'suspect'. These included the number of overhead walkways and inter-connecting exits; the position of the main entrance; the type of entrance; and whether or not the block was raised above garages or other open space. Outside the blocks, variables included the number of blocks in the scheme; access from the street; play areas and the spatial arrangements of open space.

The results showed that the five most significant variables were dwellings per entrance, dwellings per block, storeys per block, overhead walkways and spatial organisation. This last perhaps requires some explanation. By it Coleman meant the arrangement of the grounds around the blocks in ways which encourage their control and maintenance by residents. Such space would vary in its degree of privacy with some being shared by too many people to permit 'natural, unconscious self-policing'. Such an area was termed 'confused space' by Coleman.

In discussing the significance of these five variables, Coleman referred to them as the:

> ringleaders of the anti-social design gang. The last two may appear to be less powerful than the first three, but this is not necessarily so, as they lead from behind and increase the effect of the other suspects. If overhead walkways were removed completely, the worst excess of dwellings per entrance, vertical routes and interconnecting exits would be curtailed, and if residential space were re-organised to best advantage, the worst values of blocks per site and access points would also be damped down. Bad designs reinforce each other, and this will have to be taken into account when making practical recommendations.
>
> (Coleman 1985, p80)

Coleman argued that the best blocks of flats were those which were most like houses and that the building of houses in the future would obviate the worst of the design problems. She therefore studied a sample of 4,172 houses and measured instances of vandalism and abuse. The study suggested that it was not sufficient merely to build houses instead of flats, as certain types of houses were better than others. Those which scored best were from the interwar period, particularly those of a semi-detached design; this, argued Coleman, was 'the most advanced design achieved by British mass housing before natural evolution was broken off by planning control'. (p103)

From this standpoint, Coleman moved to advocate that blocks of flats should be rehabilitated and redesigned, as far as possible, to make them more like houses, with greater defensible space and greater privacy. She therefore, listed twelve 'disadvantaging' features which, she believed, should be avoided, and twelve 'socially stabilising' features which should be encouraged in their place.

To be avoided were: windows which did not permit surveillance; windows with frosted glass; porches and garages which obstructed sight lines; houses being set too far back from the road; lack of side fences between neighbours; lack of front gates; lack of front walls on to the street; rear fences exposed to access ways; back gates; culs-de-sac; houses not facing each other; and corner houses without the means to overlook both the intersecting roads. To be encouraged were designs which avoided these problems. Where housing already existed, Coleman recognised that design modifications were not always possible but, where they could be effected, then there were sixteen disadvantaging features which ought to be tackled., These included overhead walkways and interconnecting exits, which should be removed; the density of the development (storeys and dwellings per block), which should be tackled through height reduction and conversion; communal play areas which should be removed or relocated; and issues of access, doors, corridors etc which required redesign to allow for surveillance and the creation of defensible space.

Coleman concluded by attacking what she saw as authoritarianism in local government, in housing and in planning:

> Why should Utopia have been such an all-pervading failure, when it was envisaged as a form of national salvation? It was conceived in compassion but has been born and bred in authoritarianism, profligacy and frustration. It aimed to liberate people from the slums but has come to represent an even worse form of bondage. It aspired to beautify the urban environment, but has been transmogrified into the epitome of ugliness. Its redemption, after 40 years, is not only a matter of improving the buildings, but also of winning the hearts and minds of those who create and control them.
>
> (Coleman 1985, pp182–3)

Coleman was particularly critical of local planning policies, referring to density standards as 'pointless' and advocating a simplified planning system which would allow people the freedom to deal with their homes in their own way. She invoked the shanty towns of the third world as an example of such free expression — autonomy rather than regimentation.

Coleman's work was, indeed, full of rather pejorative language, referring to the 'paternalism', 'authoritarianism' or 'failure' of local authorities, and much of their work in the planning and housing fields was described as a 'failure' or 'pointless'. Her book was laid out with chapter headings such as 'The suspects', 'The evidence' and 'Case for the Prosecution'. It should not be surprising therefore that her work has attracted much criticism, centring not only on her conclusions and interpretations but also on her basic methodology.

Perhaps the most sustained attack on Coleman came from Hillier (1986a, b, c). He regarded her methodology as fundamentally flawed, not least because of her failure to allow for block size in her calculations. Thus, large blocks scored more highly for the existence of graffiti or litter but this would surely be what was expected, if there are more people in the block in the first place. Hillier went on to recalculate some of Coleman's data, for example on children in care correlated with block size, concluding, in contrast to Coleman, that the largest blocks actually had the lowest proportion of children in care (Hillier 1986a). There were further criticisms of correlation coefficients and trend lines which, according to Hillier, were inadequately calculated.

Criticisms of her methodology led to a rather acrimonious debate in the pages of the *Architects Journal*, with Coleman (1986) attempting to refute Hillier's accusation. She stated:

> So far I have found the pattern of criticism of 'Utopia on Trial' very revealing. Those who are close to the housing workforce accord it with a warm welcome as reflecting the reality of their firsthand experience. Those who are more remote are divided and some of them are more preoccupied with academic games than with the welfare of the residents.
>
> (Coleman 1986, p17)

A second major criticism of Coleman, however, has come from those who see her as romanticising the urban past and attempting to look backwards to a time before public housing was a major form of tenure. Some flavour of Coleman's views can be obtained from the opening paragraph of her second chapter:

> The twentieth century in Britain has been split in two by a great revolution in housing. The first half of the century was dominated by the age-old system of natural selection, which left people free to secure the best accommodation they could. The second half has embraced the Utopian ideal of housing planned by a paternalistic authority, which offered hopes of improved standards but also ran the risk of trapping people in dwellings not of their own choosing.
>
> (Coleman 1985, p6)

Quite apart from the doubtful historical accuracy of this statement (Malpass 1988), there is an implicit suggestion that 'natural selection' is to be applauded, regardless of the unsatisfactory workings of the housing market at that time. Coleman's praise of the suburban semi-detached harks back to some cosier past, characterised by the nuclear family and with children taught to respect property, not to drop litter and, most importantly, brought up in a loving family environment at home. Childrearing is seen by Coleman as a more important factor in colouring attitudes than poverty and unemployment.

Anson (1986) refuted this, arguing that the reason why housing deteriorated and why once houseproud families began not to care about their surroundings was simple despair, brought on by unemployment and lack of money. Solutions to the problems of certain housing estates needed therefore to be sought not just in design modifications but in job creation. Later he challenged Coleman to explain why identical design factors produced an entirely different result in each place:

> why, for example, do the unfenced tulip-lined lawns of Surbiton remain unscathed, when a similar arrangement in Hoxton wouldn't last a night?'
>
> (Anson 1989, p81)

Clearly the levels of affluence in these contrasting areas are the explanation and critics have felt that Coleman has dealt with this in inadequate fashion.

Thirdly, Coleman has been accused of a form of racism, in pandering to a fear of strangers and intruders held by many communities, and suggesting that all could be cured by the creation of defensible space. This

> relies on a profoundly reactionary belief that human beings, like certain animal species, have an inbuilt 'territorial instinct' and will only defend their own territory. The reverse side of this belief is that there can be no public or social responsibilities or obligations. The ideology of 'defensible space' legitimates a paranoid attitude to 'strangers' and 'aliens' and easily fits into racist paradigms of who 'intruders' are.
>
> (Wilson 1991, p153)

There is thus a danger in accepting Coleman's recommendations that public or 'confused' space should be broken up and assigned to individual blocks or flats to create individual territories. The effect of such modification would be to create areas where people would never go unless they had business there. There would never then be a feeling of space being used by passing pedestrian traffic and in such circumstances, the appearance of a stranger would be extremely threatening. This would be in complete contrast to the very public, traditional streets and roads which characterise the interwar suburban estates admired by Coleman. There is thus no guarantee that her modifications would work.

Finally, criticism of Coleman has been levelled by Oscar Newman himself. While welcoming fresh research on the subject, Newman appears to have been rather less deterministic than Coleman. He pointed out that he does not regard high rise housing as intrinsically bad, merely that it is frequently inappropriate for families with children, and suggested that Coleman paid insufficient attention to the social factors interacting with the physical as causes of housing design problems. What he missed in Coleman's work, according to Newman, was the fit between building type and family type (Heck 1987).

Despite the criticisms which have been heaped on to Alice Coleman during the last seven years, there is no doubt that she struck a chord with many who felt instinctively that she was right.

Many postwar housing estates were undoubtedly ugly, featureless and over-large and often these estates were precisely the ones which exhibited problems of management, with high rates of vacancies and turnover, and a high incidence of vandalism and graffiti. To link the two — as Coleman did — and suggest that the one caused the other is to argue that housing design has the major impact on resident behaviour, without necessarily taking account of the other factors involved. Nevertheless, Coleman's views have received widespread publicity, reminded us of the importance of our physical environment and led to major changes in official thinking on design.

Theory into Practice: DICE and design modification

The first local authority to attempt to put into practice Alice Coleman's ideas was the City of Westminster, whose Mozart estate was regarded as particularly problematic, with a number of large blocks, overhead walkways and a high crime rate. In 1986, the Council decided to spend money on the selective removal of the walkways, to limit the opportunities for intruders to enter the estate and to prevent the easy escape of criminals. The demolition was given central government backing and work began with the high-profile presence of Kenneth Baker, the then Environment Secretary. The intention was that a later phase of development would involve driving a road through the estate and selling the open spaces to developers to build private housing. Wherever possible, tenants would be given their own defensible space. Support for the changes was not widespread throughout the estate and, although they were backed by the local tenants' association, other tenants clearly felt that the greatest problem was not vandalism but disrepair.

Following the removal of the walkways, the Safe Neighbourhoods Unit assessed the effect of this change, with a view to providing information for the second phase of the development. They found, however, that there had been little thought given to improvements beyond the simple removal of the walkways and that the needs of residents had not been adequately considered. In particular, they found that, firstly, there seemed to be little correlation between size of blocks and crime. Indeed, burglary rates were highest in the smallest blocks. Secondly, the crime statistics showed no significant reduction as a result of the walkway removal. Thirdly, almost half the tenants stated that they would prefer the walkways to be reintroduced because of the difficulties which they faced in getting to the shops, particularly with prams and buggies (Brimacombe 1989).

Finally, the research examined the socio-economic and demographic profile of the estate and showed a particularliy high proportion of single parent households, headed by women. This, it was suggested, would increase the vulnerability of the estate to criminal activity, and make it seem an 'easy target'.

Although the design changes on the Mozart estate have therefore proved to be controversial, a number of other authorities have instigated similar adaptations. In 1988, Southwark announced that it was demolishing all the walkways on its North Peckham estate while the following year, Islington decided to take similar action, as part of a refurbishment of its Packington estate. In Gateshead, the St Cuthbert's Village estate was the subject of a major redevelopment, which also removed walkways.

Central government has played a significant role, after Alice Coleman had persuaded the then Prime Minister, Margaret Thatcher, in November 1988 to fund the setting up of the Design Improvement Controlled Experiment (DICE) at Kings College in London. Armed with an overall budget of £50 million, DICE surveyed a number of estates across the country, with a view to selecting between six and eight for design modification. The first estate chosen, and where the tenants voted in favour of the experiment, was the Rogers estate in Tower Hamlets, while two further projects agreed in 1991 were at the Bennett Street estate in Manchester and the Avenham estate in Preston. In all estates, ground floor flats are being given their own gardens, the numbers of flats sharing common entrances are being reduced and defensible space created, where possible. More controversially, DICE favours removing play areas and converting culs-de-sac into roads on the grounds that children in areas where there is no through traffic are not taught proper road safety (Morris 1989). A further four estates have now been selected for the DICE experience, in London, Birmingham, Sandwell and Nottingham.

Although not part of the DICE experiment, one authority which wholeheartedly embraced Coleman's ideas was Liverpool, when under Militant control in the 1980s. In 1983 the Council approved its Urban Regeneration Strategy (URS) and designated 17 priority areas where deprivation was particularly severe; a further five areas were added in 1987. The aim of the Council was to concentrate resources in these areas so as to improve both housing conditions and the surrounding environment.

What these areas frequently had in common was a concentration of unpopular housing, often in the form of flats or maisonettes, and this led the local authority to consider converting or replacing 'unsatisfactory' house types through a series of design principles. Subsequently, it was agreed that all new developments should be of houses and bungalows on small sites; culs-de-sac and play areas were to be avoided; and, wherever possible, dwellings should face on to existing roads. In the first four years of the URS, 7,500 flats or maisonettes were demolished or were emptied ready for demolition. In their place, around 9,000 houses and bungalows were completed or were under construction, improved or created from 'top-downing' blocks of flats (Mars 1987).

Certainly, the scale of the URS was impressive but the dogmatic and inflexible approach of the Council alienated many, particularly in the housing co-operatives, who believed that the Council's policies were not necessarily what the tenants wanted. Certainly, Mars (1987) showed that semi-detached housing in some parts of Liverpool was suffering from high void rates because, although possessing the road frontages and front and back gardens recommended by DICE, they were generally too small for many families.

The experience of Liverpool suggests, therefore, that design modification alone may not be the answer to problem estates and that management initiatives may also be necessary. It will be interesting, therefore, to assess the impact of DICE during the next few years.

Design Against Crime initiatives

Coleman's work and the subsequent launch of the DICE experiments has led to further work on crime in housing estates and to examples of what have sometimes been referred to as 'design against crime' initiatives. The professional bodies have also become involved and there is an increasing interest in the production of guidance on good practice in housing design.

Two years after Coleman's work, Poyner and Webb (1991) analysed crime on 38 housing estates in Northampton, each of which had a different layout design and a different crime profile. Those areas with the highest crime rates were all public sector housing built during the 1970s, mostly with houses laid out with backs facing fronts, with complex systems of footpaths and with garages distant from the houses. Low crime areas tended to conform to a more traditional street layout with houses facing each other to provide greater surveillance. Indeed, surveillance seemed to be the key, so that some terraced public sector housing had a low crime score, because the layout was such that roads were overlooked by the houses.

These findings serve to remind us that not all low crime areas are private housing estates. Newman's work focused on crime rates in public housing but the situation in the United States is very different from that in Britain. In the US, the proportion of public sector housing is only around 3 per cent and those living in it would generally be regarded as a socially under-privileged minority. Even after twelve years of the 'right-to-buy' and some residualisation of the council sector, such a situation is not the case in the UK. It is important, therefore, in discussing design issues not to focus solely on the public sector.

It is also important to be realistic about the actual occurrence of such criminal acts as burglary, assault and vandalism, as fear of crime may be greater than its incidence. There has been increasing pressure, during the last ten years, for police to be given access to housing plans at the design stage and many forces have appointed police architect liaison officers. There is increasing 'target-hardening' — making casual criminal acts more difficult. But misgivings about such approaches have come, particularly from those working in the field of community architecture who would argue for consultations on security taking place with local residents rather than the police.

There is also a danger of over-reliance on defensive measures:

> A 'fortress mentality' can develop where people lock themselves up in an atmosphere of isolation and mutual suspicion. Everyone's mobility and freedom is potentially hampered if they have to cope with extra keys, entryphones, closed circuit television surveillance, burglar alarm over-rides, guard dogs and falsely triggered alarms on shops and houses .... There may also be a conflict between the interests of fire safety and the prevention of unlawful access.
>
> (Stollard et al. 1989, p11)

There is a need, therefore, for a much broader approach to safety and crime prevention and no one solution to the issue. The danger is in being too deterministic because clearly no one design option is automatically 'the best' and there are no simple directives. Designing for security must also be site-specific, taking into account the nature of the site and the type of housing as well as the patterns of crime in the area (Warren and Stollard 1988).

The Institute of Housing's view concurred with this and, following a series of case studies, it took the view that there was no set of golden rules which could be universally applied. Nevertheless, they suggested that recent experience pointed to certain principles of sound practice which might be adhered to, and these were as follows (IoH/RIBA 1989, p45):

— involving residents (whenever possible) in deciding what should be done;
— concentrating effort on layout: creating an environment that dissuades a potential criminal from entering;

— avoiding screened areas where criminals can work unobserved at effecting entry;
— designing out easy entry routes: drainpipes, flat roof access to fanlights etc;
— specifying uniformly secure components: windows of substantial profiles fitted with security hardware;
— securely installing these components;
— reviewing security provisions as part of a programme for regular maintenance and being prepared to make adjustments;
— providing a residents' handbook to explain the operation of security provisions;
— combining physical security design with back-up services from the landlord, the police, youth services, voluntary organisations and residents;
— setting up a support system to ensure contacts between residents and outside agencies (NACRO, police, etc).

While there are clearly a large number of areas to be examined in any 'design against crime' initiative, there has been some scepticism as to whether crime can, in fact, ever be 'designed out' and whether we are still paying insufficient attention to other factors. It is instructive, therefore, to examine the experience of the North Tyneside Crime Prevention Project, set up by the Home Office in January 1986 and operating in two particular housing areas, Longbenton and Killingworth.

The new township of Killingworth, on the northern edge of Newcastle was designed as a 'Northumbrian Castle Town' with, at the centre, the Towers, representing a kind of ancient citadel, while beyond were the Garths, low rise housing representing the houses clustered around a medieval settlement. Like the crescents of Hulme which were supposed to replicate Bath (p81), the comparison was rather lost on the tenants and the Towers became deeply unpopular. They were demolished in 1985–6. The Longbenton estate comprised 151 three-storey blocks in a monotonous open-access layout and had previously been the subject of a housing management area initiative, involving the local tenants' groups.

Although crime rates were fairly high there was some evidence that much of it stemmed from boredom, as most burglaries were petty, with little of value being stolen and most being committed within two miles of the offender's home. With only 29 per cent of the residents of the two areas employed at the time, there was a view locally that solving the problem of poverty would solve the problem of crime (Cowan 1988).

Specifically, the evidence from the Project suggested that, firstly, any resulting changes in the local patterns of crime might only be temporary. Secondly, the Project coincided with other events in the area including related estate improvements and it was unclear as to how much the change was due to the Project and how much to other action. There was a suggestion that the Project was being much hyped and given credit for improvements which might have happened anyway. Thirdly, there was a major problem regarding cost and, given public sector spending cuts, it was unclear whether crime prevention work in the future would attract government funding. Finally, the role in crime prevention played by high standards of housing management needed to be stressed.

Thus, although the issue of crime prevention is one which must be addressed by housing designers, it is becoming increasingly clear that the built environment is only one of the factors influencing resident behaviour and cannot be considered in isolation. The relationship between good quality design and good quality management is arguably more important.

Design versus Management

Unfortunately, the relationship between design and management is often presented as one of opposition and the defensible space debate has led to the occupation of some rather entrenched positions. An example of this was provided by the *Architects Journal* in asking Alice Coleman and Anne Power, consultant to the Department of the Environment's Priority Estates Project, both to review a collection of conference papers on design. The implication was that two, quite conflicting, views would emerge, arguing respectively for changes in design or changes in management (*Architects Journal* 1988). In fact, this was far too simplistic a presentation and, although DICE and the Priority Estates Project (PEP) have approached the issue of estate improvement from different standpoints, the approaches have frequently overlapped.

The PEP has always recognised the major design problems which exist on flatted estates and the way in which communal space is simply abandoned and unused. The PEP would, however, argue that such lack of use reflects a lack of community on the estates and a lack of tenant involvement. The Project has always maintained that the key issues in resolving problems on housing estates are the level of tenant involvement and the existence of a local housing management presence. As Power stated:

> The design of flatted estates required the provision of resident custodial staff, caretakers, porters, janitors, or continental-style concierges. Many communally built estates of houses and gardens

> required an estate warden or caretaker too. Without a resident caretaker, it was impossible to maintain such areas in functioning order.
>
> (Power 1987, p147)

The Department of the Environment's Estate Action programme, which builds on the PEP, has embraced these ideas providing money for the rehabilitation of problem estates based on greater tenant involvement and decentralised management.

Roberts (1988) too, saw the presence of litter, graffiti and faeces on an estate as indicating a breakdown in municipal housekeeping rather than merely a problem of design, and argued that more resources should be spent on developing this service on housing estates. In the long term, spending on good quality caretaking could pay for itself in terms of a decrease in vandalism and voids. She recognised that, for some, there was an inconsistency in that such caretaking, on owner-occupied estates, was carried out by families themselves. She argued, however, that firstly, attempts to place the burden of caretaking on the family put an inequitable burden on women; secondly, that council housing was different in architectural form to private housing and would always tend to have more public space; and thirdly, that problems in the private sector were indeed increasing with ower-occupied properties slipping into disrepair through lack of maintenance.

Local management and maintenance are not the only solutions and Power drew attention to the role which can be played by allocation policies. Local lettings initiatives, or the restriction of lets to particular client groups can all play a part in reducing voids; such initiatives have already been introduced in previously difficult-to-let high rise blocks (see Chapter Four).

Tackling poorly-designed estates must therefore be seen as a collaborative exercise. Those who argue for either design solutions or for management ones are doing such housing a disservice. There are no absolute offenders in building types and hence no absolute panacea in design adaptations. Design and management are closely linked and:

> the efforts of architects, housing managers, maintenance officers and tenants interdependent. Ease of maintenance will depend on the use of sturdy or easily replaceable materials. Sound surveillance of housing estates by a caretaker or, more importantly, the tenants themselves, will depend on the design of layouts which can be policed .... The designer is involved at every stage, though the actual physical design may be only part of the 'package'. Designing against vandalism, therefore, encompasses everything from the manufacture of stout door hinges to the management, and self-management, of people.
>
> (White 1979, p43)

Ultimately, indeed, the tenants themselves may be the most significant weapon in tackling poor design, either through local associations, through the development of Estate Management Boards, involving tenants in the running of the estate, through resident participation on the Committees of local Housing Associations, or through a system of Neighbourhood Watch schemes, and the encouragement of informal surveillance. The advantages of such tenant-based solutions are that they are flexible, can help to reduce the fear of crime as well as crime itself and can be integrated into a collaborative, multi-agency approach.

Conclusions

The defensible space debate is one which has been ongoing for many years, indeed since Oscar Newman's work in the early 1970s. That it has become so important in the search for solutions to poorly designed estates is due almost entirely to the work of Alice Coleman, firstly in applying Newman's ideas in a British context and secondly, in obtaining central government funding to put her ideas into practice through the DICE project. Her arguments have been met with strong criticism and there are many who have attacked her as too deterministic. More recently, there has perhaps been greater recognition that solutions to problem estates should be sought not merely in the design area or in improved management but in a combination of both. The role of the tenant is increasingly being seen as crucial.

This leads us onwards in two directions. Firstly, recognising the poor designs of the past, many local authorities have issued design guidance and sought to control the type of housing being built in their areas. Chapter Seven, therefore, examines how good design can be promoted. Secondly, there have been increasing attempts to involve users in the design of their own homes, and a thriving community architecture movement has developed. This is the subject of Chapter Eight.

Chapter 7
The promotion of good design

Introduction: the importance of good design

Several of the previous chapters in this book have dealt with housing designs which, while acceptable at the time, have subsequently been the subject of substantial criticism and attack. The importance of promoting good design, therefore, lies in learning from the mistakes of the past and ensuring that housing designs which are unpopular, difficult to manage, or which otherwise fail to work are not repeated in the future.

It must be clear that there are no absolutes in housing design and some house types which work in one place may not work elsewhere. A good example of this is the flat which has never enjoyed in England, with its tradition of individual houses, terraced or semi-detached, the acceptance and popularity accorded to it in Scotland, or indeed many European countries. The poor reputation acquired by flatted dwellings probably owes its origins to the failings of some public sector high rise housing, as described in Chapter Four. The work of Alice Coleman and the defensible space debate discussed in Chapter Six has continued to focus attention on the problems of such housing.

The blame for high rise housing — or indeed any form of unpopular housing — has traditionally been laid at the door of the architectural profession, even though many of the prefabricated, system-built housing schemes had minimal architect input. There has, nevertheless, been a long-running controversy between architects and the public, such that it has been relatively easy for the Prince of Wales to strike a chord by attacking modern architecture. Housing design affects us all and the 'public view', if it may be said to exist, has increasingly articulated a desire for better design and, indeed for the controls necessary to achieve it. The public appears to be relatively conservative in such matters and:

> it is worth noting that, as far as urban design goes, amenity groups and bodies such as parish councils all pursue the same aesthetic objectives i.e. a preference for conservation and neo-vernacular construction and a desire that development should 'fit in' with local character. There are no 'comprehensive redevelopment' or 'modern movement' societies vociferously campaigning for, say, more high buildings.
>
> (Hall 1990, p9)

Local authorities, in responding to concerns about poor design, have approached the problem in two ways, firstly by providing detailed guidance to housebuilders in the form of Design Guides and secondly, by adopting planning policies which have strengthened their development control function. Both these areas are covered in this chapter.

As well as learning from the past, the other key argument for better design guidance is in dealing with the pressures of the present. During the 1980s in particular, there were enormous pressures for new housing development in various parts of southern England. In some instances, there were proposals for completely new settlements, or 'new country towns' as they were frequently described, planned by consortia of the major housebuilders, often adjacent to major road and rail routes out of London. In other instances, however, traditional villages in rural areas have been targets for infill housing, adding groups of ten or twelve houses into an existing settlement.

Such infill development has led to much debate about the impact of new housing on an old established village because, while the injection of new families can help to sustain village services, there is the danger that the new development is over-intrusive:

> The prospect of whole new 'villages' being built in the countryside generates such emotion that the idea of filling up the odd gaps left in old villages strikes many ... as relatively benign. But infill, as it is being applied today, is really the most destructive of all forms of development .... The delicate fabric of a village can be ruined in just a few years.
>
> Infill cannot work because the new houses are the wrong size .... Most old village houses are cottages ... with ... low doorways and beams on which the unwary can bang their heads: their inhabitants would not forego them. When it comes to new houses, nanny is on hand in the form of the district surveyor to ensure that no one is exposed to such perils. This alone would make the dimensions of the executive home more akin to those of the rectory; and for any village to acquire ten, twenty or fifty rectories looks odd.
>
> (Aslet 1991, p49)

It was to try and prevent such intrusion that local authorities developed design guidance and, while some guides have been criticised as being too restrictive and, indeed, conservative in the approach, nevertheless housebuilders have increasingly shown themselves willing to follow the advice that they contain.

As well as the local authorities themselves, there is a range of other professional bodies with an interest in the promotion of good design, including the Royal Fine Art Commission, the Civic Trust and the Royal Institute of British Architects. Many of these bodies help in the promotion of good design through awards systems and this will be discussed later in the chapter.

Finally, the relationship between housing management and housing design will be further discussed, in terms of the impact which management decisions may have in the design of new housing.

The role of design guides

Although pressures for housing development in rural areas were seen most recently in the 1980s, they date back to the early years of the century. The construction of railway lines in rural south east England had opened up many areas to Londoners seeking fresh air and time away from their crowded city. Many landowners, seeing the potential for selling land for holiday homes, divided their farms into plots which they sold on an individual basis. By the outbreak of the First World War, there were a number of 'plotland' developments, particularly in Essex and Sussex (Hardy and Ward 1984).

During the interwar period, the growth in speculative private housebuilding led to further sprawl, mainly along main roads and railway lines, prompting the Government to pass the Restriction of Ribbon Development Act in 1935. The legislation had only limited effect and it was only with the introduction of the present town planning system in 1947 that a greater measure of control over suburban development of this nature was established. In Essex, however, the planning policies adopted were relatively weak and tended to be highway-dominated. As a result, it was possible for speculative builders to continue with a series of housing developments, generally fronting main roads and with open plan front gardens. Although the average density was 10–12 dwellings per acre, privacy was often inadequate and rear gardens small. While commercially successful, such estates tended to lack character and variety (Neale 1984).

By the early 1970s, therefore, the County Council had become extremely concerned about the poor standards of design of much of the private housing in the area and in 1973, published its Design

Guide for Residential Areas (Essex County Council 1973). This was an important policy document which had a profound influence on housing design, not merely in Essex but in other local authorities who produced similar design guides based on the Essex model.

Recognising that Essex was a heavily urbanised county, the Guide argued for an average density of 13 to 15 houses to the acre so that 'comfortable family housing with decent sized gardens can be provided' (p22). They should normally be designed to meet Parker Morris standards (not then applicable to the private sector), with adequate attention paid to privacy, daylighting and sound insulation, while the minimum size for private gardens was set at 1,080 sq ft (100 sq m). The exceptions to this policy on gardens were houses with paved patios and houses built within a substantial area of well landscaped and maintained public open space.

As far as vehicular and pedestrian access was concerned, a hierarchy of traffic routes was proposed and, in most cases, cars and people were kept apart. The Guide did, however, recommend the use of the 'mews court' which was a combined vehicle/pedestrian area intended to cater for cars being driven at very low speeds. In part, the use of the mews court was also an attempt to move away from the highway-dominated suburban layouts which had been built up to that point. The Guide laid stress on the need to provide contrasting spaces, defined either by houses or by trees which would be of irregular shape and which would provide interest to anyone walking through them; some spaces would be culs-de-sac with the surrounding buildings grouped to provide an identifiable sense of enclosure.

One of the most significant parts of the Guide dealt with the requirement to design buildings which would fit with the existing urban fabric (pp71–2). Much new housing had been developed in a style unsympathetic to the local area and the County Council took the view that where new residential development was taking place, builders should attempt 'to perpetuate the unique building character of the country and to re-establish local identity'. To this end, housing should be designed to 'employ external materials which are sympathetic in colour and texture to the vernacular range of Essex materials' (p72).

The Guide recognised that there were three aspects to the design process of new housing. Firstly, there were the clients' requirements which related to the type of housing being provided and the market at which it was aimed. Secondly, there was the impact on design of the characteristics of the site itself. Thirdly, there was what was referred to as the 'community brief':

> Any new development forms part of and affects the community. Therefore, it is reasonable for its members to expect certain things

> from the development. The planning authority as the representative of the community in such matters provides this brief. In respect of housing, the brief is the new policy and contents of this document. [The Guide] (Essex County Council 1973, p83)

It was recognised in the Guide that the fusion of all these elements was not an easy task and the use of an architect was recommended. The Guide included various notes and examples to show how any problems might be overcome.

The publication of the Design Guide provoked two forms of response. The first, from architects, argued that planners, by involving themselves in the aesthetics of design, were stepping beyond the bounds of their professional discipline into the realm of architecture and the letters pages of the *Architects Journal*, in the period from 1974 onwards, frequently featured criticisms of the design guide concept, which it was argued would strangle creativity. Proponents of the guides pointed out that they were simply intended for guidance and were not rigid rule books; indeed they might encourage more imaginative design solutions.

In part, problems arose from the way in which the guidance was interpreted by architects and developers. The Guide included suggestions for a whole range of different design solutions including terraced housing, culs-de-sac, detached and semi-detached dwellings. But speculative builders concerned to offer homebuyers the maximum amount of privacy and perhaps also seeking to provide each house with an individual identity, opted almost exclusively for detached housing. Many of the resultant estates, of small two storied, narrow-fronted detached dwellings, possessed something of the proportions of a doll's house and were soon criticised for their Toytown appearance. Chelmer Village, on the outskirts of Chelmsford and developed by Countryside Properties Ltd, was a classic example:

> In consequence, a Countryside Properties estate, though often attractive in detail, appears restless when considered as a whole. The company's interpretation of the guide's canon is a valiant attempt to solve an exceedingly difficult problem, but their estates would be more varied, more restful and less Noddy land-like in appearance if they would soften some of their houses' hard surfaces with climbing plants, and include a substantial proportion of terraces in their projects.
>
> (Edwards 1981, pp254–5)

There is, however, a political element in this, illustrated by proposals in the late 1980s for a new settlement at Chafford Hundred within the borough of Thurrock. As the settlement was based around a disused chalk pit, the Essex country planners proposed terraced cottages to fit in with the rather unusual landscape. Thurrock's Labour Council, however, rejected this form of housing as being the type of dwelling from which working people were trying to escape and they opted instead for a more upmarket suburban form, with detached houses. 'Irrespective of the rights and wrongs of the opinions held by the respective parties, it is notable that the politicians had clear design objectives in their minds independent of that of the professional officers' (Hall 1990, p61).

The second criticism of the Essex approach was that although it appeared on the surface to be extremely comprehensive, there were nevertheless gaps. The Design Guide was overwhelmingly residential in scope and focused entirely on new build and infill development; it failed therefore to provide guidance on refurbishment of streets and older properties. Further, the guidance it contained was fairly general in its attempt to be of country-wide relevance and it therefore failed to address local issues. It resulted sometimes in a uniform 'Essex style', ironic in view of the intentions of its authors. Hall (1990) therefore, proposed that design objectives should be specified for much smaller areas, such as towns or parts of towns, while avoiding a building by building approach. Design briefs, while being more valuable than county-wide guidance were too site-specific and Hall argued for 'design areas' to be devised, showing in a case study of Chelmsford, how some forms of development were better suited to one part of the town rather than another.

Despite these criticisms, however, there is little doubt that the introduction of the Design Guide led to improved standards of development in Essex. Neale (1984) demonstrated how, in South Woodham Ferrers, a small, rather sprawling town was transformed into a new settlement of enhanced character and with a properly planned town centre, industrial and recreational areas and associated infrastructure. The Design Guide appeared to be interpreted flexibly enough for a range of house types of different sizes to be built, to suit different households, first time buyers and so on. Increasingly, developers have shown themselves willing to work within the overall framework of the Guide while seeking local flexibility; those who do not and who have taken the County Council to planning appeal have usually lost their case as the Guide has continued to be regarded as a relevant design policy document by the planning inspectorate.

The impact of the Essex Design Guide was felt beyond the county boundaries, with other local authorities deciding to publish similar guidance. A number published general planning standards on issues such as road layouts, parking and site potential while refraining from detailed guidance of building materials and built form (e.g. Cheshire

County Council 1978, 1988, 1990). Developers, however, argued that the advice contained in many guides was not based on market research and this led to conflict where builders felt that their profit margins were being eroded through the need to use more expensive materials. Elsewhere,

> it was evident that authorities were doing little detailed research on their own vernacular, and slightly modified variants of Essex vernacular were being promoted throughout the county.
>
> (Chapman and Larkham 1992, p7)

There is too the danger that Design Guides become over-prescriptive and less flexible. The Northern Ireland Housing Executive, for example, uses private sector architects in around half its schemes and each is issued with a Design Guide for housing types and details, which has been described by Murray (1989) as 'amounting more or less to a pattern book'. While there is no doubt that the system guarantees regular work for architects, there is a danger that individual style and imagination could be strangled.

Most recently, there has been a new wave of design guides which have gone a stage beyond the Essex Guide and its imitators and which have a wider approach, addressing the character of a town as a basis for how the appropriate design principles can be assembled. This is very much in tune with Hall's (1990) argument for detailed guidance for different towns and their constituent parts and a good example is the Design Guide for the historic town of Leamington Spa (Rock Townsend 1990). This guide, as well as discussing the various elements of townscape within the borough, provides advice on non-housing uses and also on refurbishment of the historic core, and is therefore more comprehensive in some respects than its predecessors.

The role of the planning system

The planning system has a role to play in a number of different ways, first through aesthetic control, as part of the statutory development control system; secondly through its published design guidance, which may or may not be part of the statutory development plan system; and thirdly, through the promotion of good quality design in planning briefs for site development.

The history of aesthetic control by planners is a long one, and can be dated back certainly as far as the seventeenth century and the controls exercised on the rebuilding of London after the Great Fire in 1666. In more recent times, a number of local councils like Liverpool, Newcastle and Bath sought to control design features on new buildings, such as height, building lines and elevations, often using specially promoted legislation such as the Bath Corporation Act of 1925 (Punter 1986, 1987). This historic precedent became the justification for the aesthetic control exercised under the modern town planning system after 1947.

In point of fact, such control was not initially an issue. Much of the housing development of the postwar years was public sector and local authorities were therefore able to exercise control throughout the design process. Later, the urgent need for housing in the 1950s and the scale of the building programme arguably led to quantity rather than quality as design considerations became subordinated to the Conservative Government's housing drive. Design control became more of an issue — particularly for the public — in the later 1960s and 1970s, partly as a reaction against high rise building and partly as a reaction against widespread clearance of older, and familiar, housing areas. There was too a growing awareness of the value of much of our townscape, which could so easily be spoiled by unsympathetic development, and which led to the passing of the 1967 Civic Amenities Act and the establishment of conservation areas.

Ministry circulars, through the 1960s, emphasised the role which planners should take in preventing bad design and encouraging good. But there were alternative views and there were frequent conflicts between the planning and architectural professions, with architects complaining that their designs were frequently being rejected on aesthetic grounds. This was wrong, according to Moro (1958) for the following reasons:

- it stifles architectural expression;
- it encourages uniformity and discourages contrast;
- it usually discriminates against those who are exercising their traditional right of wanting to live in a house of their time;
- it gives undue power of judgement to officials without aesthetic training;
- it smacks of totalitarianism and is, in fact, a characteristic adjunct of such a form of government;
- it is humiliating to the architect and makes nonsense of his professional status;
- it puts those architects into an invidious position who lend themselves to the distasteful task of sitting in judgement over their colleagues;
- it rarely stops bad conventional building;
- it often stops good unconventional building.

(Moro 1958)

Similar views were expressed by the development industry and, eventually, found sympathy with the civil servants. The election of the Conservative Government in 1979 led to attempts to dilute the town planning system on the grounds that planners were involving themselves in areas where they had little or no professional competence. There was also a belief in Government circles that planning was acting as a hindrance rather than a stimulus to development (HMSO 1985, 1988).

This belief was illustrated in the Department of Environment's Circular 22/80 which pointed out that aesthetics was an extremely subjective matter. Planners were not, therefore, to impose their tastes on developers simply because they believed them to be superior. Control of external appearance was only to be exercised when there were compelling reasons to do so. In issuing this advice, Central Government sided unequivocally with the developer, ignoring the argument that planners, through the democratic accountability of Planning Committees, were representing a much wider cross-section of public opinion than developers normally would.

In fact, though, Planning Committees have not a good record in the area of aesthetic and design control. Committees are composed of lay people, who rarely have the detailed technical or aesthetic knowledge to make informed judgements about design and have rarely discussed major design principles. In cases where local authorities have successfully imposed design controls on developments, committees have concentrated on minor details such as colours of bricks and tiles (Whitehand 1990).

There is, of course, a logic in attempting to resolve design issues in pre-application discussions with developers, so as to avoid later wranglings at the committee stage. There is, too, an argument for wider public consultation on new developments. Recent work by the RIBA, together with the House Builders Federation, has advocated public presentations and exhibitions of large scale new housing proposals because they:

- extend the democratic process by involving local politicians at an early stage (it is usually council officials who see draft proposals);
- help the developer and architect to understand the nature of local objections. If they are genuine, and not simply founded on a desire to preserve personal property values then it may be possible to make a positive response;
- remove the 'fear of the unknown', local press often publish exaggerated 'horror' stories which fuel the fears of existing residents; and
- reveal local support which would otherwise remain hidden because the nature of the consultation process and natural inertia tends to focus attention on the objectors.

(Davison 1990)

Such pre-application initiatives are useful because they place the planner in a less reactive situation. A similarly positive role for planners is through the Development Plan system, which can frequently contain design guidance. Local plans, in particular, may contain policies which make reference to design matters, in the context of the existing character of local areas and neighbourhoods. Structure plans, as region — or county-wide documents, are perhaps less concerned with detailed design guidance although many make reference to the need to take full account of the impact of new development on the existing built environment.

Many local authorities supplement their development plans with more specific design guidance, indicating which forms of development would be most acceptable to the planners. This is a particularly important issue in the context of infill development and the need to construct new buildings which are broadly in sympathy with their surroundings. Much inner city development, particularly by housing associations, is infill and it is important that, while the new building is reasonably harmonious with adjacent properties, the extra design requirements should not increase the costs of construction to the extent that resultant rents cease to be affordable.

Conservation areas are, of course, parts of our towns and cities where planning controls are particularly important. Development must preserve or enhance the character and appearance of the areas and it is usual for local planners to provide fairly detailed guidance as to the form of building and the types of material which would be allowed.

Sometimes, however, other considerations come into play, and a good example is provided by Liverpool's Urban Regeneration Strategy, discussed in Chapter Six. The design guidelines adopted as part of that strategy were based on the type of Council property which had proved to be consistently popular, namely semi-detached or terraced housing with a conventional street layout and traditional movement of vehicles and pedestrians. As a result, the Council undertook not to allow the construction of any more flats and to create, as far as possible, areas of defensible space. These design principles, it was stated, were so important that they went beyond the physical provision of a dwelling (Liverpool City Council 1988).

Unfortunately, the dogmatic adherence to such a policy led to major difficulties in the rebuilding of the city's inner areas, with architects and developers being refused planning consent for any housing above two storeys in height. This meant that new housing was not always able to blend with the surrounding area and architects were increasingly forced to make a choice between housing needs and conservation, rather than trying to combine the two. The Liverpool Housing Trust, one of the local housing associations, developed a sheltered housing complex at Upper Parliament Street which was higher than two storeys but only received consent by appealing to the Secretary of State; ironically the scheme later received a Europa Nostra award.

Similar reactions against flatted housing have occurred in Scotland whose traditions of housing design have resulted in a great shortage of houses with gardens. Much of the postwar tenemental stock is located in local authority estates on the periphery of major towns and cities and is deeply unpopular. As a result, some councils have reviewed their building programme in terms of housing mix, building form and quality of layout. Glasgow, for instance, decided in 1977 that, firstly all family accommodation should be in the form of houses with gardens or as the ground floor component of a flatted development, again with a garden. Secondly, the only flatted developments which would be allowed would be for one or two persons and defensible open space would be provided at ground level. Thirdly, the housing mix in any scheme would be such as to avoid excessive concentration of children. Glasgow did avoid the dogma of Liverpool's stance by accepting that in infill schemes, housing in excess of three storeys could be considered, but it was suggested that these would be the exception rather than the rule and would be judged on their own merits (Glasgow District Council 1978).

More recently, it has been recognised that small-scale two-storey housing has a suburban appearance which is not necessarily appropriate for certain inner city areas. Where major renewal projects are under way therefore, a bigger scale of development has been recommended within local design guidelines. Good examples are provided by some dockland and waterfront redevelopments, particularly in London Docklands, where much new housing is flatted, but also in Newcastle, Merseyside and Salford. Indeed, Salford Quays has been suggested as a good example of an imaginative and well-thought-out design framework, producing a good overall result (so far), despite the varying quality of individual buildings (Aldous 1988). Initially, schemes like Salford Quays seem to have worked, because the housing has been occupied mainly by single people and young couples who have less need for a garden. If family housing is to be encouraged, however, in order to create a more balanced social community then different housing forms will have to be adopted.

The last area in which planners have a key role to play in encouraging good quality design is through the promotion of design and development briefs. This is a valuable method of providing guidance for important sites and areas, particularly on local authority owned land, which are ripe for development. A local authority which is marketing land in its ownership in order to develop social housing can exercise quite tight control over the proposed development.

The formal approach to interested parties, either private developers or public sector bodies such as housing associations is frequently in the form of a brief, whose purpose is two-fold:

> It acts as a checklist to ensure that, within the local authority, due consideration has been given to all development-related issues which might arise. Secondly, it sets the framework within which developers (both housing associations and housebuilders) will be negotiating for the site.
>
> (Dunmore 1992, p19)

Typical briefs would therefore contain information regarding the site, planning and design requirements and the detailed housing requirements for the site. Design guidance would include information on the building form, the materials to be used and the landscaping and car parking layouts likely to be acceptable

Design and development briefs may also be produced, even if the land in question is not in local authority ownership. Local and structure plans, for example, may identify housing shortfalls in particular areas, together with sites where such shortfalls may be met. Such proposals frequently arouse concerns in local people, regarding the impact of new development on services, on roads and on the character of their area.

Planners, with experience of development management, can balance these legitimate concerns of residents with the requirements of developers through the production of a development brief, setting out a development framework acceptable to all. Healey et al (1988) provide a useful illustration of a brief in the Walmley area of Warwickshire which, essentially, advised developers of the attitude the planning authority would take to proposals coming forward and indicating to them how to proceed. The distribution of land between housing, open space, roads and other uses was determined by questions of landscape and access rather than land-ownership, and co-ordination of development between different owners proved complicated, but never insuperable. Issues of design were an important element of the brief, covering density, building heights etc.

Perhaps the one major problem with design and development briefs is that their success is closely linked to the economic climate of the day. During the 1980s, when the housing market in the north of England was fairly depressed, Aldous (1988) suggested that planners would be more likely to welcome development with open arms rather than take a particularly tough line on design standards.

Perhaps in the 1990s, similar problems have begun to affect the London housing market. At the other end of scale, the success of London Docklands in the 1980s led the Development Corporation, in its haste to promote development, to let architectural and design issues take second place. Although the Corporation had, in its second year of existence (1982), commissioned a Design Guide for the Isle of Dogs, its recommendations were more honoured in the breach than in the observance (Brownill 1990). It is to be hoped, however, that developers themselves see the value of good quality design and construction, as these will contribute towards the success of regeneration initiatives and a well-designed house will always be able to command a better price than a poorliy designed one.

The role of other bodies

Although planners have arguably the greatest impact on housing design, because of their statutory powers of development control, there are a number of advisory bodies which have had a significant effect in raising design consciousness.

One of the most important is the Royal Fine Art Commission which, with its Scottish counterpart, advises both developers and planners on the quality of design of many modern buildings. It provides general design guidance but, because of its limited staffing, intervenes only selectively in a relatively small number of cases. It has taken an increasing interest in urban regeneration and the inner city and, because of its wide remit and the collective authority of its members, may be 'the only body able to promulgate and apply "quality control" in design standards for urban regeneration' (Aldous 1988, p5).

Another body with a similar remit, set up as a result of public concern regarding the rebuilding of our cities, is the Civic Trust, again with a Scottish counterpart. One major initiative taken by the Trust has been the launch of a series of annual design awards for various categories including housing. Although the number of submissions may usually be over a thousand, only a handful receive awards, with a number of others receiving commendations. Generally, public sector housing has received the greatest share of awards with the contribution of the private sector frequently being somewhat disappointing.

A similar situation has tended to prevail regarding the awards scheme run by the Royal Institute of British Architects which similarly covers categories other than housing.

The Department of the Environment too has become involved in awards schemes and in 1981, launched a biannual scheme for housing designs, open to projects completed in England and Northern Ireland. There were four categories: private sector new housing; public sector new housing; private or public improvement or conversion; and private or public housing for the elderly. In keeping with current trends, awards have tended to be given for schemes which are generally modest in scale, use materials sympathetic to their surroundings and are often linked to or re-use existing buildings important to the character of the surrounding area.

The importance of award schemes is one of raising public and professional consciousness about good quality design and helping to make individuals more aware of what might constitute good and acceptable design practice.

One long-established body which has constantly and consistently advocated the high quality design of new communities as an antidote to urban sprawl is the Town and Country Planning Association, whose credentials go back to Ebenezer Howard. In 1991, it joined forces with the Joseph Rowntree Foundation, itself experienced in housing design through the model settlements of its founder, to promote a design competition, entitled 'Tomorrow's New Communities'. Recognising the pressures which were being exerted on green belts for new settlements, the competition set out to stimulate a number of new designs for new forms of settlement,

> which could have the success of the early garden cities, setting new standards of balanced development in which the quality of life and the adequate funding of community facilities are both the central ingredients.
>
> (Darley, Hall and Lock 1991, p27)

The competition stimulated some very imaginative entries, for mixed urban/rural developments, for small new towns and for town expansion schemes. It demonstrated dramatically the value of design competitions, as well as the important role played by advisory agencies and organisations.

The role of housing management

The relationship between housing management and housing design should be a close one but, as demonstrated in Chapter Six, this is frequently not the case. The approach to poorly designed estates with related estate management problems, has often been portrayed as a kind of 'design solutions versus management initiatives' debate.

In fact, many of the initiatives undertaken in such estates, frequently under the aegis of the Government's Estate Action programme, involve both. While it may never be possible, when designing an estate, to foresee the kinds of problems which may arise in years to come, nevertheless the involvement of housing management in the decision-making process may go some way towards averting future management difficulties.

The undertaking of any form of development is usually to meet a housing need and the first step for any housing organisation must therefore be the assessment of that need. Some needs may be satisfied by new building where the required housing, for example for special needs, does not currently exist. Some needs may, however, be met through changes to existing stock or through changes in management policies. For many years, during the 1950s and 1960s, the quantitative shortages in housing meant that needs assessments were undertaken with a view to providing new building but, now that the quantitative shortfall in housing provision is generally smaller, issues of quality and management have become more important. Needs assessments, therefore, must include considerations of firstly, the needs of all types of households (including the single, the elderly and the handicapped); secondly, the need for improvement and conversion of existing stock, as well as new build; and thirdly, the role of management policies in ensuring the most effective use of the existing housing stock.

Within any housing organisation, therefore, needs assessments are not simply statistical exercises. Housing management staff may indicate to development staff not only where they see shortfalls in housing provision, but also where existing housing designs have created estate management problems in the past. When developments are at the design stage, it is essential that, in appraising the outline scheme, the management and maintenance issues raised are fully considered. Such issues might include the density of development (and related child density), the amount of defensible space, the maintenance responsibility for communal open space, the positioning of car parking, play space and clothes-drying areas and the provision for external servicing such as refuse collection. The arrangements whicxh estate management staff can make for any new housing scheme are thus a pre-condition for its success:

> Design can, of course, assist in reducing future management and maintenance problems, but these can never be eliminated altogether .... The level of on-site management and maintenance that can be expected is therefore, an important design element. The initial brief should determine responsibility for future upkeep ... but good design ... can never be a complete substitute for regular

inspection and attention by the management agency.

(IoH/RIBA 1983, p48)

Management has an important role to play, too, once a scheme is finished. It is essential that there is feedback from tenants regarding completed housing schemes so that the information obtained may be used to correct any past failures and new designs are more closely related to residents' needs and aspirations. Such feedback may be acquired through surveys, through regular estate management visits or perhaps through an open forum in which tenants are encouraged to speak about their experiences with their housing. Management and maintenance staff must work together in these circumstances and the responsibilities must not be divided, as occurs in some housing organisations. Local offices and a local presence on estates, as advocated by the Priority Estates Project, can be used to gain information on how well designs are working in practice.

Given the importance of the links between the design and development staff and those in management, it must be a matter of some concern that the Welsh housing agency, Tai Cymru, is currently proposing that only a limited number of Welsh associations would retain development functions. In some, smaller associations, this would break the development–management link and might result in designs which were less sympathetic to the local environment.

One final area where the issues of management and design meet is in the provision of housing offices themselves. As local authorities increasingliy decentralise and seek to provide local or neighbourhood offices, there is increasing attention being paid to the design of such offices. While there is debate as to whether offices should be purpose-built, in portakabins or in empty dwellings or shops, they must have sufficient space for all staff, 'private' facilities for meeting and interviewing tenants and, if possible, it may be helpful to provide a base nearby for local tenants' organisations. This helps in liaising with such organisations and allows tenants to participate more in the decisions which affect their estate.

Within offices, it is helpful to provide a fairly open and informal atmosphere and, to this end the provision of screens to separate staff and tenants are not a good idea, except at secure cash collection counters. Access for the disabled should be essential and, if possible, public toilets and children's play areas should be provided. A more detailed discussion of the various design options for local offices is contained in Power (1991 pp57–65).

Conclusions

This chapter has sought to demonstrate the promotion of good design, learning from the various mistakes of the past. Good design must be a collaborative effort and the roles of different agencies and different elements of the housing service have been discussed. At the end of the day, however, as shown by the value of tenant feedback studies in new housing, the success of a design depends crucially on whether people like living there. In the same way that the involvement of housing management in the design process is increasingly seen as essential, so too is the involvement of the future tenants. User participation in design is increasing, often under the name of 'community architecture' and this is the focus of the next chapter.

Chapter 8
User participation in design

Introduction

Previous chapters have highlighted both the failings of some postwar housing designs and the need to promote better design solutions, through a system of planning and architectural guidance. One element in this is the growing belief that the future users of housing should have a key participating role in its design and this movement towards what is frequently referred to as 'community architecture' has been given added impetus by the support of the Prince of Wales.

Demands for participation, however, have their origins in earlier decades, particularly the 1960s with the growth of community protest and the increasing reaction against the destruction of older — and familiar — housing and well-loved local landmarks. Many of the community activists of the time rejected the traditional professional values of architects and planners and, through the provision of technical support, encouraged local people to seek control of their own built environment.

This chapter explores the antagonisms which have existed between architects and tenants and the growth of the community technical aid movement before moving on to discuss the more recent growth of community architecture. Different groups of people seek different degrees of involvement and the chapter provides examples of user participation at different levels and in different forms, in existing housing and in new build. Finally, the ultimate stage in user participation — self build — is discussed.

Users versus architects

There is no doubt that the architectural profession has frequently been blamed for the ills and failings of much of postwar housing and, however unfair these accusations may be, there is seen to be a gulf between the type of housing designed by architects and the type of housing that people actually want to live in. The profession is seen by many as remote, with little attempt being made to understand the needs of users.

Certainly, architects themselves seem to have very stereotyped images of the types of households for whom they are designing. Research by Darke (1984a, b, c) in which she interviewed the architects of a sample of six public sector housing schemes in London, showed, for example, that only a limited range of household types was envisaged, namely nuclear families and elderly people. Little thought was given to other forms of household while even with a 'traditional' married couple household, it was clearly assumed that the woman would be at home, making friends with neighbours and helping to develop a cohesive community. Such a limited perspective on the nature of households is not, of course, confined to architects and many of the central government Design Bulletins of the postwar period have similarly focused on the nuclear family. But it remains strange that architects should have so little appreciation of the range of household requirements for which they were designing.

Most of the architects interviewed claimed that they relied on personal experience in arriving at an image of users' needs, although this clearly assumes that users would be much like themselves. A relatively minor contribution was made by information from clients (Housing Departments), direct information from users themselves and by research reports. Indeed, there appeared to be a great deal of suspicion of much of the research carried out on housing estates, particularly if done by sociologists.

> To follow their own intuition and to use their own experience as a guide seemed to them an entirely normal and accepted procedure.
>
> (Darke 1984, p415)

The issue of community was an important one for architects. They believed that the development of a community spirit was important in ensuring the success of the estate and, to this end, tended to design houses with gardens, rather than flats (which were seen as being more impersonal), and to arrange the houses around shared open spaces accessible from the gardens of each house. They did not seem to reflect on whether it was right that architects should aim to meet such social goals. To be fair, there is certainly some evidence that residents did prefer houses to flats, partly for the better defensible space which they provided, but architects themselves conducted little in the way of feedback surveys, beyond the customary maintenance inspection, six months after completion.

This lack of feedback and a lack of awareness of how residents actually use the houses in which they live, leads to misunderstandings about the things which residents value. In a Cardiff study (Edwards 1974), a comparison was made between furniture items, as arranged by 232 tenants, and the arrangement expected by 28 architects involved in the design of similar housing. There was a high degree of consistency in the tenants' arrangements but they were accurately predicted by less than half the architects. Figure 8.1 shows the actual and predicted arrangements for dining tables and illustrates the disparity. Interviews revealed that architects valued circulation space and had a tendency to regard rooms as having various 'activity zones; tenants simply wanted to create a pleasing display.

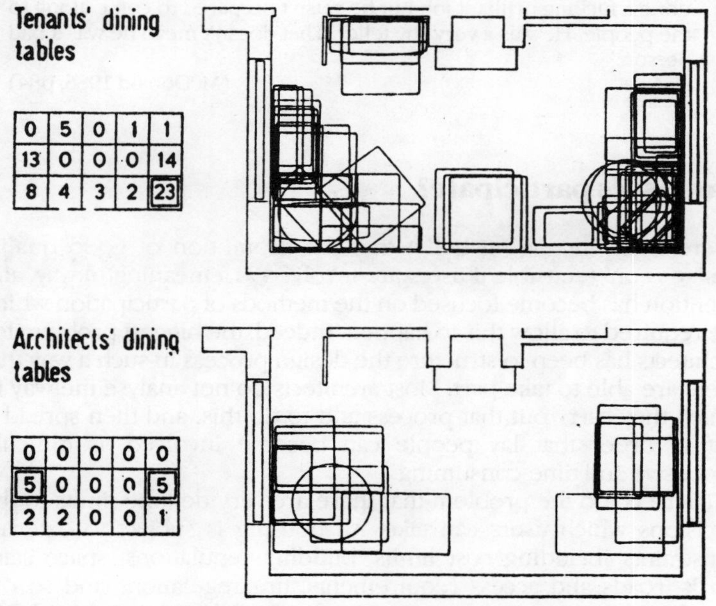

Figure 8.1 From Edwards, m (1974)

There was, therefore, a conflict within the architectural profession in relation to housing design. Although expressing a belief in the value of creating a community and frequently designing with this aim in mind, architects did not always appreciate the values of tenants and found it hard to listen to what they had to say. This conflict has surfaced particularly clearly in relation to the growth of housing cooperatives who have taken on the task of designing their own homes.

There are examples of co-operative formed through stock transfer from local authorities, who, in seeking an architect to design their refurbished homes, have interviewed the local authority's own Architects Department. But the step from designing for tenants to designing with tenants is sometimes too difficult to make. An excellent example of this is provided by the Weller Streets Housing Co-operative in Liverpool and their search for a sympathetic architect, prepared to work in a different way:

> One of the architects who came for interview . . . virtually ruled himself out by his interpretation of what it meant. Paul Lusk says, 'They said, our idea is we design the houses and you hold the pen. he wasn't happy with that.' Kevin Byrne remembers him more sympathetically: 'He wasn't prepared to come to meetings. He'd have done a fucking brilliant job but he wasn't prepared to come along to the people. He was a very shy feller. That doesn't mean he was a bad person!'
>
> (McDonald 1986, p84)

Can users participate?

There is an increasing belief that the promotion of good quality design is only sensible if users are involved in a meaningful way, and attention has become focused on the methods of participation which are required to allow this to happen. Indeed, the biggest problem for architects has been to structure the design process in such a way that users are able to take part. Most architects do not analyse the way in which they carry out that process and to do this, and then spread it out in order that lay people can become involved, is difficult, expensive and time-consuming.

There is too the problem that there are very definite limits to the decisions which users can take. All housing is subject to external constraints including cost limits, building regulations, space standards, roads and access requirements, fire regulations and so on. The design process is thus a complex one and there can be no doubt that in these, more technical areas, an architect may be in a better position to take decisions than users. It may be necessary therefore to accept that users cannot be involved in absolutely every decision and issues are presented to residents' design groups only when there is real room for manoeuvre. Disappointment will therefore be avoided when residents make a decision which conflicts with an externally-imposed regulation.

Certainly, there seems little doubt that residents will respond enthusiastically to the opportunity for involvement where the decisions they take are meaningful and will impact on the final design. Exercises in 'consultation' where tenants have simply been informed of design changes being made to their estate and offered the opportunity to choose colours of paint have, quite rightly, led to minimal response. But where residents have been able to work hand-in-hand with technical and professional staff, the results have been much more satisfying. This is particularly true in relation to the redesign and refurbishment of existing but unpopular estates, where the process of involving residents to a high degree has opened the way for the estates to receive substantial resources from central government, through schemes like Estate Action. Government may be reassured by the high level of resident commitment, even when they may have had reservations on other grounds, and projects have been subsequently recommended for funding. (Co-operative Development Services, nd).

Within such estates themselves, the establishment of design groups has often had long term benefits in relation to future management. Residents have been able to address other, related problems such as the repairs service, refuse collection and security, and structures can be established for allowing residents' representatives to contribute to the development of strategies for the management of the whole estate. Such developments help to break down antagonisms between tenants and landlords, and to rebuild communities. They provide useful examples of the continuing links between estate design and estate management.

The key to meaningful participation in the design process must be training, because residents, professionals, councillors and committee members require skills and awareness not necessarily needed in the traditional design process. Training must focus in particular on residents because, while the skills of professionals may increase with experience, participation in design may be a one-off exercise for residents. Therefore, the ability of residents to contribute to the design process must be developed and optimised quickly (IoH/RIBA 1988).

There are four key areas where new skills may be needed and the first of these is in communication. Written forms of communication may be appropriate initially as a means of getting residents involved, in the shape of leaflets, posters and newsletters. Later, however, different media will become necessary to enable residents to understand the design process. A major problem which all design groups face is in the area of site plans and drawings, as they can be confusing and complex to a lay person:

> Designers sometimes act as if the bird's-eye view they have of a building from its plan is somehow transmitted to the users, and

> hence there is a need to make that plan look as neat and formal as possible. The mere fact of attention suggests that this is a spurious exercise as no user of the building can ever be aware at a given moment in time of all the aspects which make up the plan. At a more specific level, any designer using a coding system for identifying parts of his building or routes within it, which had more than six or seven elements, should not be surprised if many of his building users are confused, on their first attempts to use the code.
>
> (Canter 1974, p41)

Sketches and perspectives may therefore prove more effective, particularly if users find it difficult to visualise three-dimensionally from a plan. Models are valuable, while site visits to other housing estates can provide residents with some ideas of the range of options which might be available. More recently, there have been developments in computer-aided design where a computer can 'plan' and then portray on screen a three-dimensional image of what the finished scheme might look like inside and out. Because such images can be changed and options explored at the touch of a button, this is in many respects more participative than using a model.

A second skills area where training is needed to allow participation is in groupwork. Many residents are unfamiliar with what is required to establish a group, conduct meetings, take minutes and follow procedures for making decisions. Where tenants' associations are already in existence, or where design is part of the work of a housing co-operative, where decision-making structures are already in place, then the task is easier.

The third and fourth skills areas are in decision-making and in negotiating. Decision-making is never easy and ways must be found to enable design groups to identify options and choose between them and to enable them to achieve some kind of consensus. Inevitably, there may be conflicts and differences of opinion may need to be reconciled. Varying proportions of persuasion and compromise will be needed (IoH/RIBA 1988).

Technical Aid

Support for local people and local communities to allow them to take a more active role in the creation of their housing and their environments began in the late 1960s with the setting up of local action groups and projects. One of the most significant was Shelter's Neighbourhood Action Project (SNAP) in the Granby area of Liverpool in 1969 where, perhaps for the first time, architects worked in the neighbourhood for a committee which included local residents. SNAP led to the setting up of other organisations in Liverpool aimed at improving the accessibility of professionals to users and some, like Neighbourhood Housing Services, have expanded to offer technical support to a number of co-operatives within the city.

In Glasgow in the early 1970s, similar concerns led to the setting up of ASSIST by a group of architects and students from the University of Strathclyde. Seeking to demonstrate how local residents could be actively involved in the improvement of their homes, they set up a Tenement Improvement Project in Govan which later led to the foundation of Central Govan Housing Association. Since the 1974 housing legislation, a substantial community-based housing association movement has developed in Glasgow and ASSIST has continued to work with resident-controlled committees.

Later developments in the field of technical aid had their origins in the Planning Aid system, operated by the Town and Country Planning Association since 1973. In 1979, The TCPA set up in Manchester the first organisation actually calling itself a Community Technical Aid Centre and two months later, the first publicly-funded centre — COMTECHSA — was set up in Liverpool, funded through the city's Inner City Partnership Programme. COMTECHSA (the Community Technical Services Agency) is a non-profit making members' co-operative, with the bulk of its membership drawn from community and residents' groups. Much of its activity has been in carrying out feasibility studies for building to enable client groups to take forward applications for funds on a sound basis (Forsyth 1988).

A similar organisation, in Glasgow, is the Technical Services Agency set up with Urban Aid funding in 1984. With Scottish Office approval came two conditions: first that the Agency should operate only in Areas for Priority Treatment (deprived areas designated by Strathclyde Regional Council) and second, that any income was to be re-invested in the extension of services (TSA 1987). Most of the TSA's activity has been in helping tenants' associations to campaign for better housing conditions and against, for example, dampness. In so doing, however, the TSA has provided a valuable training and education service so that tenants have gained extensive technical knowledge. This is proving to be a valuable resource as more and more tenants set up co-operatives and take over ownership of their own homes from the local authority.

In order to provide a forum for people working in the field of technical aid to share experience and, collectively, to campaign for more resources, the Association of Community Technical Aid Centres (ACTAC) was set up in 1983. Since its launch, membership has increased to some seventy member organisations but there is a striking regional imbalance. In England, Greater London and the

North West are well served, a reflection of where central government has seen the greatest problems and where Urban Programme money has been available (Bailey 1991). Thus, in 1984, an attempt to set up a Technical Aid Co-operative in Sheffield failed because the Department of the Environment would not provide the funding; presumably it saw other cities as having priority.

In Scotland, Glasgow is well served but there are only limited facilities available in other cities. Northern Ireland is served by Community Technical Aid (NI) Ltd, which, while based in Belfast provides technical assistance to community groups throughout the province.

The growth of technical aid services has perhaps been a response to landlord disputes (for example, over dampness), to unsympathetic redevelopment proposals and to a desire to develop local community facilities. It did not, initially at any rate, see its role as providing support for user groups to work up designs for new housing. But as more tenants take over housing from local authorities, set up co-operatives and increasingly take control of their own environment, the technical training and advice provided by ACTAC members will prove invaluable in enabling greater user participation in design and technical matters.

Byker: the first community architecture?

Byker is in east Newcastle-upon-Tyne and was originally developed as working class housing in the late nineteenth century. Most of the property was in the form of Tyneside flats (see Figure 1.2 earlier) and lacked one or more of the basic household amenities. By the 1960s, the area featured in the city's slum clearance programme and some clearance had begun; the intention was to rebuild Byker completely by 1976.

Newcastle in the 1960s was led by T. Dan Smith, who began to pursue a vision of a revitalised city, leading the north-east region into the twenty-first century (Malpass and Murie 1990). As part of this renewal, the city had developed a substantial urban motorway programme, which included an eastward running motorway planned to pass through Byker. The proposal had a blighting effect on the area and, although clearance continued apace, no new houses were started. By the later 1960s, there was considerable local agitation for new housing in the area which it was felt should be allocated locally in order to prevent the break up of the Byker community. In 1968, the Conservatives won one of the council seats in Byker, previously a Labour stronghold, after campaigning on the slogan 'Byker for Byker people'.

The Council decided to accede to local demands and finally acknowledged that the community was one which should be preserved. They therefore 'decided to use Byker to represent a break with the familiar 'numbers game' in public housing and to emphasise instead redevelopment based on the existing community' (Malpass 1979). The architect Ralph Erskine was appointed in 1968 to draw up a rehousing scheme which, he stated, he intended to do through collaborating with the residents. First he opened an office in the middle of the redevelopment area using an old shop, into which local people were encouraged to call. Second, he demonstrated to the Council that, by reducing the size of clearance areas, it would be possible to provide greater opportunity for local rehousing. Third, he began a pilot scheme in which prospective tenants were involved with the architects in the design of their homes.

The first new housing to be built in the area took the form of the now famous 'Byker Wall', designed to screen the rest of the site from the proposed motorway. Although this motorway was eventually scrapped, the line reserved for it was subsequently used by the Tyne and Wear Metro system. The wall was built in a sinuous ribbon for over half a mile, with its height ranging from five to eight storeys; its form was broken down, however, into identifiable sections, distinguished by different coloured brickwork and timber balconies.

Within the wall, housing was mainly low-rise, comprising a mixture of terraces and maisonettes.

> ... much attention has been given to circulation space, roads, playgrounds, shopping and social facilities. Shops and offices have been inserted into small housing blocks, providing a normal urban mix. Variety and surprise, planting and creative use of what would otherwise be left-over space, have all been achieved within normal housing cost-yardsticks. Despite the inventive and unconventional design of the new building, familiar landmarks, such as churches and pubs were retained and incorporated into the community. Byker even won an award for the 'Best Kept Village in Britain', a unique achievement for a mass housing scheme.
>
> (Knevitt 1985, p114)

Because Byker was the first large redevelopment scheme in which local people had had any kind of involvement whatsoever, it has tended to pass into folklore as the start of community architecture. Certainly, Erskine himself was lauded for his work, subsequently winning the RIBA Gold Medal, and it has proved difficult to separate out the myth from the reality.

Malpass (1979) posed two key questions in an attempt to analyse the real achievements of Byker, namely whether the community had been retained and whether the people had been closely involved in the design of their homes, and he suggested that the answers to both were in the negative. The retention of the community was prevented by simple density constraints; the old Byker had had a population of over 17,000 in 1960 and it would never have been possible to build houses to modern standards within the clearance site to house such a large number of households. In the event, the 1979 population after completion of the scheme was only 4,400, a quarter of the 1960 total.

As far as user participation in the design process was concerned, Malpass suggested that what was actually built was not the result of Erskine and the local people sitting down together but did nevertheless take account of comments made by local people. Part of the problem was the inability of tenants, particularly in the first phase, to visualise the finished product; at least tenants in subsequent phases could see what had been built and had some idea what to expect. Perhaps the Byker redevelopment then was not exactly an exercise in user participation but more a broadening of the architect's view of the right way to conduct relations with their primary clients:

> Erskine, and in particular his Byker-based colleagues, have led the field in promoting ways of involving the public and ... have achieved some definite progress .... Perhaps the most important lesson to be learned from Byker is that, even though progress has been made, the real power to decide what should be done and when, lay outside the community, in the Civic Centre.
>
> (Malpass 1979, pp968–9)

In point of fact, Byker was not the only place where such community-based renewal projects were being undertaken and there are examples elsewhere. The Jericho area of Oxford, for example, experienced a mixture of renewal and selective demolition and infill, although the area was also undergoing a process of gentrification (Gibson and Langstaff 1982). Nevertheless, Byker illustrates better than most the distribution of power between the architect and the residents and the local authority. Indeed, it shows clearly the difficulties faced by an architect, inclined to involve the users, but who is ultimately answerable to a corporate client (the local council). Much of the subsequent energies of the community architecture movement have been directed towards resolving this basic issue of where the power actually lies.

The community architecture 'movement'

The approach to design used by Ralph Erskine at Byker had a significant impact in changing attitudes within the architectural profession. But the approach to urban renewal was also changing and the unsympathetic clearances and redevelopments of the 1960s had led to important legislative changes. The 1969 Housing Act, for example, which established General Improvement Areas in England and Wales, made it clear that rehabilitation of existing property rather than clearance and new build would become the norm. Since this would often involve existing tenants and owners, new consultative practices would have to be evolved by local authorities and by their architects.

The other significant change was the setting up of the Housing Corporation in 1964 to foster the growth of housing societies and associations as an alternative arm of housing provision. Particularly after 1974, the vountary sector began to attract larger amounts of funding and took on substantial tasks of inner city renewal. Architects were forced to respond to these changes by evolving new working practices with the new, often locally-based associations. Community architecture may therefore be seen as a response from within the profession itself to internal pressures for change and to a set of changes involving the nature of work and the sources of funding (Sharples 1987).

During the late 1970s, there was increasing local involvement in renewal in places like Birmingham (Gibson and Langstaff 1982) and a number of architects began to embrace the idea of user participation, because of a genuine belief in the need for community involvement. As well as Ralph Erskine, architects who have been identified with community architecture are Edward Cullinan and Rod Hackney. Hackney, in particular, has become the movement's most articulate propagandist.

Rod Hackney first came to prominence when living in Black Road in Macclesfield in 1972 as a student. His house, a 'two-up, two-down' property had been built for local factory workers and was structurally sound but lacked an inside toilet or bathroom. On applying to the local authority for a grant for the installation of a wash hand basin, he was refused on the basis that the whole area was to be cleared within five years. Hackney formed the Black Road Action Group to fight the Council's plans on the grounds that the properties, while officially unfit because of their lack of amenities, were nevertheless structurally sound and capable of being upgraded.

Hackney campaigned for the Council to use the powers, granted by the 1969 Act, to declare a General Improvement Area so that the area as a whole could be upgraded and, after long and sustained pressure the local authority finally agreed in March 1973. Hackney himself became the architect for the scheme and, partly to keep things within budget, residents themselves began to participate in the building work, demolishing the toilets and washhouses and tackling repair and plasterwork inside the houses. The work on all 33 homes was completed by the end of 1974.

Politically, Black Road was a success, demonstrating the enormous resource value of local people, as well as the merits of renewal compared to clearance.

> The real story was the triumph of the people. The scheme has boosted their morale and self-respect, as well as giving them the responsibility of a mortgage. There had been 18 per cent unemployment in the area before work began; by the time it was completed many of the previously unemployed were able to use their newly acquired skills to set up their own businesses or find jobs — a feat which would have been impossible without the personal confidence acquired through the self-help scheme.
>
> (Hackney 1990, p77)

Subsequently, Black Road received a number of awards for its imaginative approach to renewal, a supreme irony for an area once threatened with wholesale demolition.

Although, during the 1970s, a number of architects practised what might be termed 'community architecture', it was often regarded in professional circles as something of a fringe activity. There were periodic boosts to the movement, such as the establishment of the Covent Garden Forum in London in 1974, the publication of Colin Ward's *Tenants Take Over* also in 1974, and the establishment of local architectural aid schemes, providing technical advice to local people. In 1976 a Community Architecture Group within the RIBA was formed.

There is no doubt, however, that the greatest fillip to the movement occurred in 1984 when the Prince of Wales, at a RIBA gala dinner, used the opportunity to castigate the architectural profession for its apparent arrogance and indifference to the wants and needs of the people. He singled out for praise certain 'community' architects, including Hackney, who subsequently became the Prince's architectural adviser.

Although the Prince of Wales had initially reserved his criticism for some of the proposed new buildings in central London, including the National Gallery extension and Peter Palumbo's proposed redevelopment at the Mansion House, he later extended his concerns more generally to the inner cities and to poor quality housing. He appeared to have been vindicated in October 1985 when riots occurred on the Broadwater Farm estate in London, depressingly similar to those in Brixton in 1981. The following year, Lord Scarman, author of the report into the Brixton disorders, the Prince of Wales and Rod Hackney all appeared on the stage of London's

Astoria Theatre at a major conference entitled 'Building Communities' and billed as the first international conference on community architecture, planning and design. The Prince of Wales used the conference to launch the Inner City Trust and its fund-raising arm Inner City Aid and made a plea for planning to take place 'from the bottom up'.

During the last five years, community architecture has become one of the most significant areas within the profession, helped in part by the election of Hackney as President of the RIBA in 1987.

> Architects, burdened with cultural baggage, borne down by regulations, overheads and a massive overseeing bureaucracy, had simply become incapable of responding to downmarket demand. A vast cottage industry of irregular, undocumented home improvement work had grown up beneath their competence in the wake of the great public sector housing crash, when local authority new house construction dropped from half the national annual total to less than 10 per cent. Jettison their decisions of grandeur, get their boots muddy, the community architecture propaganda said, and all that business and more could be theirs again.
>
> (Pawley 1987, pp14–15)

Although, clearly, community architecture means different things to different people, certain characteristics can be discerned. First, that there is user control over the built design, second that the designers or architects support wholeheartedly the principle of user control, and third, the designer has direct accountability to the users. The value of this approach lies, similarly, in three main claims, first that deprivation is, in part, due to a lack of access by low income groups to professional resources and that the involvement of architects in the local communities will help to solve these problems; second that if users are able to participate in the design of their housing, they are more satisfied with the result; third, that if people are involved in developing their local environment, they will look after it better. (Woolley 1986). None of these claims can be supported absolutely and much research still needs to be done on the successes — and failings — of community designed housing. Nevertheless, the most successful projects have appeared to be those where local residents have been able to take the initiative and it is necessary to examine some of these in more detail.

Involving users: existing housing

Involving users in design issues where existing housing is concerned is generally more extensive and more complicated than it is in the case of new build. The level of partcipation clearly varies according to the type of dwelling and a range of different households will have different views and different priorities for design and renewal. Generally speaking, tenants in flatted dwellings are more likely to want a greater degree of involvement than those living in estates of semi-detached and terraced houses where each house has its own front and back door, if only because flatted housing, by the nature of its construction, generates numerous complaints about its design.

When an area is being considered for renewal, it is important for all the parties involved — residents, elected members and professionals — to define what are seen as the main problems involved. Residents should have the opportunity to express each and every concern they have about their estate, as well as being encouraged to suggest solutions; in this way the first proposals for tackling the renewal of the housing will emerge. In order to obtain more structured information, it may be useful to conduct a social survey covering all residents, not only to ask about problems but to obtain basic data concerning the households actually living on the estate. In the case of the public sector, technical information on the houses and management information, on allocations, voids and estate management issues should also be collated at this point.

The second stage must be to provide residents with the opportunity to participate in further decision-making. Residents will need to be given information about the funding which is available, the constraints which may exist, and the options which may be available. It is also important at this stage to identify local communities, or areas where there is a natural community of interest. This may necessitate using a variety of techniques of involvement, ranging from individual streets to much larger areas and so on, up to the whole estate (Co-operative Development Services, nd).

Preliminary proposals and options can be developed by architects in conjunction with residents and first reactions obtained. Once general agreement has been reached on the overall proposals for an estate, this then requires to be discussed with individual residents so that everyone appreciates the impact which design changes will have on their particular house. It should then be possible for residents to choose options to meet their specific requirements, particularly in regard to types of bathroom and kitchen fitments and forms of heating. The whole process is slow and time-consuming but it maintains resident interest, maintains accountability and is a long-term learning process for all concerned.

There are now several examples of housing areas where local residents have participated in the redesign of their properties and these cover the local authority, housing association and owner-occupation sectors. As far as the local authority is concerned, one of the best examples is provided by Lea View House and Wigan House, both in Hackney and renewed in different ways, one with tenant involvement, the other without. Both blocks had been built in 1939 and were five storeys high, consisting of 300 units. The flats had full amenities and communal facilities were generous, including a community hall, bowling green, tennis courts, laundry, several porters and a resident caretaker. By the end of the 1970s, however, poor maintenance and staffing cuts had rendered the estate difficult-to-let and the majority of tenants had applied for a transfer.

At the end of 1980, the architects Hunt Thompson were appointed by Hackney Borough Council to improve Lea View House and, after considerable campaigning by the tenants, the design stage became a collaborative one. A social survey identified the needs of the tenants while a physical survey showed that, while the structure of the blocks was basically sound, kitchens required modernisation, balconies were unused and there was a major problem of dampness.

The solution adopted by the design team was to restructure the blocks internally by creating two-storey maisonettes with front doors leading directly off the street for families, while above them, flats were refurbished with larger kitchens and with sizes varying to reflect differing household needs. Some flats were designed specifically for the elderly and some for the disabled and tenants were given a choice regarding decoration. The courtyard was landscaped, new lift towers were added and the roof and all windows were replaced. In particular, walls were specially lined internally to prevent condensation and to retain heat.

The scheme was a huge success. Work was carried out by Hackney's Direct Labour Organisation, for whom the tenants held a 'breakfast party' on the first day, and was to a high standard. Tenant satisfaction remains high. But in Wigan House, on the same estate, refurbishment took place at the same time and to similar standards but without involving the tenants. Within six months, the block had reverted to being difficult-to-let.

Lea View House is an often-quoted example of the success which can be achieved through tenant participation but it is not the only one. On Merseyside, Co-operative Development Services have conducted similar exercises with some of the most problematic peripheral estates within Knowsley Borough Council's area. Design groups were set up with tenants and key issues identified were the demolition of the most unpopular housing (usually maisonettes) and the creation of defensible space. In many areas the Radburn layout was abandoned and the designs of roads and parking areas changed. Even more importantly, the refurbishment of the estates has led to improved working relationships between estate residents and local housing management staff and a sense of partnership has begun to prevail (Co-operative Development Services, nd).

There are further examples of user participation, from Glasgow, involving both private owners and housing associations. The Scottish tenement is a housing form which, by its nature, leads to co-operation. Many blocks were once owned by one individual and flats rented out but where flats were privately owned, owners were required to co-operate to deal with maintenance of the common areas — the roof, the staircase, and the back garden or court; usually the maintenance was carried out for the owners by a 'factor' or private property agent. During the 1970s and 1980s Glasgow District Council actively promoted and administered generous repair and improvement grants and this led many owners collectively to organise repairs schemes, involving new roofs, renewal of stone-work, stonecleaning and back court improvements. The owners were ultimately in control and made decisions collectively about the changes, often with much debate about the design of the back court, although much of the administration of the projects was handled by the local authority. Although there were frequently high levels of participation, it was essentially a 'one-off' situation for the owners and

> there were no real learning opportunities for the participants which would have allowed them to develop a deeper understanding of the design process. On the other hand, particularly with backcourt improvements, the owners quite often had very strong views on what was required. The greatest demand on the architect was the ability to respond, in design terms, to strongly felt needs.
>
> (Jack 1991, p79)

In many parts of Glasgow where levels of home ownership were low and tenement property was privately landlorded, the condition of the housing was generally much poorer. The approach to renewal was through the declaration of Housing Action Areas but the renewal work was not carried out by the local authority itself. Instead, the Council began to enlist the energies of local voluntary organisations to act as their agents in improvement schemes (Robertson 1989) and a network of community-based housing associations developed in the city.

The primary activity of these associations has been the rehabilitation of tenement property and they have proved to be an effective vehicle for user participation. Committees are made up of local people who have usually become tenants of the association as their properties have been acquired. They have had full control over the appointment of architects and consultants and many newer architectural practices such as ASSIST, referred to earlier, have grown with the movement. Because of the long involvement with rehabilitation and later new build, committees have become well informed and able to participate fully in the design process.

A key issue in Glasgow has been the support of the local authority and this has led to a voluntary housing association sector of considerable size. In that sense, there are some differences with housing co-operatives in cities like Liverpool, discussed later, where although there have been many successes, they have been achieved despite, rather than because of Council policy.

Involving users: new build

In some respects, the involvement of tenants in the design of new build housing is relatively straightforward in that the process is not complicated by the constraints of existent dwellings; it may be easier to start with a clean sheet of paper, as it were. On the other hand, residents may have little to go on and are less able to progress the design without considerable professional support. User participation in new build also assumes that pre-letting of the houses has already taken place and an immediate consideration for the housing organisation will be to decide the proportion of potential tenants who should be involved. If the scheme is a large one, there may be a temptation to involve as many people as possible but experience suggests that participation is best limited to around 40 households as this is the maximum that can naturally operate as one group (IoH/RIBA 1988). Even smaller groups of around 25 households may be preferred but the likelihood of some households dropping out during a long process means that there is a danger of the group which remains becoming unrepresentative. Whoever becomes involved, the design process may take considerable time and this creates a dilemma for households urgently requiring housing. This is regarded as a stumbling-block to successful tenant participation in new build work.

Among the best examples of such participation is the work of the former Scottish Special Housing Association (SSHA) in Glasgow, first at Kirkland Street, Maryhill and then at Dalmarnock 'B', in the Glasgow Eastern Area Renewal area. The Kirkland Street scheme consisted of 144 houses, designed and built between 1981 and 1985. The tenants selected to participate in the design constituted only four per cent of the future households in the scheme and the design process took around 19 months, partly because techniques of participation were still being learned, on both sides. The original layout, envisaged by the SSHA's architects, was for the houses to be built in rectangular blocks, following the traditional street pattern but with the main entrances and the living rooms facing the inner courtyard which would also be the location for car parking. This was rejected by the tenants who felt, particularly strongly, that their living rooms should face outwards on to the busy streets. Apart from the desire to see the natural hustle and bustle of city life, tenants felt that the courts would attract children and encourage vandalism. The entire layout was thus turned round, in accordance with tenants' wishes.

At Dalmarnock 'B' the techniques used by the SSHA at Kirkland Street were refined and, as a result, the design process took only ten months. The design group comprised 36 per cent of future households and carried out its work between October 1985 and July 1986. The group met weekly or, at least, fortnightly and as well as using sketches and plans, three-dimensional models were also available to help tenants come to decisions. As with Kirkland Street, tenants rejected layouts which contained courts and opted for traditional street layouts. The addition of bay-windows to the living rooms met with approval as this provided the opportunity for surveillance and also harked back to the traditional Victorian tenement.

Of particular interest was the attitude of tenants to privacy. SSHA architects had proposed private individual entries to houses and flats but tenants instead opted for communal entrances similar to the traditional tenement 'close'. Housing management staff had preferred individual entries to avoid the problem of managing common areas but tenants argued that closes offered greater security, opportunities for social interaction and mutual assistance, safety and convenience, and this view prevailed (Brown 1991).

Another example of user participation in new build is provided by the 1550-house extension to the Blackbird Leys estate in Oxford, begun in 1986. The City Council decided that it wanted to initiate a scheme involving tenants in the design of their dwellings and, after local publicity, 50 tenants from the waiting list came forward to participate. Later the number increased to 67. As a result of involving the tenants, the range of house types was quite extensive, although each individual house was not especially unusual. The point was, however, that while the built form may not have been very different, tenants perceived their houses as being special because of having been so closely involved in the decision-making. There are long-term advantages in management terms, because Blackbird Leys had previously gained a poor reputation within Oxford. Tenants moving in to the new phases, by virtue of working together on the design, had been able to get to know each other and form a community, and this was ultimately to the benefit of the whole estate.

Co-operative housing: full user involvement?

The key argument for user participation is that user and client are not synonymous and architects have tended to take account of the client's wishes but not necessarily the user's. User participation ensures that the views of future residents can be taken into account. But housing co-operatives take the process a stage further by combining the client and user roles. The user is given the client functions and is budget holder as well as having responsibility for future management and maintenance.

There are advantages in this. Having played a key role in the design process, co-operative members will have a clearer understanding of why certain decisions were taken, particularly those which were affected by external constraints such as planning and finance.

> These are the advantages of incorporation — the idea that a bad decision is more acceptable if it has been made by, rather than for you. This may be true, but more positively, co-ops can avoid bad decisions. The briefing process is enhanced (and perhaps extended but certainly given more importance); the users are more likely to get what they want; and they are therefore more likely to be happy with the resulting housing.
>
> (Thomas 1990, p76)

Work carried out by Thomas in Liverpool suggested that tenant satisfaction levels were particularly high in co-operatives. In the case of the Portland Gardens Co-operative which he studied, respondents were asked if they were happy with the final designs and 90 per cent stated that they were. This was a remarkaby high figure, particularly given the inevitable compromises which had taken place along the way, and indicated that the architects had been successful in establishing and maintaining relationships with their clients (Thomas 1990).

The city of Liverpool has a long history of co-operative development, sometimes in the face of considerable local political opposition, and many have been new build co-operatives. The earliest, in 1977, was the Weller Streets Co-operative, for whom the architect was Bill Halsall. In their desire for equality, the Co-operative took two key decisions regarding the design of the scheme. Firstly, they decided to restrict the number of house plans to six and to standardise fittings and other details, so as to simplify future management of the housing. Secondly, they divided the estate into ten courts, each court forming a sub-group for management purposes, and having some degree of autonomy. The courtyard plan was opposed by the City Council who believed that they were too restrictive to allow proper access for bin lorries and delivery vehicles; as a result the Council refused to adopt the roadways within the courts and they remained the responsibility of the Co-operative (Quiney 1986).

The Hesketh Street Co-operative came into being in 1979 and had a similar history to Weller Streets, with all 40 households participating in the design process. Instead of the small courts of Weller Streets, Hesketh Street adopted a layout which consisted of a large irregular square built around a central vehicular access. The houses were designed as a 'fixed shell' with the opportunity for occupants to organise the internal layout to suit themselves. A system of 'thrust' porches was adopted in order to remove the hall from the living room and provide extra space. Interestingly, co-operative members appeared to have been less concerned about the provision of landscaping as this was felt to be too reminiscent of a council estate, and it was left to the architects to argue the case for perimeter planting around the edges of the scheme (Ospina 1987).

Figure 8.2 shows the layouts of some of the Liverpool housing co-operatives and demonstrates the enormous variety which has been achieved by different groups. All, however, produce a strong sense of enclosure and in all cases, there is only one point of access to the housing. This cul-de-sac arrangement has produced maximum defensible space and surveillance and would accord with the design principles espoused by Alice Coleman; cynics might suggest that the layouts simply betray the influence of television's 'Brookside'.

The largest, and possibly best known of the Liverpool co-operatives is the Eldonian Housing Co-operative set up in Autumn 1984 in the City's Vauxhall district and built partly on the side of the former Tate and Lyle sugar refinery. Like Hesketh Street, the houses were designed as shells with variations of layout within them to allow for different household structures and preferences. Similarly, the layout of the scheme itself displays a variety of approaches. The co-operative found itself unable to choose between terraces and courtyards and clusters and eventually a compromise emerged, guided by the architect Bill Halsall. Some residents objected to rear access on security grounds but others were quite happy with this arrangement. In the event, most houses had some form of secondary access and those on the edges of the site could have garden gates on to the surrounding roads. Bungalows for the elderly were provided adjacent to the main road on the east of the site in order to be close to shops and public transport.

Such an expression of variety is perhaps peculiar to a co-operative scheme and sprang, in part, from a desire to provide housing which was better, in every way, than that provided by the local authority. Although the housing had a close fit to the requirements of

Figure 8.2 The layouts of some of the Liverpool housing co-operatives estates showing the great variety of enclosures achieved by the different blocks of houses
Source: Quiney 1986

households, needs will change and management will need to be flexible in the future, in allowing transfers within the scheme (Owens 1988). This is a problem for all co-operative schemes where the housing is tailored to a particular users, as any future allocations may be constrained by the design of the property.

There is another problem too in that while space standards conform to Parker Morris, which was still in force when the earlier co-operatives were designed, the cost yardsticks appear to have produced housing which is relatively small. Many halls lead straight into living rooms and staircases rise from living rooms. As children became teenagers and need space of their own, such houses will soon began to feel cramped.

Liverpool, of course, is not the only area where a co-operative approach to new building has been adopted and an excellent example is provided by the Coin Street community builders in London. This development, which has taken place on 5.4 ha of land on the South Bank is unique in that the land is owned entirely by the local community, which implemented the redevelopment according to its own set of priorities. In addition, until March 1989, Coin Street had its own architectural design team, working solely on the project in a purpose-built office on the site.

The form of the housing emphasises the community and the first phase comprised 56 dwellings of three to five storey terraced housing around a private communal garden. It provides a suitable environment for young children, giving each dwelling a view overlooking open space and allows pedestrians to take precedence over cars. It is very much a revival of the London square, as an ideal residential layout.

Self-build housing

Perhaps the ultimate form of user participation in housing is self-build and this can be traced back to the various plotland developments in England between the wars. Numerous settlements like Peacehaven near Brighton, and Jaywick in Essex testify to the skills, determination and perseverance of those early self-builders (Hardy and Ward 1984). After the Second World War, the introduction of more stringent planning legislation made such developments more difficult to achieve and it is only in the last two decades that there has been an upsurge in interest. The idea itself is not particularly new, however, and has its origins in the work of N J Habraken, in Holland in the early 1960s, and his critique of mass housing. Although he accepted the need for industrialised and mass-produced housing, he argued for users to be given the responsibility for designing their own home within the overhall housing structures. His work led to the setting up of architectural research programmes in Holland and the development of a kit system of housebuilding. A separation was made between the support structure or 'shell' and the internal slotting in of divisions which would create either separate dwellings or separate rooms within dwellings. This was called the 'primary support system and housing assembly kit' or PSSHAK.

The system was used in 1976 in a GLC pilot scheme at Adelaide Road, in the Chalk Farm area of London. Tenants were pre-selected and the participation period was fairly intense, with tenants opting for a variety of designs. The scheme was relatively successful as far as the tenants were concerned but difficulties were experienced in obtaining supplies of the kit and foreign contractors were eventually used by the GLC. Habraken envisaged users themselves participating in the construction process but, because the Adelaide Road scheme was a public sector estate, the GLC's own builders were used. In that respect, PSSHAK in Britain failed to live up to its promise as a method of self build.

Much more successful — and now the most commonly used method of self-build — is that devised by Walter Segal, using a type of timber-frame construction. The method is simple because it uses materials and techniques which are readily available, rather than manufactured for a particular system, and individuals need little more than basic carpentry skills and rudimentary knowledge of 'do-it-yourself'. Building board materials such as plasterboard are used to enclose the rooms, within a basic framework provided by standard sections of timber, and are assembled using simple bolts and screws. There is therefore no need for building skills such as bricklaying and plastering, and foundations and groundworks are kept to a minimum. The construction process itself can be relatively quick, depending upon the time which the household has available to undertake the work. Various types of houses can be produced, of one or two storeys and of different designs, and they are very adaptable and easily extended (Broome 1986).

Segal himself died in 1985 and in 1988 the Walter Segal Self Build Trust was established to offer advice and support to households, particularly those on low incomes and in housing need, to build homes for themselves. The Trust has sought to foster self-build groups throughout the country and to co-ordinate these groups with sympathetic local authorities, financial institutions and architects in order to create a network which can provide mutual support.

One of the most sympathetic local authorities and the one which perhaps provided the greatest boost to the self-build movement was the London Borough of Lewisham. In 1976, the Council agreed to support some pilot self-build schemes, aware of the potential which they could offer for households on their waiting list. Four sites were selected, with a capacity for a total of 14 houses, and waiting list applicants were then invited to meetings with council officers and Walter Segal himself. Eventually 14 households were selected by ballot with others on a waiting list for further projects.

Once a site start had been achieved, all the building work was carried out on a collaborative basis, the exception being roofing which was done by an outside contractor, to ensure the buildings were watertight. To simplify financial arrangements and to allow the houses to qualify for DoE subsidy, the houses were built as council houses with the self-builders effectively 'contracted' to build them. On completion, the housing was partially sold to the households on a shared ownership basis; the self builders could staircase up to full ownership in 10 per cent instalments (Ospina 1987).

In 1984, a second Lewisham Self-Build Project was launched, completed two years later. Rather than using separate sites throughout the borough, this second scheme used one site with a capacity for 13 houses. The average house size was just under 900 sq ft (80–83 sq m), larger than some contemporary council housing.

Further self-build schemes have been constructed, in Milton Keynes, in Stirling, Brighton, Bristol and Birmingham. The London Docklands Development Corporation has also actively promoted self-build for around 200 homes, using equity-sharing arrangements. In Liverpool, building work began in 1990 on an 83-house self-build project on the site of a former comprehensive school. Three self-build housing associations co-operated in the project which was funded largely by building society finance.

The scale of self-building has increased dramatically. By the late 1980s, around 11,000 houses per year were being built by this method, a larger output than any of the volume builders, and the movement has been aided by various books of plans and designs which provide guidance. Although some people are undoubtedly fired by the attractions of alternative lifestyles of community philosophy, most self builders are simply seeking to provide themselves with a home, designed to suit their own circumstances. Indeed, self-build has a particular attraction in rural areas where the availability of housing is restricted, and various forms of kit houses have now been developed. The process is not a simple one and the questions of land availability and finance are ones which are not always easily resolved, but the end result is frequently a source of great pride to the household concerned.

Conclusions

The scale of the self-build movement and the burgeoning of community architecture are clear indications that, for many households, town hall paternalism is no longer acceptable. The reaction against the butalism of much of 1960s municipal architecture and the search for other 'user friendly' alternatives found a sympathetic ear in those architects whose training in the late 1960s and 1970s taught them to respect the community view. User participation in design can never be a panacea, not least because of the external constraints within which decisions have to be taken, but it is a major step towards greater accountability to users on the part of the architectural profession and a redefining of the relationship between client and user. As housing policy changes and public sector housing is broken up in favour of smaller associations and co-operatives, such user participation is likely to increase. The result will hopefully be housing that people genuinely want to live in.

Chapter 9
Designing for all

Introduction

Many of the design issues and much of the design guidance to which we have so far referred has focused on what is often termed 'mainstream housing provision'. More cynically this could be translated as housing for younger, able-bodied families, designed, in the main, by men. It is immediately obvious therefore that there are numerous groups who may find themselves excluded, ranging from the elderly and the disabled, who may have particular support needs, through to those who have been able to have only limited influence on the design process, including most women, young and single people.

People with support needs have the same varied needs as others and the same rights to have them met, but these ordinary and positive life experiences have often been denied, because of a failure on the part of housing designers (and managers) to see such people as 'ordinary'. Disabled people seem to be particularly affected by this and, despite United Nations Declarations of Rights for the disabled to live independently and to be self-reliant, the provision of housing for the disabled falls far short of the need. Pressures from our European counterparts to overcome the social exclusion of certain groups has also been important.

This chapter explores the design requirements of those groupings for whom most 'mainstream' housing is, in some way, unsatisfactory. As well as the elderly, the frail elderly, the disabled and those with sensory impairments, the chapter will also look at the ways in which women have been ignored by the essentially male-dominated design process. Finally, the chapter looks at ways in which the range of housing needs could be catered for through improving the flexibility of existing designs, rather than seeking separate solutions for so-called 'special' needs.

Designing for older people

With improved living and working conditions, and with advances in medical science, larger numbers of people are now living to an advanced age. For many elderly households, there is no reason why they should not continue living where they are, provided some adaptations to their houses are made, but for others different forms of housing may need to be provided. The need for such accommodation, either in the form of 'amenity' housing or 'sheltered' housing, depends on physical, psychological and social factors. Physical factors refer, simply, to the degree of mobility and capacity for independence for the elderly individuals concerned; mobility in particular may be a problem, especially where stairs are concerned. The psychological dimension of need derives from feelings of loneliness, boredom and isolation, and the social dimension relates similarly to the extent of social contact with other people. Elderly households who are in an apparently isolated situation may feel that they need or would benefit from the greater communality and opportunities offered by sheltered housing (Scottish Development Department 1976).

The elderly are not, of course, a homogeneous group. They require different levels of care and support and these requirements will change as they grow older. Indeed, as the residents of any sheltered housing scheme age, the importance of the warden service will increase and the use made of communal facilities is likely to decrease. There are therefore important management issues raised by the proportion of frail elderly and infirm residents in any one scheme.

Sheltered housing schemes generally comprise around 30 dwellings, as this number has been found to make optimum use of the warden's services and to produce an economically viable scheme. Some schemes are linked to other types of housing such as one- or two-person dwellings which might be let to elderly people, or small residential homes. Where sheltered housing forms part of a larger housing scheme, this enables neighbours to participate in social activities and ensures that the sheltered scheme is part of the community.

The general location of sheltered housing is important and proximity to shops, buses, post office etc should be considered as part of the site selection process. Proximity to mainstream housing is also important, as the elderly do not necessarily want to be separated from younger families, although they may not wish disturbance from noise. The location of children's play areas, footpaths and the view of street activity which can be obtained from a communal lounge should all be taken into consideration.

The two design considerations which are specific to sheltered housing are, firstly, the provision of a warden service and secondly, the provision of common rooms and ancillary accommodation. A warden's dwelling will therefore be required within a sheltered housing development or in an existing dwelling nearby. Within each resident's room, there should be an alarm system, usually in the form of pull-cords, located so that it is possible to call the warden from living room, bedroom, kitchen or, in particular, the bathroom. The most effective alarm call systems tend to be those which allow the warden and tenant to speak to each other by means of two-way communication boxes, activated by the pull-cords.

The common room in sheltered housing is intended as the focus of social activity and may be combined with television lounge, kitchen or hobbies room. The minimum aggregate floor space allowance for communal space is 1.5 sq m (16 sq ft) per elderly person's dwelling. For a 30-dwelling scheme this would imply common facilities of 45 sq m or 485 sq ft.

Important design issues are aspect and, internally, floor coverings, lighting and furnishing. Other communal provision in sheltered schemes might include a laundry room to allow residents the independence of doing their own washing without relying on a commercial laundry, and guest bedrooms to allow relatives and friends to stay overnight. A reasonable provision would be two guest rooms for a 30-unit scheme.

Many elderly people do not, of course, live in sheltered housing but, instead in 'amenity' housing, designed to similar standards but without a resident warden or communal facilities. The recommended minimum space standard for a one-bedroom dwelling for the elderly is 33 sq m (350 sq ft), with 48 sq m (520 sq ft) for a two-bedroom property. Many houses will be provided as single storey dwellings, to avoid internal stairs, although two-storey houses are not uncommon.

External access should be level or ramped with level access preferred, as ramps can be dangerous to elderly people, particularly in icy weather. Internal stairs should have fairly wide and shallow steps with the recommended maximum pitch of a flight being 35°. Handrails and bannister rails are essential.

Particular attention must be paid to the design of the bathroom and the kitchen because of the safety aspects involved. Elderly people need space to walk around when using walking aids and this results in a need for slightly larger bathrooms and kitchens. Within the bathroom, the design should allow for both a bath and a shower. The bath should be flat-bottomed with handgrips on both sides or, alternatively, on the wall; the bottom of the bath should have a non-slip surface. Some elderly people find it easier to use a walk-in shower and this may also be provided. The hot water supply to showers should be thermostatically controlled with shower roses both adjustable and removable for hand-held operation.

The rim of the wash-hand basin should be approximately 800 mm above the floor and the bottom of the bowl around 600 mm from the floor. It is useful if it can be reached easily from the WC. Grabrails also need to be provided close to the WC. Taps and the cistern flushing mechanism should both ideally be operated by lever action as these are often easier to manipulate.

The design of kitchens in amenity housing will not necessarily be very different from that of general needs housing but with two provisos. The first is that, ideally kitchens for the elderly should accommodate a seated person, in which case it is useful to provide knee space below the sink and worktop. Access to the kitchen window should not be obstructed by the kitchen units. Secondly, a relatively compact layout is helpful in order to minimise difficult movements.

Other design considerations in elderly persons' housing are as follows:

(a) Ventilation. Catches to all windows need to be easily opened and opening windows should be at a safe height for anyone leaning out. In living rooms, because elderly people spend time sitting looking out of windows, lower sill heights are recommended of 600 mm but with a safety rail provided. Similarly, in bedrooms, the windows should be low enough for elderly people to see out, when lying in bed. All windows should be able to be cleaned both internally and externally. Mechanical extractor fans will be necessary in both kitchen and bathroom.

(b) Doors. Entrance doors need to be secure, with a peephole to allow residents to see callers, covers to letterboxes and mortice locks fitted. The recommended width for doors is 775 mm which allows reasonable clearance for the less mobile elderly. Lever handles are the easiest to use.

(c) Floors. If floors are concrete, they will need to be tiled. Non-slip tiles should be provided in bathrooms and kitchens.

(d) Electrical installations. Socket outlets should have rocker switches and be fitted at a height of between 700 mm and 900 mm above the floor, except in the kitchen, where 1,150 mm is recommended. Light switches should also be of the rocker type, or touch sensitive, requiring only light pressure.

(e) Heating. Central heating should be provided to give an even temperature of 21°C (70°F) throughout the dwelling. Radiator positions need to be carefully thought out at the design stage so as not to conflict with movement within the dwelling or likely positioning of furniture.

(f) Insulation should be to a high standard, particularly against sound.
(g) Telephone points should be provided in most rooms to allow maximum flexibility in the positioning of the instrument.

(IoH/RIBA nd)

Outwith the dwelling, the provision of open space needs to be carefully planned. Many elderly people will not be able to undertake gardening themselves although for some, this will be an enjoyable recreation. In both sheltered and amenity housing schemes, a compromise design may be to provide communal open space, managed and maintained by the landlord, with a number of areas, perhaps in the form of raised beds, which the residents themselves can look after.

As far as external car access is concerned, provision should be made for taking cars to all houses and shared and paved pedestrian/vehicular cul-de-sac may be an appropriate way of achieving this. Car ownership among the elderly is likely to be low, however, and a sensible provision of parking is 1 space per 4 dwellings. There are local authorities which insist on a higher standard than this, because of visitor parking, but generally this is unnecessary. Dropped kerbs are important to assist the less mobile, when alighting from cars.

Further reading on designing for the elderly may be found in Department of the Environment (1969, 1970, 1975a) and Scottish Development Department (1980).

There have now been a considerable number of amenity and sheltered housing developments since the beginning of the 1960s and some of the design issues are beginning to change. At the inception of sheltered housing, the focus was on enabling those with impaired mobility to lead lives which were as independent as possible. But as the elderly population itself has continued to age, other problems such as failing eyesight and hearing and the onset of dementia have become more common and sheltered housing itself has needed to adapt to a more dependent clientele.

The designs needed for housing for the more dependent have not as yet received the same attention in Britain as in countries like Germany and Scandinavia. As awareness of the problems has increased, however, sheltered housing has proved sufficiently flexible for traditional designs to be adjusted to take them into account (Phippen 1992).

One of the biggest providers of housing for the elderly, and which is now developing a different pattern of provision, is Anchor Housing Association. Their 'Housing with Care' caters for frailer elderly people who can no longer cope on their own and require both personal care and the provision of meals.

The current design concepts are as follows:

(a) Every resident in a Housing with Care scheme has an individual 'flatlet' or bedsit to ensure privacy and independence;
(b) Each flatlet has a minimum area of 16 sq m (175 sq ft) with a minimum clear living area of 10 sq m (110 sq ft);
(c) Each flatlet has its own WC and wash-hand basin and many have an en-suite shower;
(d) The schemes are designed to mobility standards and aim to create a pleasant, domestic environment.

(Tindale 1992)

The costs of such schemes tend to be higher than traditional sheltered housing because of higher staffing levels and the need to design for reduced mobility. There is therefore much debate about certain aspects of design, particularly where they may be contributing to this extra expenditure. Areas of debate include the overall size of the scheme, the amount of communal space which should be provided and the size of the flatlets, since a larger flatlet would allow residents to bring more of their own furniture and reduce usage of the communal space. In order to explore some of these issues, Anchor Housing Association commissioned an ideas competition in 1990, with entrants required to produce designs for future 'Housing with Care' schemes.

The competition attracted 174 entries and amongst the issues affecting design and which may be considered in future developments were the following:

(a) The provision of community facilities is desirable on social grounds and may be of different kinds, in different parts of the scheme. Most importantly, the building should be easy for residents to move around and to comprehend.
(b) Flatlets ought to be as large as possible to allow residents to use their own furniture and belongings. A living area of 30 sq m (325 sq ft) is not too generous.
(c) Entrance halls and circulation areas need to be inviting and spacious. Institutional style corridors could be avoided and internal streets or atria might be considered.

(Tindale 1992)

During the 1990s, the number of very old people will increase and OPCS projections suggest that by 2001, there will be 1.1 million people over the age of 85, an increase of 22 per cent in 10 years. The needs of the frail elderly will therefore assume greater significance and the design requirements for care housing will change. The work of bodies like Anchor Housing Association in raising awareness of some of the design issues has therefore been of major importance.

Designing for the disabled

Physical disability can take many forms. It can include those with mobility problems, due either to an illness such as arthritis or to loss of a limb, and also those who are completely wheelchair-bound. It can also include those with sensory disabilities, that is the deaf and the blind. This section, however, deals with mobility issues, and those with sensory impairments are considered later in the chapter.

Most disabled people in Britain are old, and more than a third of those over 75 suffer from some kind of impairment. For these people, sheltered housing or care housing may satisfy their housing needs, especially as such housing is usually built to mobility standards. But for younger individuals who are wheelchair-bound or suffer from mobility problems, alternative forms of housing provision are necessary.

There are perhaps three types of housing provision which are specially relevant for the physically handicapped. The first is ordinary housing with ground floor access and suitable alterations and adaptations for the user, including handrails, sliding doors, etc. The second is specially designed housing for wheelchair users which is maintained as a pool of dwellings for allocation to households containing persons who are wheelchair bound. The third is 'sheltered' or supervised housing for younger disabled people, allocated on the same criteria as for the elderly in that it helps to maintain them in some form of independent living and obviates the need for institutional care. This section looks specifically at the second type of housing, that is specifically for wheelchair users.

Housing for wheelchair users should be interspersed amongst other housing and small infill sites are useful for this purpose. Sites should be as level as possible and close to amenities and the whole of the housing scheme should be accessible to wheelchair users, so that individuals do not become isolated. The starting point therefore is 'the principle that disabled people should be able to gain independent entry into the homes of their friends, relations and others, as well as their own.' (Thorpe 1985, p1). Ramped access is an alternative to level access but with a gradient of around 1:20; where changes of direction occur small landings need to be provided, and a level area is also required in front of the door. Lobbied entrances are useful, but the space between the doors needs to be large enough to allow for wheelchair manoeuvre. Security is an important issue for disabled people and the design of locks and handles and the provision of spyholes needs to allow for the occupant to feel secure, while allowing helpers to gain access in cases of emergency.

Many disabled people use cars and disabled parking should be provided adjacent to the house or no further away than 60 m (650 ft) of level access. One parking space per wheelchair house is recommended and spaces should have dropped kerbs to allow for access to the vehicle.

In some authorities, particularly in urban areas, disabled persons are allocated houses in blocks of flats (Voutsadakis 1989). This should not be a problem because the lift can provide level access at the ground floor and at the level of the dwelling. Lifts need to be relatively large (the equivalent of 12 person carriages) to accommodate wheelchairs, and the control panel needs to be located no more than 1,200 mm above the floor of the lift. Within houses, lifts may also be provided to allow access to an upper-storey and there are numerous designs which attach to stairs and which can be relatively simply installed.

A key area in any form of housing lived in by disabled people is the bathroom, which should be fitted out with grabrails and other special fittings once the exact requirements of the occupant have been established; the participation of the occupant and the occupational therapist in the design process are therefore essential. There should be space for a wheelchair and also for a helper at the side of all the fittings, and floors and baths should have non-slip surfaces. Wash-hand basins need to be at a height of no more than 750 mm to allow for their use by a person sitting in a wheelchair. All controls for bath, shower and WC need to be in an accessible position. In particular, the wall, floor and ceiling construction of the bathroom need to be strengthened to allow for the secure fixing of equipment.

Similar decisions need to be taken regarding the layout of the kitchen, another key area, and one which requires the participation of the occupant. In particular, space under worktops is essential for wheelchair users and some form of mobile central storage may be considered, as this may be easier to access than fixed units. The height of kitchen appliances, the opening mechanisms of cupboards and the installation of specialist controls are all crucial elements of design.

As far as other aspects of the dwelling are considered, floor finish is a design aspect requiring careful thought, although there is no universal type of flooring suitable to disabled users. Too pronounced a texture or too resilient a material may make wheelchair movement difficult; on the other hand, materials must be able to withstand the wear and tear caused by wheelchairs and walking aids.

Everywhere in the house, the question of controls needs to be carefully considered, ranging from the positioning of power-points, through simple manual controls of windows, to door-opening mechanisms and alarm switches. All should be positioned in such a way as to be easily accessible from a wheelchair, or from a bed, assuming that the occupant may be confined to the bedroom for part of the time.

The Department of the Environment makes a distinction between housing which is built to mobility standards for people who find movement difficult and that which is built to wheelchair housing standard with full provision of ramps and lifts. In practice, many authorities, in providing the former, will ensure that the design is adaptable enough to be upgraded to full disabled standards at a later stage. This is necessary where future tenants cannot be identified at an early stage and the landlord concerned wishes to ensure maximum flexibility for the allocators of the housing; also to allow the property to be relet at some point in the future to another tenant whose needs may be different. A flexible approach in design is essential to overcome difficulties in allocation, ease future adaptation, control initial expenditure and minimise subsequent costs (Voutsadakis 1989).

Further details on housing for the disabled may be found in Department of Environment (1974, 1975b), Thorpe (1985), Voutsadakis (1989), Scottish Development Department (1979), and Habinteg Housing Association (1988).

Designing for sensory impairment

A common mistake, frequently made when discussing the needs of the disabled, is to equate such people with wheelchair users, an image encouraged by the symbol used on 'disabled' stickers. Current Building Regulations refer to 'disabled people' as those with 'a physical impairment which limits their ability to walk or makes them dependent on a wheelchair for mobility'. Although the provision of access and facilities for physically disabled people in certain new buildings is now mandatory, no such requirement exists for people with sensory impairments, such as deafness or blindness.

The needs of the two groups are, of course, quite different.

> And measures which are suitable for some disabled people are not necessarily appropriate for others. A public building with a large flat floor (like Euston Station) is fine for people in wheelchairs, but a nightmare for blind people, who often prefer stairs or solid physical obstacles which make it easier for them to orientate themselves.
>
> (Spicker 1986, p22)

An estimated five million people are hard of hearing, including one in every three elderly people. About 135,000 people, of whom 75 per cent are over 65, are registered blind although, if partially sighted people are included, the figure rises to around 250,000.

About 3,700 blind people use guide dogs (Thorpe 1986), while others will use sticks and other senses to get around.

Access routes to housing should be as simple as possible, with edges clearly defined to guide blind people, featureless paved areas should therefore be avoided. Visual, aural and tactile cues and landmarks can be used, with the texture of floor surfaces being a key feature; this could be changed to give warning of any possible hazards such as steps or doors. Projecting features such as oriel windows or porches, which may look attractive on some housing, could be highly dangerous to a blind person.

Front doors themselves could be made more distinguishable from the rest of the house frontage by the use of colour and indeed, the use of bright colours in various parts of the house, such as the kitchen, can help partially sighted people find their way around. Thresholds of all doors should be flush and single steps avoided, and glazed doors can help to ensure maximum visibility. Door handles should be large, clearly identifiable and easy to grasp.

Within the kitchen, as well as the use of colour, the grouping together of certain fittings and switches can be helpful as it obviates the need for a blind person to move around too much and become disorientated. Worktops and surfaces should be carefully detailed to contrast with adjacent areas and with other kitchen items. Lighting should be positioned to illuminate work surfaces, while avoiding both excessive glare and excessive shadow. Temperature controls on water supplies and radiators may be advisable to avoid risks of accidental scalding, and taps should be identified by both colour and relief symbols.

In flatted dwellings, adaptation of the lifts would be most important, with embossed buttons within the cars and a sound system to indicate arrival at particular floors.

The deaf and hard of hearing have fewer specific requirements for housing; indeed, deafness is a subtle form of disability and one which is not readily apparent. In housing, visual aids are the most important, with flashing lights and colours of particular assistance. Illuminated signs in lifts, for example, are recommended. Designing good housing environments for the sensorily impaired therefore requires imagination but, above all, attention to detail.

Designing for women

In much the same way as the needs of the disabled were, for a long time, largely ignored by an able-bodied architectural profession, so too has the profession — predominantly male — ignored the housing needs of many women. Such a situation may perhaps be understandable in the case of wheelchair users given that their numbers, at around a quarter of a million, are relatively small, but the lack of attention to women's needs is much less understandable and far less excusable.

Throughout the many government reports on housing design, such as Tudors-Walters, Dudley and Parker Morris, the role of women was largely seen as a domestic one. The kitchen was always located at the rear of the house, away from the main rooms, with women the keepers of this domestic environment. The house became synonymous with the nuclear family unit, although clearly the majority of households no longer fitted this model, and there was an assumed separation between paid work outside the home and leisure within it.

Outside the home, the design and layout of many housing estates, while attractive in themselves, were geared towards parking and the use of the car for journeys to and from work. The daytime needs of parents (usually women) who were at home with children, were rarely considered:

> The physical patterning of this 'natural' setting contains many assumptions about women's role outside the home. It leads, for instance, to housing layouts based on 'rural' meandering paths which imply that the journeys of women, children and old people are without purpose .... The resulting layouts only serve to underline the physical distance between homes and shops or workplaces, in turn making journeys for women with children or old people even longer. Many different housing forms seem to work in a similar way to exaggerate the distances of facilities from women at home, whether in the lifts, stairs and lobbies of high rise flats or the cul-de-sacs and winding roads of surburban layouts.
>
> (Matrix 1984, p47)

As space standards in housing improved during the last century, families chose to use those gains largely for the benefit of their children, who often gained reasonable-sized 'bedsits' within the house. Previously, children's bedrooms were small and there was an assumption that they would simply join in family activities in the main living areas. This change in attitude to the use of space was reflected in the recommendations of the Parker Morris Report, discussed previously. Most recently, the abandonment of Parker Morris standards and the reduction in the size of many modern houses has led to a fresh examination of the way in which that space is used. Once again, adults appear to have sought to protect the space used by their children, while accepting a reduction in their own, or perhaps the family's, living area. It is now common for a house to have only one living room, rather than separate dining room and lounge, thereby removing once and for all the distinction between the front and back of the house enshrined in the Tudor Walters notion of a 'parlour' house. The result, however, is that adults have little privacy from each other and this may be particularly hard for women who generally spend more time in the house than men and might be expected to welcome a space to which they could retreat (Munro and Madigan 1993). Thus, while children may use their bedrooms as private, independent space, there is no room for adults to pursue separate activities, escape from the television or talk privately to friends.

Even though single living rooms are sometimes quite large, any expansion in size can usually only be bought at the expense of the kitchen/dining area. As a result, kitchens have tended to become quite small.

> The rise of the small fitted kitchen coincided with an increase in women's paid employment. Design lends credence to the confidence trick, that implies that modern housework can be done 'at the flick of a switch', so that women can be expected to take on paid employment without relinquishing any domestic commitments. Perhaps one of the key differences in women's and men's attitudes to housing is that for most women, the house remains a significant place of work. Most women still feel responsible for the tidiness and cleanliness of the house, compounding the difficulties of having just one room for all purposes, from feeding children to entertaining visitors. Such an arrangement demands higher standards of the housewife, as everything is open to public view.
>
> (Munro and Madigan 1989, p58)

There are two discernible design trends which are relevant to women's specific needs. The first, springing from the growing women's movement of the 1960s and 1970s, is a growth in women-only architectural practices, involving women and designing for them. In 1978, the Feminist Design Collective was formed in London which, two years later, became Matrix, and they developed ways of involving women at all design stages, making decisions collectively. Early work included children's centres and women's workshops and the architectural collective sought to create a more equal relationship between builder, client and architect.

The second trend has sprung from the growth in the Women's Aid movement and the related increase in the numbers of women fleeing domestic violence as nuclear families fail. Accommodation provided by Women's Aid for such women was initially in the form of refuges and offered a secure haven from a violent partner. Many women's groups have now gone beyond simple refuge provision and have set up women's housing associations, to obtain funding for longer term housing. Examples include Culdion Housing Association in Scotland and Tai Hafan in Wales. What has been unique about the schemes which have so far been developed is the inclusion of communal space, for use by the women for meetings and self-support groups and by their children for play. In that sense, these schemes have similarities to sheltered housing but without warden support; in most cases the day-to-day management of the communal space is undertaken by a committee formed from amongst the women themselves. Usage of the communal space varies from scheme to scheme and, in some cases, there has been pressure to convert an under-used resource into much-needed extra flats. But its existence illustrates a new approach to design — and one that has women in mind.

Flexible housing

Although housing designers recognise the needs of the elderly, the disabled and others with particular requirements not normally met by mainstream housing, such 'special' needs have usually been catered for by schemes which are separate and identifiable from family housing. While this may be understandable, it serves merely to suggest that those with special needs are somehow different from the rest of us, whereas it is, of course, we who change as we get older and less able to look after ourselves, and our housing needs change with us. Attention is now beginning to focus on ways of ensuring that houses too can change, or be changed, in order that families can stay where they are, without the upheaval of moving into separate forms of accommodation, moves which often involve giving up one's own furniture and leaving behind old friends.

In the case of elderly people, there are now a number of 'staying put' schemes, which aim to adapt existing houses, while providing alarm systems linked to a central control unit. There are also a number of 'care and repair' initiatives which have helped elderly people to maintain their existing property. Similar schemes have now been applied to disabled people, a recognition that disability takes many forms and that people with disabilities may be parents with children, or children themselves, for whom simple adaptations of existing houses are the most appropriate design responses (Morris 1986).

Housing therefore needs to be adaptable, in order to suit the huge variety of people whose needs may be subject to unforeseen changes:

> Present housing policy is based on a false premise, namely that all human beings are physically fit, reasonably agile and of 'average' size and height. What architects and planners need to recognise is that most people experience change as a natural part of the human condition, if not through traumatic injury, illness or disease, then certainly as a direct result of the ageing process. The whole concept of the way the built environment is designed needs to be re-examined.
>
> (Lewis 1992, pp27–8)

Few authorities, however, have begun to think in this way. A survey conducted by Morris in 1989 for Shelter (Morris 1990) showed that local authorities did not have much information about their local populations of disabled people or as to whether appropriate housing provision existed. Social services departments seemed to have taken more of a lead in developing policies on independent living but there was little co-ordination between housing and social services departments. Morris suggested that space standards were declining and this was to the detriment of disabled people; she argued that the housing association and private sectors should do much more to create barrier-free environments.

The term 'barrier-free design' is one which is becoming more common and may be defined as the provision of an environment and housing which is accessible and usable by as many people as possible, whether disabled, elderly, sensorily impaired or simply pushing a pram. It is not about designing a special environment for people with disabilities but about designing in such a way that a wide range of people can move freely around and use all the facilities provided (Martin 1992).

Barrier-free design should take account of a number of key issues. These are:

(a) mobility and limited reach, an issue of importance not only to those who use wheelchairs, sticks or zimmers but also short or overweight people or children. Design features which help such people are level access, wide doors and controls which are carefully positioned to be within easy reach;

(b) manipulation limitations, which affect people with arthritis and various forms of paralysis, and amputees. Large handles on cupboards and easily operated switches are needed here;

(c) sensory impairment, as described earlier. Embossed and textured surfaces and the use of colour are important;

(d) disorientation, affecting people who experience dementia, learning difficulties or mental health problems. The important issue for the designer is whether the layout of the house makes sense, and the provision of distinctive and familiar features is therefore of paramount importance.

Barrier-free housing should take account of all of these issues, so that it becomes usable and accessible to all, regardless of the form of disability experienced by a particular household.

Martin (1992) identified four categories of barrier-free housing provision, as follows;

(a) Negotiable. The most basic desirable standard which allows a wheelchair user access (sometimes assisted) to the lowest level of a house, but not all facilities (including the WC) may be accessible;

(b) Visitable. The preferred minimum standard which allows an independent wheelchair user unassisted access to the lowest level of a house, and which has an accessible WC;

(c) Universal. A house designed to full wheelchair standard throughout.

The appeal of barrier-free housing is that it creates housing that is more flexible and better suited to a wider client group. Within the private sector, it provides an opportunity to appeal to a wider market. A similar approach has recently been adopted by the Joseph Rowntree Housing Trust in its garden village of New Earswick at York, under the term of 'lifetime housing' (Lewis 1992). These are houses which are designed from the outset to be flexible and adaptable as the needs of the households change. They can therefore accommodate a wide variety of differing needs and lifestyles. They allow for modification of facilities, the installation of partitions to create extra rooms (such as a ground floor bedroom) and for the installation of stair lifts. If all dwellings could be designed in this way as 'lifetime homes', and made accessible to all, then 'special needs housing' as a separate entity would disappear.

Conclusions

This chapter has emphasised the importance of ensuring that housing is designed to cater for all forms of households. While there is no doubt that designers have sought to accommodate the needs of the elderly and, to an extent, the disabled, we are already becoming conscious of the need to amend designs as needs change and as our perceptions change. In the case of the elderly, the ageing process has ensured that standard forms of sheltered housing will have to be supplemented by designs which cater for the frail elderly. In the case of disabled people, there is a growing recognition that not all forms of disability are being catered for and it is wrong to equate disability with wheelchair use; designing for sensory impairments is therefore achieving a higher profile.

There are, too, groups who may no need 'special' designs but who have requirements which are different from the average household. This would include, for example, Asian families, who may simply require slightly larger dwellings to cope with a larger household size, or HIV and AIDS sufferers, who can use ordinary mainstream housing but who may require additional support at particular times. Most importantly, therefore, there is increasing attention now being focused on the need to make housing designs as flexible and barrier-free as possible, so that housing can be used by as many people as possible with the minimum of adaptation. It is important that such housing can cope with change in the longer term future and there may be planning issues to be resolved. Although such housing is still in its relative infancy, the enthusiastic embracing of the concept, particularly in the voluntary sector, is heartening and provides a good omen for the future.

Chapter 10
Current issues in housing design

Introduction

The history of housing design is one which is linked inextricably to changes in housing policy and to changing public concerns. Thus, in the nineteenth century, the growing awareness of the need for improvements in public health and the campaigns by philanthropists like Rowntree and Cadbury against working class housing conditions led to changes in legislation and housing standards. In 1919, the experiences of the First World War and the poor medical condition of many of the men conscripted into the army, was one of the factors which influenced the Tudor-Walters report and the post-1919 housing legislation.

In the interwar period, population pressures in areas like south east England led to a major expansion of private housing, much of it suburban sprawl. This was eventually contained by green belt and planning legislation while the poor standard of some of the housing was a spur towards the later development of design guidance by local authorities.

More recently, we have seen housing policy shift dramatically from clearance and redevelopment in the 1960s to rehabilitation and renewal in the 1970s and 1980s, and with these changes have come changes in design approaches, from large scale system building to small scale infill. The greater involvement of residents in the renewal programmes led to greater recognition of the user's role in the design process and the spread of 'community architecture'.

These issues have been dealt with in earlier chapters. This chapter, therefore, seeks to explore some of the issues which are of concern to housing designers in the 1990s. It begins with an examination of the changes in housing designs during the Thatcher government and the effects of the abolition of Parker Morris standards. Secondly, it looks at the increased use of design and build packages and the advantages and disadvantages of standard designs. Issues of population pressure and the role of the housing market in the south east are still of concern and the development of private sector new town designs is dealt with. Finally, in a period when 'green' issues are increasingly coming to the fore, the chapter closes with an exploration of some of the changing designs which seek to improve energy efficiency.

Changing housing standards

The Parker Morris Report of 1961 was a landmark in the debate about housing standards because of the way in which it analysed carefully the use which households made of the dwellings in which they lived. The Report began, therefore, by recognising the various activities in the lives of any household, and their relative importance, before going on to assess the space and conditions necessary for their pursuit. This approach was continued by the resultant Design Bulletin which set out to do three things:

> to illustrate some of the main family and personal activities for which the design of a house has to cater; to set out in quickly accessible form suggested space and furniture requirements related to activities; and to provide a specimen analysis of a house plan to illustrate the approach and the standards recommended in 'Homes for Today and Tomorrow' [the Parker Morris Report].
>
> (MHLG 1963, p1)

There is no doubt that Parker Morris standards led to good quality housing, and various studies demonstrated that tenants were more likely to be satisfied with the space available in Parker Morris dwellings. Rooms were larger, storage space was more generous and heating systems generally superior to houses built earlier. But none of this was achieved without cost and the main objections to Parker Morris for many years were on the grounds of costs, particularly in construction. Parker Morris standards, on their own, were not responsible, but the combination of mandatory standards and the cost controls of the Housing Cost Yardstick led to economies being made in materials and building quality, to keep within the yardstick while achieving Parker Morris standards and rapid building rates.

Standards became a target for attack, not necessarily because they were unrealistic but because any capital investment in housing is expensive at times of financial stringency. Thus, as early as 1966, when the Wilson government was facing economic difficulties and the prospect of devaluation, Richard Crossman as Housing Minister was forced on to the offensive against schemes which he regarded as too expensive to build. He chose to make an example of a development at Basingstoke, the planning of which was already well advanced:

> I had begun to realise that largely as a result of accepting the Parker Morris standards, council housing is already becoming dangerously expensive. I felt here was an opportunity to set an example by refusing to allow the Basingstoke Group to exceed our Ministry cost yardstick by such a huge amount . . . . I said I knew I was doing this terribly late in the day but I had to make an example of one scheme and I had selected Basingstoke because the architecture was good. If we allowed this one, all the other much worse architects would say that they would have the right to go beyond Parker Morris standards and to exceed our Ministry yardstick. I added I would never again permit our Ministry people to let a scheme get this far, without exerting our sanction.
>
> (Crossman 1975, p543)

The debate surrounding Parker Morris continued through the 1970s, with contrasts being drawn, frequently unfavourably, with the private sector whose space standards were lower. Parkinson (1976), for example, referred to the situation in Sefton where the borough were given consent to build at private sector standards; it was suggested that the saving per dwelling was of the order of £1,600. Goodchild and Furbey (1986), however, pointed out that there was a tendency to publicise only those public sector schemes which had been particularly expensive. Building costs are influenced by all sorts of factors, including the nature of the site, the specifications of the developer and the local and national tendering climate. It was unwise therefore to generalise from a small sample of schemes, especially from a sample of one.

There seems little doubt that, in the most general terms, council housing was more expensive to build than private housing. For some, therefore, the issue was a quantitative one. At a time when housing needs were increasing, yet public expenditure was under threat, surely it made sense to cut standards, in order to allow more homes to be built for the same resources, precisely the arguments which Macmillan had used in 1951, as he launched his housing construction drive? Others saw the dangers in this approach, pointing out that tenant satisfaction was higher in Parker Morris housing and that these were the houses which were most likely to be sold to sitting tenants. While it was acknowledged that smaller private housing was selling, nevertheless the average household size in the private sector was smaller than in the council one, so there was less danger of overcrowding and unsatisfactory living conditions (Alton and Crofton 1979).

In the event, changing political ideology led to the abandonment of mandatory Parker Morris standards in 1981, with the Conservative government preferring to leave standards of new housing to the producers themselves. The system, however, is not totally deregulated and there are still certain minimum standards to be observed (Karn 1992). For new construction, the most important are the building regulations which lay down certain minimum provisions based on considerations of health and safety. In recent years, regulations have been used as a means of raising insulation standards in housing and there is consideration of their covering access for the disabled. Building regulations also link to statutory standards of 'fitness' (in England and Wales) and 'tolerability' (in Scotland). Local authority planning guidelines, as expressed for example through Design Guides, also influence housing designs and standards and, although not statutory, may be upheld in any planning inquiry or appeal.

In housing associations, there are added controls exercised through guidance provided by the Housing Corporation, Tai Cymru and Scottish Homes, and in England, through the Total Indicative Cost (TIC) system. These cost indicators are based on average unit costs for broad space bands; unfortunately their effect seems to have been to squeeze space standards to the bottom of each band, particularly on more expensive sites (Karn 1992).

Within the private sector builders need comply only with the statutory building regulations but in order to provide purchasers with a recognisable seal of quality, they would have to meet the standards of the National House Building Council (NHBC). In contrast to Parker Morris standards, these do not have floor space minima but heating, kitchen layout, storage, WC provision and the number of electric socket outlets are included. Houses should be constructed to a high finish and requirements are updated regularly to take account of the more common failures reported to the Council (Tutt and Adler 1979).

Although it is clear that regulation of housing standards still exists, there is no doubt that the move towards a market-led situation poses considerable risks. Some would argue that a fall in space standards is unimportant if housing design itself is of a high quality, while some consumers may be happy with less space if this implies a saving which could then be used on other aspects of the dwelling, its fittings and its surroundings. On the other hand, a balance needs to be struck between short-term acceptance of lower standards and the production of housing with long-term usefulness. This is the classic contradiction which has affected so much of the debate on housing design and takes us back to Aneurin Bevan in the 1940s and his refusal to expand the building programme at the expense of any reduction in standards; for Bevan, the needs of future generations were as important as those of the present one.

The problem is illustrated very clearly by the growth in the construction of starter homes in the 1980s, in response to the government's encouragement of low cost owner-occupation. Some houses were remarkably small, with examples in the London area having a total floorspace of 24 sq m (260 sq ft); some second bedrooms were barely 3.7 sq m (40 sq ft). Builders were able to sell them, partly because of the package of incentives which could be offered, including domestic appliances, carpets and other fittings, but their resale price was often lower than the original purchase price. Thus,

> the very fact that private developers had to include a wide variety of incentives to make starter homes sell on a large scale indicates that, if judged on grounds of design alone, these small dwellings were generally less attractive to purchasers than older property of equivalent price.
>
> (Goodchild and Furbey 1986, p93)

As well as reducing levels of floorspace, many builders in the 1980s sought to cut costs during the construction process. A classic example of this was the use of the timber-frame method of construction, by which houses were built using a wooden frame, which carried the main load of the roof. Because the brickwork which was used to face the walls was not load-bearing, unskilled labour could be used and developers dispensed with the services of trained bricklayers. The timber-frame method was not necessarily problematic in itself and had been used extensively in Scandinavia and North America for many years, but it was relatively untried in Britain. As a result, the need to keep the timber dry at all times was not always appreciated and careless site practices led to concerns being expressed about the risk of future moisture problems in the housing. In June 1983, a television programme by the 'World in Action' team broadcast these concerns and there was an instant effect on the housing market. It took some time for the market to recover and there began a move back towards more traditional materials such as brick.

Brick had always had its supporters but, during the 1960s, the increasing use of system-building methods led to its relative decline. Some areas, however, continued to use it in an attempt to retain a local vernacular approach to design:

> There used to be a map on the wall of the Department of Education and Science showing the education authorities, coloured according to which of the various consortia for system-building of school construction they had joined. A white patch in the middle stood out as a reproach. This was Buckinghamshire, which went on building purpose-designed schools of brick, timber and pitched roofs, and was finally vindicated when its simple, durable and cheaply-maintained brick buildings gave about fifteen per cent more school for the money.
>
> (Ward 1985, p33)

A similar trend can be seen in housing, as the fashion swung back from system-building and new methods like timber-frame to brick. The Essex and other design guides discussed in Chapter Seven were influential here, in encouraging the appreciation and recognition of the value of traditional building materials.

By the end of the 1980s, builders had moved substantially away from both cheaper homes and cheaper materials and begun to build rather more upmarket developments. Even here, however, the total floor space remained small and the quality variable. Kitchens were frequently too small to have a dining area and bedrooms were too small for children to use as 'bedsits'. Because circulation space was kept to a minimum, tight internal layouts often resulted, with rooms sometimes having irregular and awkward shapes, creating problems for furniture layout. Such houses like the starter homes, have sold, but may experience similar resale difficulties in years to come. These houses will have to last for many years, at current rates of replacement, but it is hard to see how they can meet future needs satisfactorily.

The problem is that there is no nationally set target for housing standards and quality, and the nearest thing we have is a commitment to bring all housing above the levels of fitness and tolerability. In contrast to, for example, the Scandinavians, we have thought little about what we would like our housing to look like in fifty years' time and what needs we wish it to serve. There is now some increasing interest in this area, and studies are underway, backed by the Joseph Rowntree Foundation; there are at last, therefore, some signs that public and political awareness of the issues are being raised.

Design and Build

In the same way that house sizes have tended to become smaller in recent years, so too has the variety of house types been reduced. Within the social rented sector, this variety had come about for a number of different reasons. Most local authorities had their own architects and, as each new build development was planned, an individual design could be formulated, taking into account local needs and local building styles and materials. Even in the 1960s, when many authorities were using system building, councils often insisted on changes being made to standard designs, a habit which Crossman, as Housing Minister, felt jeopardised the success of the system building programme (see Chapter Four). Housing associations, on the other hand, did not always employ their own architects, but the types of schemes with which they were frequently involved — infill projects and rehabilitation schemes — demanded ingenious and individual approaches to design.

In the 1990s, most new build development is in the housing association sector but is constrained by the 1988 legislation which requires that associations become more cost efficient. As a result, associations have made increased use of design and build packages, whereby family standard house types, developed by private house-builders, are purchased by the associations, with the builders then undertaking the work. As with many initiatives in housing, there are both advantages and drawbacks. On the positive side, the design and building processes can be co-ordinated from the outset, while any risk involved is more likely to be borne by the builders. Associations can therefore obtain certainty of cost and of the development programme and play to Housing Corporation rules without bearing the risk themselves (Hillier 1992).

Secondly, the use of standard house types which have been developed by the private sector for social renting can help to remove the stigma from rented housing, given that it will be indistinguishable from ower-occupied property. There may also be substantial savings realised by using standard types as this removes the cost of designing a new house type. Many builders offer a range of the different house, bungalow and flat types most commonly used by associations, costed to appropriate HAG bands. The system can thus help associations meet requirements for minimum Housing Corporation grant input (Thompson 1992). On the other hand the use of design and build does substantially limit the input which associations can have into the planning of their own housing. As well as a reduced role for development staff, there is a reduced role for committee members and, in smaller associations in particular, committees may resent the lessened contribution which they can make.

Perhaps most seriously, the architecture of the housing association movement reflects a changing set of ideals. Earlier development, being more individualistic, was perhaps of a more responsive and sympathetic design.

> What essentially distinguished the housing produced by the voluntary housing movement was its small scale. The essentially incremental nature of the urban fabric was fully recognised and understood by designers, and the very nature of the voluntary movement, made up of a variety of small charitable and other groups without statutory powers encouraged variety and innovation. The funding system, based on project specific annual allocations of capital, discouraged thinking on a grand scale, and these constraints, applied both to small scale infill schemes and to rehabilitation programmes in the inner city, contrasted vividly with the massive estates of municipal housing.
>
> (Moseley 1992, p9)

What changed all this was the 1988 legislation which has led to a more market-orientated approach to housing. The larger associations especially, are now operating much more like private developers, making use of private developers for the design of their housing. Moseley (1992), for instance, discussed a scheme carried out in Chingford for Circle 33 Housing Trust on a design and build basis. In appearance, the housing had a very conventional and suburban layout and was composed of a limited range of standard house types; it was indistinguishable from a similar estate built for owner-occupiers. While such schemes seem to be popular with tenants, there was a danger that such an approach to housing, in the long term, would not produce good quality designs which would last.

Indeed, there is already evidence that house sizes in the housing association sector are getting smaller. Recent research for the National Federation of Housing Associations (Walentowicz 1992) showed that reduced HAG levels had resulted in a 10 per cent reduction in space standards in newly built homes. In 1987/88 the average floorspace of new housing association dwellings was 62 sq m (670 sq ft) but by 1989/90, this had fallen to 56 sq m (600 sq ft). Similarly, homes built before the 1988 legislation were above the Parker Morris yardstick whereas by 1989/90, they were 9 per cent below it.

The situation is particularly advanced in Wales, where Tai Cymru has sought to rationalise housing associations' development programmes and, indeed, limit the number of associations which will be allowed to undertake development. Tai Cymru confirmed its intention, early in 1993, to introduce standard or 'pattern book' internal designs for new housing association dwellings, along the lines of those used by private sector volume builders. From April 1994, all Welsh associations will be expected to use the pattern book, whenever appropriate, and it is anticipated that savings will result. Already 80 per cent of new build schemes are procured using design and build forms of contrast (Cahill 1993) and this is likely to increase.

Within the pattern book, space standards are significantly below those of Parker Morris. Thus a pattern 2-bedroomed 3 person bungalow will have a floorspace of 54 sq m (580 sq ft) compared with a Parker Morris standard of 61 sq m (660 sq ft). A 2-bedroomed, 4 person house will be 69.5 sq m (750 sq ft) compared with 76.5–79 sq m (825–850 sq ft); and a 3-bedroomed, 5 person house will be 84 sq m (900 sq ft), compared with a Parker Morris range of 86.5–98.5 sq m (930–1,060 sq ft). It is clearly vital that the introduction of these standard types, on a design and build basis, does not herald a decrease in overall quality and diversity of provision. Standard house types may not be appropriate for the needs of rural areas, or for rehabilitation and for special needs projects and careful monitoring and feedback from associations will be necessary once the system is in place.

New country towns

Perhaps one of the reasons why the use of design and build packages involving private sector house types has aroused concern is because the private sector does not enjoy a good reputation in the area of housing design. Space standards have usually been poorer than in the rented sector, and often comparatively little attention has been paid to areas of the estate outside the dwelling. The result, from the 1930s onwards, was suburban sprawl, with local authorities increasingly trying to encourage developers to do better, armed latterly with Design Guides and planning legislation.

Developers could, of course, plead in mitigation that they were meeting a pressing need for housing and that the public, as the ultimate arbiter, must be satisfied, as the houses sold. Increasingly, as environmental concerns begin to move up the political agenda, such arguments have become less effective and both planners and politicians have sought ways of containing the spread of urban areas.

In seeking to achieve this, a system of sticks and carrots was adopted, the stick being the designation of Green Belts around all major British cities and the imposition of strict planning controls, the carrot being the identification in Structure and Local Plans of sites suitable for housebuilding, which could be offered to the volume builders. The problem, however, for many builders was the location of these sites, many in inner city areas where the private housing market was less buoyant, and they continued to argue that they should be allowed to build beyond the limits of the built-up area, in places where new dwellings could command high prices. During the 1980s, the pressures on housing, particularly in the south east of

England, lent some weight to their arguments and housebuilders began to explore locations for new settlements. It became obvious, however, that many politicians were reluctant to support large scale development in the Green Belt, not least because of the fears expressed by local residents, and a new acronym was coined — NIMBY or 'Not in my backyard' — a motto adopted by many local groups seeking to fend off new housing in the countryside.

The builders' response was to seek to promote a new form of housing solution, based on the New Towns, developed so successfully in the postwar period. These 'New Country Towns' were designed to be freestanding new settlements with the emphasis on environmental quality, an attempt to conserve the best of the countryside while seeking to meet development pressures. It was suggested that this option had the advantage of relieving speculative pressures and defusing local political opposition aimed at more piecemeal land allocations (Shostak and Lock 1984). The volume builders, in order to progress these ideas, formed themselves into an association and campaigned as Consortium Developments Ltd.

The first proposals for new country towns were at Tillingham Hall in Essex in 1985 and at Foxley Wood in Hampshire in 1988. Both were rejected on appeal by the Secretary of State, the first as it lay within the Green Belt, the second on environmental grounds. What was interesting about the proposals was their scale, each town consisting of 5,000 houses and with a target population of 12,000–15,000 people. At an average rate of building of 500 homes a year, plus associated infrastructure (the rate suggested by Consortium Developments) they would each have taken ten years to complete. They represented a substantial investment to the areas concerned.

Although detailed designs for the housing were not prepared, at the outline planning stage it was clear that, as the settlements were to be self-contained, there would be little through traffic and a system of neighbourhood units could therefore be created. The proposals therefore bore a resemblance to New Towns themselves, although it is likely that the detailed designs would have been influenced by the culs-de-sac and mews courts of the Essex Design Guide. The intention was to have a mix of tenures and special needs housing was also to be included.

Consortium Developments proposed further new country towns, at Stone Bassett in Oxfordshire, at Waterfenton, north of Cambridge, and at Peterborough. At the time of writing, none has received planning consent, and, in any case, the slump in property prices in the south east and the failures of certain property companies have tended to cast doubt on the viability of major new developments such as these. Nevertheless, they represent an important new approach to the provision of housing in a congested region and are an indication that the private sector is becoming more conscious of the need for proper settlement planning.

Energy efficient housing

The environmental concerns which have influenced the debate over the location of new housing have also had a major impact on our approach to energy efficiency. At the present time, there is a basic problem concerning fuel poverty and deprivation, with poor households being forced to use more fuel in order to try and heat cold, damp houses, but attention is now being turned to preventative measures which ensure that houses can be heated much more cheaply and efficiently. There are, however, two schools of thought on appropriate investment strategies. One argues that, because investment has already been made in existing stock, there should be a presumption in favour of retention, so long as refurbishment or upgrading is less costly over, say 60 years than new build. The second argues that this is merely tinkering with the problem and that it would be better to demolish and rebuild — to start with a clean slate, as it were — and that the enormous costs involved would be recouped through energy savings (Brooke 1991).

What will inform this decision will be the nature and form of the housing stock itself. Research has shown that the greatest levels of energy consumption are in detached and semi-detached houses, or in houses at the end of a terrace. Flats in the middle of a common structure use by far the least energy, but are clearly less popular with residents. There is thus an immediate problem in that the house type most preferred by residents is the least energy-efficient.

> In making 'green' investment decisions, we must consider the present and potential energy efficiency of the basic built form, its orientation and layout, the ease and cost effectiveness of bringing groups of dwellings up to adequate standards of energy efficiency and the future capital investment which a dwelling might require to ensure a minimum 60 year life, such as the replacement of lifts and cooling systems.
>
> (Brooke 1991, p15)

In practice, housing policy makers have proved reluctant to pursue widespread demolition and new build and most demolitions have concerned blocks of flats suffering from irremediable dampness. In most cases, energy-efficient refurbishment has seemed to be a more attractive option. One such example is Haden Court in the London Borough of Islington which was used as the focus for a study of energy conservation options, funded by the Building Research Establishment's Energy Conservation Unit (Clarke and Myer 1986). The estate, a group of postwar deck access blocks, was built mostly of brick with single glazed windows and without central heating; unsurprisingly the flats and maisonettes were difficult to heat.

Four different packages were presented as options to the council. The first, a basic package, simply involved the upgrading of the heating systems but this, without any related measures, would have rendered the heating system too costly for many tenants. The second, upgraded package also included draught stripping and flat roof insulation, while a further insulation package added in extractor fans, floating floors and double glazing. Finally, a solar package involved the addition of a conservatory and enclosed access gallery, and a pitched roof. The value of the different packages depended not only on the saving in energy but on the value given by landlords to added amenity value and affordability. The architects themselves recommended the solar package because although, in some respects, it was not cost effective because of the extra expense involved in building the conservatories, it offered additional space within the flats and offered the potential to enliven drab-looking dwellings.

The use of solar energy has been particularly successful in the Easthall housing scheme in Glasgow, an estate of some 1,000 postwar tenement dwellings. Although of traditional construction the houses suffered from damp and were poorly heated, and tenants campaigned for remedial action to be undertaken. In 1987, they held a 'Heatfest', organised in conjunction with the Technical Services Agency, aimed at finding innovative but practical energy saving measures for thermally substandard postwar stock. The winning idea involved cladding and insulation with the addition of a south-facing conservatory to provide a suntrap. This not only channelled warm air into the flat but provided an area for drying clothes which would be separate from the airing space, thereby cutting down on condensation (Humble and Hughes 1990). The scheme proved successful in practice and the City Council was able to secure European funding for the refurbishment of six blocks of housing to the same design.

Solar energy should not, of course, be considered in isolation and an example of a wider package of energy saving measures in housing has been demonstrated in Leicester, which has earned for itself a reputation for being environmentally conscious. The Leicester Ecology Trust has, for a couple of years now, supported the Eco House as a show home for alternative technology and energy efficiency (Jones 1991). A large conservatory in front of the house acts as a suntrap and keeps the heat in through triple glazing, while draught proofing and high levels of insulation in floor and walls also contribute. Internally, materials are all from replaceable softwoods and low energy lighting is used. The house demonstrates that all sorts of energy saving measures can be incorporated into design, if the will is there to do so.

Another authority which has taken a lead in energy-efficient design is the new town of Milton Keynes, which has conducted a number of experiments in this area. Two schemes are worth discussing. One, at Linford, consisted of eight detached houses built to solar designs and with cavity wall insulation, double-glazing, draught stripping and full central heating. Given that this is the house type which normally uses most energy, there was considerable interest in how energy-efficient these houses would be. The second scheme at Gifford Park, consisted of a housing co-operative development of 36 flats and houses with similar levels of heating and insulation and with conservatory-style living room extensions. Both schemes were monitored and the results were slightly disappointing. In neither case was the solar design particularly cost-effective and some elements of the package (such as the water heating) were uneconomic; it was suggested that the payback period from mass production of the housing would be around 45 years. Thus, while there may be environmental considerations which could justify such a programme of building and adaptation, they were difficult to justify on straightforward economic grounds. The need for south-facing windows also imposed significant constraints on house plans and site layout (BRECSU 1992).

Conclusions: future directions

The history of housing design in the twentieth century has, to a considerable extent, been one of repetition. At particular points in time, government reports (Tudor-Walters, Dudley, Parker Morris) have recommended improvements in standards, which have subsequently been enacted, usually by Labour governments. In each case, this has been followed by a period of retrenchment when, in order to safeguard overall housing production, the standards of individual units have fallen. The pattern can be seen in the 1930s, the 1950s and the 1980s. The continuing decline in space standards, particularly in the starter home market, must be a matter of concern and there is currently a serious danger that we are bequeathing to the next generation, housing which will have a limited life span and which will be unable to meet the needs of future households. There are some signs of optimism, such as the growth of barrier-free housing which could be adopted for a wide range of household needs, and such flexibility must be encouraged.

One of the problems which we ourselves face is the lack of flexibility in some of the stock we have inherited, particularly the system-built, flatted housing of the 1960s. Although criticism of her methodology has been fierce, there is no doubt that Alice Coleman, in her critique of such housing, has struck a chord with many people. It seems inevitable therefore that such housing will continue to be adapted, that overhead walkways will continue to be demolished and that housing authorities will launch more initiatives to try and create defensible space and crime-free environments.

Perhaps one of the most significant changes in housing policy in the 1980s has been the growth of co-operatives, and the increasing popularity of self-build, both signs that individuals have begun to take greater control of their housing. Local authorities too, long regarded as bureaucratic in the area of housing design, have begun to involve users in the design process to a quite considerable extent. The success of such participation provides a number of lessons for the future and the most popular designs with residents have often been those in which they have been most involved.

For all tenure sectors, however, and for all aspects of housing design, the key issue remains one of resources. Local authorities now build little housing for themselves, while in the housing association sector, reductions in HAG levels threaten the viability of association schemes and are already leading to declining space standards. Initiatives like energy-efficient adaptations of housing are having to prove their viability, yet there may be all sorts of unquantifiable reasons for introducing them. Resources have always been the key to good quality housing and, all too often, governments have been forced to choose between quality and quantity. For some politicians, like Aneurin Bevan, there was never any question that quality should come first and history would probably judge him to be correct. What is now needed is a government, whose housing policy makers are prepared to adopt a similar long term perspective on the issue of housing design.

Bibliography

Aldous T (1988) *Inner City Urban Regeneration and Good Design* London: Royal Fine Art Commission/HMSO

Alton D and Crofton B (1979) Standards of Conduct *Roof* **4**(6), 182–3

Anderson R Bulos M A and Walker S R (1985) *Tower Blocks* London: South Bank Polytechnic/Institute of Housing

Anson B (1986) Don't shoot the graffiti man *Architects Journal* **183**(28), 16–17

Anson B (1988) Frankie goes to Liverpool *Architects Journal* **189**(27), 79

Anson B (1989) Bending the facts to fit? *Architects Journal* **190**(24), 81

Architects Journal (1988) Home is home *Architects Journal* **188**(43), 30–31

Ash J (1980) The rise and fall of high rise housing in England, Ungerson C and Karn V (eds) *The Consumer Experience of Housing: Cross-National Perspectives* Aldershot: Gower, 93–123

Aslet C (1991) *Countryblast* London: John Murray

Bailey C (1991) Community building *in* Robertson D and Sim D (eds) *Glasgow: Some Lessons in Urban Renewal* Glasgow City Council, 69–71

Barker A (1990) Keeping up appearances *Inside Housing* **7**(27) (13 July), 8–9

Barrett H and Phillips J (1987) *Suburban Style. The British Home 1840–1960* London: Macdonald & Co

Beattie S (1980) *A Revolution in London Housing. LCC Housing Architects and their Work 1893–1914* London: Architectural Press

Begg T (1987) *50 Special Years. A Study in Scottish Housing* London: Henry Melland

Bell C and Bell R (1972) *City Fathers. The Early History of Town Planning in Britain* Harmondsworth: Pelican

Benwell CDP (1978) *Slums on the Drawing Board* Newcastle: Benwell CDP

Betjeman J (1937) Slough *Continual Dew* London: John Murray

Boneham F (nd) Sheltered high rise *Housing and Planning Review* 23–4

Bottoms A E (1974) Review of Newman O *British Journal of Criminology* **14** 203–206

Brimacombe M (1989) Beyond design *Housing* **25**(7), 11–15

Brooke J (1991) A housing manager's guide to saving the planet *Housing* **27**(1), 14–17

Broome J (1986) The Segal method *Architects Journal* **184**(45), 31–68

Brown L (1991) People power in design *in* Robertson D and Sim D (eds) *Glasgow: some lessons in urban renewal* Glasgow: City Council 73–76

Brownill S (1990) *Developing London's Docklands. Another great planning disaster?* London: Paul Chapman Publishing

Bryant R (1979) *The Dampness Monster. A Report of the Gorbals Anti-Dampness Campaign* Edinburgh: Scottish Council of Social Service

Building Research Establishment Conservation Support Unit (1992) *Energy Efficiency in New Housing* Good Practice Case Study 91, London: BRECSU

Bulos M A and Walker S R (1987) British high rise housing in context *in* Bulos M A and Walker S R (eds) *The Legacy and Opportunity for High Rise Housing in Europe: The Management of Innovation* London: South Bank Polytechnic 5–21

Burnett J (1986) *A Social History of Housing 1815–1985* (2nd edition) London: Methuen

Cahill P (1993) Standardised house design *Inside Housing* **10**(5), 10–11

Canter D (1974) *Psychology for Architects* London: Applied Science Publishers Ltd

Chapman D and Larkham P (1992) *Discovering the art of relationship: Urban design, aesthetic control and design guidance* Birmingham: Polytechnic Built Environment Research Paper 9, Birmingham

Cherry G E (1988) *Cities and Plans. The shaping of urban Britain in the nineteenth and twentieth centuries* London: Arnold

Clarke D and Myer A (1986) *Energy efficient rehabilitation: a feasibility study based on Haden Court, Islington* London: BRESCU

Coleman A (1985) *Utopia on trial. Vision and reality in planned housing* London: Hilary Shipman

Coleman A (1986) Utopia debate *Architects Journal* **184**(32), 16–17

Cook J A (1968) Gardens on housing estates. A survey of user attitudes and behaviour on seven layouts *Town Planning Review* **39**(3), 217–234

Cooney E W (1974) High flats in Local Authority Housing in England and Wales since 1945 *in* Sutcliffe A (ed) *Multi-storey Living: The British Working Class Experience* London: Croom Helm 151–180
Co-operative Development Services (nd) *Resident Led Estate Action — A Practical report on the process of community controlled estate re-design* Liverpool: CDS Ltd
Cowan R (1988) Prevention but no cure *Architects Journal* **187**(1), 32–39
Crossman R (1975) *The Diaries of a Cabinet Minister, Volume One. Minister of Housing 1964–66* London: Hamish Hamilton/Jonathan Cape
Cullen G (1953) Prairie planning *Architectural Review* **114** July
Darke J (1984a) Architects and user requirements in public sector housing: 1. Architect's assumptions about the user' *Environment and Planning B: Planning and Design* **11** 389–404
Darke J (1984b) Architects and user requirements in public-sector housing: 2. The sources for architects' assumptions *Environment and Planning B: Planning and Design* **11** 405–416
Darke J (1984c) Architects and user requirements in public-sector housing: 3. Towards an adequate understanding of user requirements in housing *Environment and Planning B: Planning and Design* **11** 417–433
Darley G Hall P and Lock D (1991) *Tomorrow's New Communities* York: Joseph Rowntree Foundation
Daunton M J (1983) *House and Home in the Victorian City: Working Class Housing 1850–1914* London: Arnold
Davison I (1990) *Good Design in Housing* London: House Builders Federation/RIBA
Department of Environment (1969) *Aspects of Designing for Old People* Design Bulletin No 1, London: HMSO
Department of Environment (1970) *Space in the Home* Design Bulletin No 6, London: HMSO
Department of Environment (1972) *The estate outside the dwelling. Reactions of residents to aspects of housing layout* Design Bulletin 25, London: HMSO
Department of Environment (1974) *Mobility housing* Housing Development Directorate Occasional Paper 2/74, London: HMSO
Department of Environment (1975a) *Housing the Elderly. The size of Grouped Schemes* Design Bulletin No 31, London: HMSO
Department of Environment (1975b) *Wheelchair housing* Housing Development Directorate Occasional Paper 2/75, London: HMSO
Department of Environment (1981) *A survey of tenants' attitudes to recently completed estates* HDD Occasional Paper 2/81, London: HMSO

Department of Environment/Department of Transport (1992) *Residential Roads and Footpaths. Layout Considerations* Design Bulletin 32 (second edition), London: HMSO

Department of Health for Scotland (1948) *Planning our New Homes. Report by Scottish Housing Advisory Committee on the Design, Planning and Furnishing of New Houses* (the Westwood Report), Edinburgh

Department of Health for Scotland (1956) *House Design* (Scottish Housing Handbook part 3), Edinburgh

Dunleavy P (1981) *The Politics of Mass Housing in Britain, 1945–1975* Oxford: Clarendon

Dunmore K (1992) *Planning for Affordable Housing. A Practical Guide* Coventry/London: IoH/House Builders Federation

Edgar W Rowbotham R and Stanforth J (1992) Dundee's Housing 1915–1974 *in* Whatley C A (ed) *The Remaking of Juteopolis* Dundee: Abertay Historical Society

Edwards M (1974) Comparison of some expectations of a sample of housing architects with known data *in* Canter D V and Lee T R (eds) *Psychology and the Built Environment* London: Architectural Press

Edwards A M (1981) *The Design of Suburbia* London: Pembridge

Esher L (1981) *A Broken Wave. The Rebuilding of England 1940–1980* Harmondsworth: Penguin

Essex County Council (1973) *A Design Guide for Residential Areas* Chelmsford: Essex County Council

Foot M (1973) *Aneurin Bevan* Vol 2, London: Davis-Poynter

Forsyth B A (1983) Conquering inner space *Housing* **19**(8), 20

Forsyth L (1988) The Community Technical Services Agency (COMTECHSA) Limited *Town Planning Review* **59**(1), 7–17

Gaskell S M (1986) *Model Housing, From the Great Exhibition to the Festival of Britain* London: Mansell

Gerry U K and Harvey G P (1983) *The Abatement of Wind Nuisance in the Vicinity of Tower Blocks* London: Greater London Council

Gibson M S and Langstaff M J (1982) *An Introduction to Urban Renewal* London: Hutchinson

Glasgow Corporation (1947) *Review of Operations 1919–1947* Glasgow: Glasgow Corporation Housing Department

Glasgow District Council (1978) *Housing Plan 2* Glasgow

Goodchild B (1987) Local authority flats. A study in area management and design *Town Planning Review* **58**(3), 293–315

Goodchild B and Furbey R (1986) Standards in housing design: a review of the main changes since the Parker Morris report (1961) *Land Development Studies* **3**, 79–99

Habinteg Housing Association (1988) *Habinteg Design Guide* London: Habinteg Housing Association

Hackney R (1990) *The Good, the Bad and the Ugly. Cities in Crisis* London: Muller

Hall A C (1990) *Generation of Objectives for Design Control* Chelmsford: Anglia College

Hardy D and Ward C (1984) *Arcadia for All: The Legacy of a Makeshift Landscape* London: Mansell

Healey P, McNamara P, Elson M and Doak A (1988) *Land Use Planning and the Mediation of Urban Change. The British Planning System in Practice* Cambridge: Cambridge University Press

Heck S (1987) Oscar Newman revisited *Architects Journal* **185**(14), 30–32

Hellman L (1988) Paradise regained. Housing Renewal, Wirral *Architects Journal* **187**(31), 33–44

Henslowe P (1984) *Ninety Years On. An Account of the Bournville Village Trust* Birmingham: BVI

Higgins S (1986) Old Visions, New Twist *Architects Journal* **183**(6), 30–36

Hillier B (1986a) City of Alice's dreams *Architects Journal* **184**(28), 39–41

Hillier B (1986b) Hard science or hard sell, letter to *Architects Journal* **184**(33), 14

Hillier B (1986c) Coleman debate, letter to *Architects Journal* **184**(42), 39

Hillier T (1992) Designer shopping *Housing* **28**(9), 15–16

HMSO (1985) *Lifting the Burden* Cmnd 9571, London

HMSO (1988) *Releasing Enterprise* Cmnd 512, London

Horsey M (1990) *Tenements and Towers. Glasgow Working Class Housing 1890–1990* Edinburgh: Royal Commission on Ancient and Historical Monuments of Scotland

Howard E (1902) *Garden Cities of Tomorrow* 1985 edition, Builth Wells: Attic Books

Humble D and Hughes J (1990) Homefront *Roof* **15**(6), 40

Hurd R (1957) Customer's Choice: The Bungalow *Saltire Review* **4**(11), 41–3

Hutchinson M (1989) *The Prince of Wales: Right or Wrong? An architect replies* London: Faber and Faber

Institute of Housing/Royal Institute of British Architects (nd) *Housing Design Brief: Housing for Elderly People* London: IoH/RIBA

Institute of Housing/Royal Institute of British Architects (1983) *Homes for the Future. Standards for New Housing Development* London: IoH/RIBA

Institute of Housing/Royal Institute of British Architects (1988) *Tenant Participation in Housing Design. A Guide for Action* London: IoH/RIBA

Institute of Housing/Royal Institute of British Architects (1989) *Safety and Security in Housing Design. A Guide for Action* London: IoH/RIBA

Jack A (1991) Community architecture: the people's chameleon *in* Robertson D and Sim D (eds) *Glasgow: Some lessons in urban renewal* Glasgow City Council 77–81

Jacobs, J. (1961) *The Death and Life of Great American Cities* New York: Random House

Jephcott P (1971) *Homes in High Flats* Edinburgh: Oliver and Boyd

Jones S (1991) The Green House Effect *Housing* **27**(1), 18–21

Karn V (1992) British housing standards: time for a new approach? Design Supplement to *Housing Review* **41**(6), 4–5

King A D (1984) *The Bungalow. The production of a global culture* London: Routledge & Kegan Paul

Kirby D A (1971) The inter-war council dwelling. A study of residential obsolescence and decay *Town Planning Review* **42**(3), 250–268

Knevitt C (1985) *Space on Earth. Architecture: People and Buildings* London: Thames Methuen

La Dell T (1986) Retaining trees on development sites *Architects Journal* **183**(8), 65–69

Lancaster O (1983) *A Cartoon History of Architecture*, London

Le Corbusier (1936) The Vertical Garden City *Architectural Review*, Reprinted in *Architects Journal* (1987) **185**(10), 48–50

Le Corbusier (1947) *When the Cathedrals were White* first published in English 1964, New York: McGraw-Hill

Levitt D (1982) Standards past and future *Architects Journal* 17 Nov

Lewis B (1992) A home for life *Search* **14**, 27–30

Liverpool City Council (1988) *Housing in Liverpool. The Director of Housing's Annual Report* Liverpool

Local Government Board (1918) *Report of the Committee on Building Construction in connection with the provision of dwellings for the working classes in England, Wales and Scotland* (the Tudor-Walters Report) London

McAlister G and McAlister E G (1941) *Town and Country Planning. A Study of Physical Environment: The Prelude to Post-War Reconstruction* London: Faber and Faber

McDonald A (1986) *The Weller Way* London: Faber and Faber

McKean C (1987) *The Scottish Thirties. An Architectural Introduction* Edinburgh: Scottish Academic Press

McNaughtan A (1967) The Jeely Piece Song *in* Whyte H (1983) (ed) *Noise and Smoky Breath* Glasgow: Third Eye Centre

McWilliam C (1975) *Scottish Townscape* London: Collins

Maizels J (1961) *Two to Five in High flats* London: Housing Centre Trust

Malpass P (1979) A Reappraisal of Byker. Magic, myth and the architect *Architects Journal* **169**, 961–9, 1011–1021

Malpass P and Murie (1990) *Housing Policy and Practice* (Third edition) London: Macmillan

Markus T A (1988) From Tudor-Walters to Parker Morris: prescription in housing design *in* Teymur N Markus T A and Woolley T (eds) *Rehumanizing Housing* London: Butterworth 32–52

Mars T (1987) Mersey Tunnel Vision? *Roof* **12**(6), 25–29

Martin F (1992) *Every house you'll ever need. A design guide for barrier-free housing* Edinburgh: Edinvar Housing Association

Matrix (1984) *Making space. Women and the man-made environment* London: Pluto Press

Ministry of Health (1944) *The Design of Dwellings. Report of the Design of Dwellings Sub-Committe of the Central Housing Advisory Committee* (the Dudley Report), London

Ministry of Health (1944) *Housing Manual* London

Ministry of Health (1949) *Housing Manual* London

Ministry of Housing and Local Government (1952) *Houses 1952. Second Supplement to the Housing Manual 1949* London

Ministry of Housing and Local Government (1953a) *Houses 1953, Third Supplement to the Housing Manual 1949* London

(1953b), *Design in Town and Village* HMSO, London

Ministry of Housing and Local Government (1958), *Flats and Houses 1958* London

Ministry of Housing and Local Government (1961) *Homes for Today and Tomorrow* (the Parker Morris Report) London

Ministry of Housing and Local Government (1963) *Space in the Home* Design Bulletin 6, London: HMSO

Ministry of Transport (1964) *Traffic in Towns* (the Buchanan Report) London: HMSO

Morgan N J (1989) £8 cottages for Glasgow citizens. Innovations in municipal house-building in Glasgow in the interwar years *in* Rodger R (ed) *Scottish Housing in the Twentieth Century* Leicester: Leicester UP

Moro P (1958) Elevational control *Architects Journal* **127**, 203

Morris B (1989) Design missionary *Inside Housing* **6**(49), 7–8

Morris J (1986) Housing disabled people — providing for us all *Housing* **22**(10), 8–9

Morris J. (1990) *Our Homes, Our Rights. Housing, Independent Living and Physically Disabled People* London: Shelter

Moseley L (1992) What architecture do we deserve? Social housing, funding regimes and their effect on design', Design Supplement to *Housing Review* **41**(6), 9–10

Munro M and Madigan R (1989) Do you ever think about us? *Architects Journal* **190**(25), 58

Munro M and Madigan R (1993) Privacy in the private sphere *Housing Studies* **8**(1), 29–45

Murray C (1989) Design by the pattern book *Architects Journal* **189**(9), 17

Muthesius S (1982) *The English Terraced House* New Haven: Yale UP

NACRO (1988) *Growing up on housing estates. A Review of the play and recreational needs of young peole* London: Nacro

Neale C (1984) *South Woodham Ferrers — the Essex Design Guide in Practice* RICS Planning and Development Case Study 3, London: RICS

Newman O (1972) *Defensible space. People and Design in the Violent City* London: Architectural Press

Oliver P Davis I and Bentley I (1981) *Dunroamin. The Suburban Semi and its Enemies* London: Barrie and Jenkins

Orwell G (1939) *Coming up for air* London: Gollancz

Osborn F J and Whittick A (1969) *The New Towns. The Answer to Megalopolis* London: Leonard Hill

Ospina J (1987) *Housing Ourselves* London: Hilary Shipman

Owens R (1988) Parker Morris in the pub *Architects Journal* **187**(26), 52–61

Parkinson K R (1976) NHBC Council dwellings; an exercise in common sense *Housing Review* **25**(2)

Pawley M (1971) *Architecture versus housing* London: Studio Vista

Pawley M (1987) Charlie's angels *New Society* 3 April 12–15

Perry C S (1929) *Regional Survey of New York and its environs. Vol 7. The Neighbourhood Unit* New York

Pharoah T and Russell J (1989) *Traffic Calming* London: South Bank Polytechnic

Phippen P (1992) Better design for the frail elderly *Housing Review* **42**(1), 14

Power A (1987) *Property before People. The Management of Twentieth-Century Council Housing* London: Allen & Unwin

Power A (1991) *Housing Management. A Guide to Quality and Creativity* London: Longman

Powers A (1989) Worlds apart, 60 years on *Architects Journal* **190**(10), 50–56

Poyner B (1983) *Design Against Crime. Beyond Defensible Space* London: Butterworth

Poyner B and Webb B (1991) *Crime-free housing* London: Butterworth

Punter J V (1986) The history of aesthetic control, part 1: 1909–1953 *Town Planning Review* **57**(4), 351–381

Punter J V (1987) The history of aesthetic control, part 2: 1953–1985 *Town Planning Review* **58**(1), 29–62

Quiney A (1989) *House and Home. A History of the Small English House* London: BBC
Ravetz A (1974) *Model Estate. Planned Housing at Quarry Hill, Leeds* London: Croom Helm
Ralph E (1987) *The Modern Urban Landscape* London: Croom Helm
Roberts, M. (1988) Caretaking — who cares? Teymur N, Markus T A and Woolley T (eds) *Rehumanising Housing* London: Butterworth
Roberts M (1991) *Living in a man-made world. Gender assumptions in modern housing design* London: Routledge
Robertson D (1989) The regeneration of Glasgow: the contribution of community-based housing associations to Glasgow's tenement improvement programme, 1964–1984 *Scottish Geographical Magazine* **105**(2), 67–75
Robinson H and Browne K R G (1936) *How to live in a flat* London: Hutchinson
Rock Townsend (1990) *Leamington Spa Design Guide* Leamington Spa: Warwick District Council
Rodger R (1989) *Housing in Urban Britain 1780–1914: Class, Capitalism and Construction* London: Macmillan
Sayle, A (1928) *The House of the Workers* London: Fisher Unwin
Scoffham E R (1984) *The Shape of British Housing* London: George Godwin
Scottish Development Department (1976) *Local Housing Needs and Strategies. A Case Study of the Dundee Sub-Region* Edinburgh: HMSO
Scottish Development Department (1977) *Scottish Housing Handbook 3. Housing Development: Layout, Roads and Services* Edinburgh: HMSO
Scottish Development Department (1979) *Scottish Handbook 6. Housing for the Disabled* Edinburgh: HMSO
Scottish Development Department (1980) *Scottish Housing Handbook 5. Housing for the Elderly.* Edinburgh: HMSO
Scottish Office Building Directorate (1987) *A Guide to Non-traditional and Temporary Housing in Scotland 1923–1955* Edinburgh
Sellers S (1988) *Sunlighters. The Story of a Village* London: Unilever
Sharples S (1987) The myth of community architecture *Bulletin for Environmental Education* **197**(8), 36–39
Sherlock H (1991) *Cities are good for us* London: Paladin
Shostak L and Lock D (1984) The need for new settlements in the south east *The Planner* **70**(11)
Simpson M A and Lloyd T H (eds) (1977) *Middle Class Housing in Britain* Newton Abbott: David and Charles
Spicker P (1986) Disabled myths *Housing* **22**(3), 22

Stollard P (ed) (1991) *Crime Prevention through Housing Design* London: Spon

Stollard P, Osborn S, Shaftoe H and Croucher K (1989) *Safer Neighbourhoods* Institute of Advanced Architectural Studies Working Paper. York: University of York

Swenarton M (1981) *Homes Fit For Heroes. The Politics and Architecture of Early State Housing in Britain* London: Heinemann

Tarn J N (1973) *Five Per Cent Philanthropy. An account of housing in urban areas between 1840 and 1914* Cambridge: Cambridge UP

Technical Services Agency (1987) *Evaluation Report 1984–1987* Glasgow: TSA

Tetlow J and Goss A (1965) *Homes, Towns and Traffic* London: Faber and Faber

Thomas A D (1990) *Falling Tenements: the rise of community rehousing* Liverpool: Merseyside Improved Houses

Thompson C (1992) Birth of a scheme *Housing* **28**(9), 19

Thorpe S (1985) *Housing Design Sheets* London: Centre on Environment for the Handicapped

Thorpe S (1986) *Designing for people with sensory impairments* London: Access Committee for England

Tindale P (1992) *Towards 2000. Designing housing for frail elderly people* Oxford: Anchor Housing Trust

Turnbull L and Womack S (nd) *Home Sweet Home. A Look at Housing in the North East from 1800 to 1977* Gateshead: MBC

Tutt P and Adler D (eds) (1979) *New Metric Handbook: Planning and Design* London: Butterworth

Voutsadakis S (1989) *Housing for people with disabilities. A design guide* (second edition), London: Islington Council

Walentowicz P (1992) *Development after the Act: the Housing Association development programme 1989/90* London: NFHA

Ward C (1974) *Tenants Take Over* London: Architectural Press

Ward C (1985) You're a Brick, Angela!' *The Planner* **71**(7), 31–33

Ward D (nd), Energy efficient refurbishment *Housing and Planning Review* 6–7

Warren F and Stollard P (1988) *Safe as Houses* Institute of Advanced Architectural Studies Working Paper, York: University of York

Wheatley J (1913) *Eight Pound Cottages for Glasgow Citizens* Glasgow: Glasgow Labour Party

Whitehand J W R (1990) Makers of the residential townscape: conflict and change in outer London *Transactions of the Institute of British Geographers* NS **15**(1), 87–101

White D (1979) Vandalism in housing estates: where it occurs and how it can be prevented *in* Sykes J (ed) *Designing against vandalism* London: Design Council

Wilson S (1980) Vandalism and defensible space on London housing estate *in* Clarke R V G and Mayhew P (eds) *Designing out Crime* London: Home Office Research Unit HMSO

Wilson E (1991) *The Sphinx in the City. Urban Life, the Control of Disorder, and Women* London: Virago

§Wolfe T (1981) *From Bauhaus to our house* New York: Farrar, Straus and Giroux

Woolley T (1986) Community architecture — an assessment of the case for user participation in design' *in* Scott J and Jenks M (eds) *What is the point of community architecture?* Oxford Polytechnic Department of Town Planning Working Paper No 95, 9–22

Worsdall F (1979) *The Tenement. A Way of Life* Glasgow: Chambers

Index